T3-AME-260

Real Bread

a fearless guide to making it

MAGGIE BAYLIS and CORALIE CASTLE
Drawings by Maggie Baylis

101 Productions, San Francisco

Second Printing, February 1981

Copyright 1980 Maggie Baylis and Coralie Castle
Drawings copyright 1980 Maggie Baylis
All rights reserved. No part of this book may be reproduced
in any form without the permission of 101 Productions.

Printed and bound in the United States of America. Distributed
to the book trade in the United States by Charles Scribner's
Sons, New York.

Published by 101 Productions
834 Mission Street
San Francisco, California 94103

Library of Congress Cataloging in Publication Data

Baylis, Maggie.
    Real bread.

    Includes index.
    1. Bread.   I. Castle, Coralie, joint author.
II. Title.
TX769.B27   641.8'15   80-21929
ISBN 0-89286-179-7

Contents

Alexander Dumas said it. "I've finished my play. Now all I have to do is write it down."

That's where we are. All that experience and months of testing, and we're ready to write down all the things that will answer your every question, so that you can walk right into the kitchen, rub the bread pan and the resident genii will hand you a brown loaf of great beauty. Right?

Well, not quite. That's not how plays get written or breads rise. There is simply no way we can promise you a perfect production the first time or any time you make bread. But if we can give you a lift past some of the trouble spots, some encouragement from the fact that we too have had some whopper failures even the birds snub, then perhaps you'll relax and read on to see how it all ends. Happily baking ever after, we hope.

If you have procrastinated about dipping your fingers into this dough business, perhaps a little push is all you need—and admission that you're afraid of failure. That may sound blunt, but it is the most common reason for saying "Oh, I couldn't bake bread." Folks have been known to risk 100 shares on an obscure plutonium mine or to buy a condominium because they liked the color of the bathtub, yet they've put off baking that first loaf for fear of making a botch out of a batch.

That is why we want to share with you what we know works, and unless your kitchen is in the path of a tornado, volcano or some other disaster, your chances of baking up your own storm with these guidelines are very good. Success will sit there, hot in you hands, waiting for applause.

Home breadmaking is back and on the rise. Flour mills have never had such heavy demands, and not only for familiar kinds, but for the heavily nutritious ones like wheat germ, rye meal, triticale and even the hard berries of grain for sprouting. The eating public is more aware than ever of the relationship of good grains to healthy bodies, of vitamins and fibers, of natural foods without preservatives. (Bread made at home needs no time-stretchers because it will disappear fast.)

Breadgiving has taken on new meaning. Once you bake regularly, friendship naturally gets into the act, and to share a warm loaf, wrapped in a pretty napkin, with a broken-hip neighbor, or a pan of sourdough scones with a Sea Scout troop is to merit a gold star on The Big Board Upstairs.

Breadforming is the deep-down best part of breadmaking at home, in the boonies or at anchor. It's the sly cure-all for aggression-prone moments when you get into kneading and pummeling a wheaty dough. It's the handy spot-remover for your depression when you dredge the top of a fancy-pan *Kugelhopf* with eye appeal. It's gratification by the liter when you can braid a four-strand egg bread, or deliver 24 gorgeous hot croissants to the bunch for brunch.

It's positive; it's downright exhilarating. It's *real bread,* and you made it. And you've faced the fact that bought bread, from now on, is only for (1) those without imagination, (2) lame excuses like I-don't-have-the-time and (3) the sick and the hapless.

There is no limit about who makes a baker. Kids love teasing dough. Men have always been the professional bakers—amateur status is now wide open. Grandmothers, teenagers, phi beta kappas and tug boat captains—even editors make good bakers. So what's keeping *you*? We've debunked the mystery of how-to and you have a fearless guide to making bread right in your hands: Make your pride rise!

The Anatomy of Bread: Ingredients

FLOUR POWER

Without drying up too much of your patience for history, it's worth noting that grains have been the main link of survival since the beginning. Prehistoric man, the hunter, supplemented his meat by collecting and eating grasses and seeds. Then came fire and roasting of seeds, the crushing and mixing with water to make a gruel, and the forming of little cakes to eat raw or bake on hot stones or in the ashes (as we still do tortillas, *pao ping* or oatcakes).

The earliest recorded reign of grain was by the Egyptians (Chinese tales tell of grains and the blessing of wild yeasts in the dim, undated past). Funerary murals in the pyramids show men carrying grain and water in big jars, others treading dough in troughs; builders of the pyramids were paid with three loaves and two jugs of beer a day and workmen under Ramses pulled off a massive strike when he cut their wages. Rulers found they could run everything by merely controlling the grain crop, which only goes to prove history repeats itself when one considers how much grain America grew for world use.

The Greeks and Romans developed the first "machinery," or rotary mill, about 1,000 B.C., and it wasn't until the first century B.C. that the "donkey" mill was born, the donkey hauling in a circle the stones used for grinding. Sifting the crushed grain was another matter. In the beginning it was coarse, often mixed with grit and dirt. Then the Romans found they could sift it through very fine linen, and the white powder that came through made a finer bread than ever before. White became socially and politically powerful: The rich and the leaders were separated from the poor who lived on leftovers that were adulterated with bonemeal, chalk, slaked lime, ashes. Milder additions through the centuries were pipe clay, lots of boiled potatoes, peas, beans and rye flour. Even as recently as 1941, the English wartime gray bread was transfused with chalk. Today, our all-purpose flour is "enriched" (original components partially restored), with chemicals.

bread is delivered daily into Tahiti mailboxes

THINGS TO KEEP IN MIND ABOUT FLOUR IN GENERAL

- Freshly ground flour of *any* kind is the key to flavor and texture in any flour. A home grist mill, or kitchen mill, is the only way to be sure of freshness since there is no way of checking shelf freshness of bought flour, even that purchased at natural-foods stores. These flours are obviously going to make good bread. We're not putting them down. It's just that home milling is now possible and worth considering (see Equipment, page 33).
- Commercial stone-ground flours have fresher taste and higher nutritive value than flour milled at high speed and high temperatures. The lower temperature of the stone-ground process preserves natural assets.
- Wheat flour high in gluten (whole wheat, cracked wheat, wheat germ, gluten flour) must be stored in the refrigerator or freezer, in containers with tightly fitting lids, because fats in wheat become rancid in a very short period. Always return to room temperature before using. Even with careful storage, whole-grain flours lose flavor and nutrients.
- Don't store any flour in a damp, warm place, or high on a shelf where the temperature could reach 75°F (23°C). It may mold or invite bugs. Don't use flour that smells musty.
- Flour absorbs and retains odors. Protect it from cheese, onions, garlic, coffee.

Easy cleaning of excess flour from work area: Sprinkle salt over flour, wipe with a damp sponge—flour will wash right out.

7

millstone grooves keep the flour cool

- Unless indicated, do not sift flour before measuring; if it has been in a container or bag for a long time and has compacted, stir with a fork to loosen before measuring.
- Humidity changes requirements for amounts of flour in yeast breads, so exact amounts cannot be indicated. A rainy or humid day or a very dry one will mean you have to adjust—either more or less. Also, whole-grain flour absorbs more moisture than unbleached white or all-purpose.
- Too little flour makes a slack, or soft, yeast dough, which is more likely to collapse when baking.
- Substituting to achieve new tastes is possible. Soy flour, triticale, bran, rye flakes, rye meal, etc. may be added in small amounts (see formulas under these ingredients below).
- Dough made with hard-wheat flour must be kneaded longer than that made with unbleached white to develop the greater amount of gluten.
- Do not add new flour to old.

BACK TO THE OLD GRIND

Modern commercial milling is done on high-speed steel rollers and sieving the flour after removes bran and germ from the starch or endosperm, if it's to be all-purpose white flour. High heat generated by the speed destroys nutrients, which are then chemically replaced. The flour is "enriched" back to what it might have been though obviously *not* exactly.

The other method of milling is strongly linked to the past and its high-protein, unbleached flours are gaining favor with more and more home bakers. The grain is crushed between stone buhrs (burrs), grinding slowly so the germ is pressed into flour, not lost on machinery or vaporized by heat. The stones have a network of quartz cavities that keep grinding surfaces sharp; the closeness of stones determines how fine the grain will be milled. Grooves ventilate to keep flour cool. The final product is labeled "stone ground."

Kitchen-mill grinding has reached a very practical stage and the units are compact, self-cleaning, lightweight. You may save the price of the mill in one year if you grind bread flours, cereals and flour for cakes and cookies for an average family. The mills give you whole-grain flour from coarse to very fine, with all the ingredients intact because they do not generate heat. The Magic

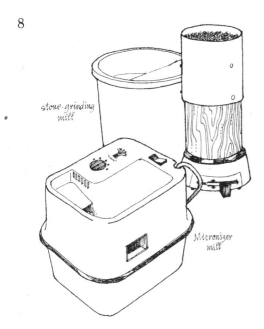

stone-grinding mill

Micronizer mill

Mill utilizes the Micronizer© process used in the pharmaceutical industry to explode solids by impact into uniform particle sizes. The All-Grain mill uses the stone-ground system, precision cut and diamond-dressed, with a special cooling system. Old flour cannot accumulate to tease insects. The mills are fast and use little energy.

WHEAT AND ITS SIBLINGS

A grain or kernel of wheat is really a dry "fruit" or "berry," made up of the *endosperm* (white, starchy basis of white flour), the *germ* (live part of the wheat berry, rich in vitamin E, fat, enzymes) and the *bran* (outside shell or husk, vitamin B$_1$). *Gluten,* a word used often in the yeast section of this book, is an elastic protein within the endosperm that stretches like bubble gum when wet and expands to hold the gas that yeast generates. Whole-grain contains ten times the vitamin E of bright white flour.

    What is really in a grain of wheat?
- *Carbohydrates:* starch and sugar, sources of energy. Unfortunately, the first thing many people leave out when dieting is bread, because of the carbohydrates. Doctors and experts insist that the nutrition from one slice of bread is essential daily.
- *Proteins:* necessary to rebuild tired cell structure, to build up and replace tissue and muscle.
- *Minerals:* necessary for strong bones, teeth; furnish calcium and iron, among other things.
- *Fats:* provide an extra energy supply.

SORTING OUT THE WHEAT FAMILY

There are three main strains of wheat grasses, and the most important are the "hard" wheats, *Triticum vulgare,* from which commercial breads are made. They are grown in cold-winter Canada, in America's Midwest and in Texas. The kernels are sharp, tough, difficult to cut, with a strong gluten that is stubborn. Another strain, "soft" wheat, is made into flour for cakes and pastries, and the third, *T. durum,* usually finds it way into French and Italian breads and into pasta.

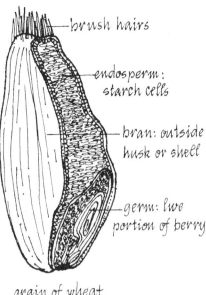

grain of wheat

brush hairs

endosperm: starch cells

bran: outside husk or shell

germ: live portion of berry

9

Coarse, low-gluten flour will slow the rising of dough— in fact, dough may not reach double bulk. Sweet doughs take longer to rise than others.

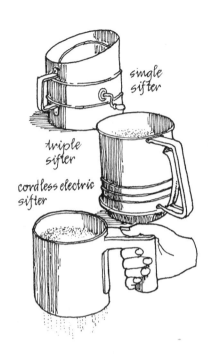

single sifter

triple sifter

cordless electric sifter

Zucchini and farmer's cheese make a moist, tempting loaf.

HARD WHEAT: Brand-name commercial bakers depend on hard-wheat flour. It gives a fine-textured, uniform bread, but must be made on heavy mixing machinery and with controlled humidity. This combination eliminates the home baker's chance of making anything that resembles "bakery" bread—an advantage, when you consider *some* of the squeezin' loaves on the shelves of a supermarket. If you decide to experiment with hard-wheat flour, however, you'll find it is scarcer than a luau without pineapple. Natural-foods stores may be able to locate some for you. Better still, look for hard-wheat berries and grind your own in a kitchen mill. The last alternative is mail order. See Sources, page 232, for names of home grist mills that will mail you small amounts. Just be prepared for a longer, harder kneading to develop the gluten; you'll find the flour takes more moisture also.

Major suppliers of flour discovered the renewed interest in home baking after World War II and developed a blend of flours that has adequate gluten for breadmaking, yet will also make cakes—"all-purpose" flour. More about that later.

SOFT WHEAT: Flour made from soft wheat is low in gluten and not a workable bread flour. It is, however, ideal for biscuits, muffins, quick breads, cakes and pastries. (To make an even more delicate flour for the last two, replace one tablespoon [15 ml] with one of cornstarch and blend well.) White pastry flour cannot be used to make yeast breads unless a large amount of the total flour in a recipe has adequate gluten; used in pastry, as the name suggests, with butter and eggs, it produces the desired flaky texture.

WHOLE-WHEAT FLOUR: Contains 100 percent extraction of the wheat kernel, including all the nutrients and bran fiber. It's the bran and germ that give whole wheat its color and provincial lustiness. Bran and germ also have a softening effect on the protein in the flour, and limit the rise of whole-wheat breads; texture will be denser than in white-flour breads. Whole grain needs more kneading to absorb moisture and you'll find dough is stickier than white-flour dough. Stone-ground wheat preserves flavor that is impaired during the high heat of the steel-roller milling. Always store whole wheats in the refrigerator in tightly covered containers to prevent fats from going rancid and destroying vitamins.

GRAHAM FLOUR: Also called whole meal. Similar to whole wheat, but is not 100 percent extraction: all the germ but only part of the bran remains. It is milled to a coarser, more mealy texture, makes a lighter bread than whole wheat and imparts a noticeably different flavor. To substitute in a recipe, limit amount in a loaf to one-half to one cup (125 to 250 ml). It is a refreshing addition to any buttermilk yeast bread. Remember, no matter what you hear, it is *not* the same as whole-wheat flour.

WHOLE-WHEAT PASTRY FLOUR: A new direction to lead your pastries. It is milled to a very fine texture and thus is a positive addition to coffee cakes and soda breads. It is not recommended as replacement for whole wheat in yeast recipes because the gluten will not respond, but it does give a wheaty taste to bland pastries.

WHEAT BERRIES: Unmilled and hard; must be soaked or cooked to soften. Soaking ovenight in warm water or sprouting the berries (see Sprouting, page 56) will do the trick. You may want to grind softened berries used in bread.

WHEAT GERM: Tiny flakes that contain the major nutrients of wheat: polyunsaturated fats, vitamins E and B, iron and amino acid lysine. Wheat germ also adds color and texture to white flour. It is available both untoasted and toasted. We suggest you buy untoasted by the pound and keep it stored in the refrigerator. It can be toasted *lightly* in the oven to give breads a nuttier flavor. Substitution of up to one-half cup (125 ml) for white or whole-wheat flour enriches any recipe; too much will limit the rising of yeast bread.

WHEAT, BRAN AND TRITICALE FLAKES Available at natural-foods stores, are coarse, and used mostly to add rough texture and extra nutrients to breads.

CRACKED WHEAT: The kernel is cut rather than ground. It adds a nutty, crunchy flavor. Is also called bulghur in Middle Eastern and Greek cooking.

UNPROCESSED BRAN: Husk of the grain, taken from the first "breaks" of the rolling process. It is high in fiber content and difficult to digest (but much needed to stimulate elimination).

Rub flour between your thumb and fingers. Good wheat flour has a granular feel; soft, slippery feeling comes from soft wheat or a blend.

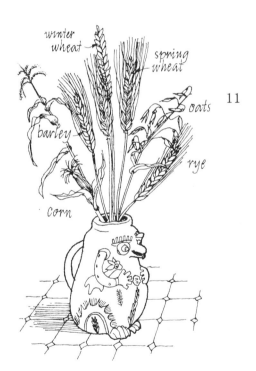

winter wheat
spring wheat
oats
barley
rye
corn

11

Bran inhibits the rising of yeast breads: limit substitution to one-half cup (125 ml). Keep bran in tightly covered container in the refrigerator for adding to breads or for sprinkling on the top of loaves ready to go into the oven (an egg white wash will make it stick). Do not use breakfast-food bran as substitute.

The trick to kneading is to handle the dough so that it doesn't stick to your hands or the board without adding too much flour.

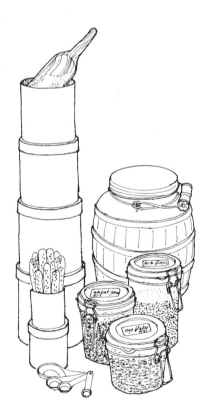

UNBLEACHED WHITE FLOUR: Throughout this book you will sense our missionary zeal when we preach *unbleached* over all-purpose flour. Of course, you may substitute and experiment, but we can tell you before you start, the resulting breads will *not* equal what we proved by many tests were outstanding yeast and quick breads. Bleaching of flour is done chemically to eliminate any color residue in the milling process, forcibly wiping out nutrients. The "enrichments" hailed on bags of all-purpose flour are *some* of these things, which have been chemically put back in. We like ours natural, unbleached, thank you. And that means breads that are gospel white—warm white, on the creamy side—without additives.

Unbleached white gives lightness and increased workability to rye and barley flours, even in small added amounts. If whole-wheat dough is sticky, an injection of unbleached will make it behave. Supermarkets, grocery stores and natural-foods stores make it easily available.

ALL-PURPOSE FLOUR: A basic white flour, about 70 percent extraction of the wheat, with some of the bran and germ left in. Obviously, the phrase "all-purpose" has made this the most salable flour in America. It is a scientific, safe blend, it has enough gluten to make a good yeast bread, yet it can bake a dream wedding cake. Is it any wonder that it is popular? *Only,* as we said above, there's always another answer, and "unbleached" is the challenger.

WHITE PASTRY FLOUR: Often sold as cake flour, it is milled from soft wheat, and has the finest texture of all, with little or no gluten. Indispensible for some crackers, pastries, cake mixes.

"INSTANT" FLOUR: Trademarked *Wondra* by General Mills, it has a grainy texture that allows liquid to enter its porous structure quickly and blends ingredients better than all-purpose (as in sauces and gravies). It is similar to soft-wheat European flour, and you may find it ideal for non-yeast, old-country recipes. Otherwise, it is expensive and not particularly important in breadmaking.

SELF-RISING FLOUR: Medium-strong flour, made from wheat or corn, to which leavener has been added at the mill, usually baking powder and/or baking soda. It is a time-saver with quick breads, although we still prefer the control of exact amounts of leavening as indicated in our recipes. We did include a few which are offbeat and may become standbys in your family, particularly Beer Bread (page 185).

GLUTEN FLOUR: Pure gluten is processed from the wheat berry (it is sold under trade names like "Do-Pep," but is not easy to find). It is not readily usable until it is blended with whole-wheat or bread flours in a ratio of two parts gluten to three parts flour. This is then called *pure gluten flour,* and is added to the recipes in amounts indicated.

When gluten is mentioned other than in recipes in this book, it is an element integral to the development of tough cells in yeast breads that will hold the gases that make bread light. Wheat has more gluten than other grains. Rye has some, but grains like barley, rice, corn and oats are "glutenless," and must be used with wheat flours to develop yeast breads. It is not soluble in water, but will absorb liquids that will cause it to swell and do its work. It is off-limits to people with allergies, but a boon to those on starch-free diets.

Gluten flour should never be added to pastries or cakes. Keep it refrigerated in an airtight jar and bring to room temperature before using.

PROPRIETARY FLOURS AND MEALS: There are packaged flours of wheat and wheat blends available to make special breads, Roman Meal, Wheatena, Zoom, Malt-O Meal, Cream of Wheat and many others. What they offer is flavors of another dimension, particularly for muffins and quick breads.

13

In yeast breads, add the high-gluten flours first and last to develop the gluten, and add the other flours in between.

NON-WHEAT FLOURS

BARLEY FLOUR: Coarse-ground grain that has been hulled. It makes a sweet, malty, moist loaf, but has no gluten, so it must be used with a wheat flour. Taste is improved by very light toasting in a hot oven: Stir often until color begins to change; don't scorch or it will turn into a strange mistake. Limit substitution to one-third to one cup (75 to 250 ml) of white flour.

BROWN-RICE FLOUR: Is not readily obtainable, but if you can find it, will deliver a dense, moist, dark side to breads (it's a favorite of Tibetans). Brown rice plays the heavy, so don't overplay your part, even though the rice is loaded with nutrients. If you are going to use the whole grain it must be steamed and cooled; one-half cup raw (125 ml) equals two cups (500 ml) cooked.

buckwheat

BUCKWHEAT FLOUR: Buckwheat is *not* a member of the wheat clan, but is a different grass, related to sorrel. It is triangular in shape and has tough brown rings surrounding the kernel. The flavor is pungent, distinct, and some claim it delicious. It's outstanding characteristic is that it develops "warmth," as in pancakes on a snowy campout (that probably explains why the Soviet Union grows much of the world's supply—and uses most of it too). Substitute no more than two tablespoons (30 ml) in one cup (250 ml) unbleached white flour.

Leftovers in the refrigerator? Cooked kasha, rice, sausages may inspire you to invent a new loaf.

14

CORN FLOUR: Commonly called cornmeal because it is gritty in texture. It comes in several grinds, but stone- or water-ground retains the germ. Refined (usually a finer grind) is shorn of nutrients. *Avoid* buying *degerminated* cornmeal because you'll get all that starch without any food value and the bread will be very crumbly. Cornmeal is also called Indian meal because the first Americans ground their corn on stones, making a chewier, nuttier bread. Depending on the color of the corn ground, it can be either white cornmeal or yellow. White has more flavor, is favored in the South for hush puppies and spoon bread; yellow is higher in vitamin A. We recommend grinding dried corn fresh in a kitchen mill to get the finest flavor treat of all (see Equipment, page 33). Store whole-grain ground corn in the refrigerator.

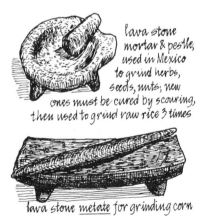

lava stone mortar & pestle, used in Mexico to grind herbs, seeds, nuts; new ones must be cured by scouring, then used to grind raw rice 3 times

lava stone metate for grinding corn

GARBANZO FLOUR: Stone-ground dried chick peas. One of the best in taste and texture of all the legume family.

GRANOLA: A high-energy mixture of grains, nuts, coconut, raisins available at supermarkets and natural-foods stores. The best mix is the one assembled to your own taste. Flavor is excellent when fresh, tends to be elusive as the mixture ages. See recipe for basic mixture, page 93.

MASA HARINA: A flour made from corn and used in tortillas. The corn kernels are parched, cooked in unslaked lime and water, then soaked and ground to a smooth consistency to make a *masa,* which is then dried and stored. Do not try to substitute cornmeal; it will not work.

MILLET: Often called the poor man's rice, millet is very easily digested. It is a grass that probably originated thousands of years ago in Africa; the Spaniards introduced it to the New World. It is high in calcium, lecithin and riboflavin, and is a good source of available proteins. Grinding in blender releases flavor.

OATS: Oats are richest of all grains in proteins and minerals. They are not commonly made into flour but are steel-cut into tiny bits, or rolled into the familiar flakes of the breakfast cereal. The groat, or berry, has a hull that must be removed by heating to make it brittle. Old-fashioned oatmeal is the dehulled groat; the quick-cooking type has been cut into smaller bits. They blend into batters better if soaked in boiling water briefly (with shortening) and cooled before yeast or baking powder is added. Rolled oats make a chewy, moist, slightly sweet bread. You can make a coarse flour of old-fashioned oats by whirling in a blender for 60 seconds. Barley flour, chopped walnuts or hulled sunflower seeds add a brightening to oatmeal bread. Substitute one and one-third cups unprocessed oat flakes (325 ml) for one cup (250 ml) whole-wheat or unbleached white flour per loaf.

POTATO FLOUR: The potato is cooked, dried whole and then ground into flour which is of no good use to bread unless blended with other flours. Also, blend it with sugar or shortening before adding to any batch. (Potato flour is used mostly for thickening soups and sauces.) Substitute one-fourth to one-half cup (60 to 125 ml) for one-fourth to one-half cup (60 to 125 ml) unbleached white flour in one of the cups (250 ml) per loaf.

Oatmeal bread takes on a new charm when sweetened with maple syrup and combined with a little graham flour.

15

Frozen croutons: Cut ends from loaf into cubes and freeze in plastic bag; shake out as needed, brown in butter, drain on paper towel. Use in salads, soups.

PEANUT FLOUR: High in protein, is an additive and like potato flour, not used alone. Substitute two tablespoons (30 ml) for two (30 ml) of unbleached white flour in each cup (250 ml).

RICE FLOUR: Not much used in breads, but it will complement non-yeast recipes using eggs. Rice flour is milled from both white and brown rice grains. The dark gives a hearty rich character with small volume and close texture. Rice has no gluten-forming proteins and is recommended for gluten-free diets. Substitute seven-eighths cup (210 ml) for one cup (250 ml) unbleached white flour per loaf. Note: Avoid *sweet* rice flour. It's a waxy substance and cannot be used for baking bread.

RYE FLOUR: Rye has a limited gluten content, but it is good friends with the wheats. It is rich in flavor, dark, earthy, sour, spicy. Rye is an economical crop, flourishes in poor soil, as do oats and millet. Light rye is most easily available; look for stone-ground unbleached for your breads, or preferably, grind your own. Minnesota rye has a red tinge and makes a darker loaf. Rye is a sticky-working flour and needs the help of gluten from whole-wheat or white flours. The more rye used, the lower the volume. Rye flour gives bread a fine texture and a chewy crust. Substitute one-fourth cup (60 ml) for one-fourth cup (60 ml) wheat flour in one cup (250 ml).

Rye meal is a coarser grind and can be used in place of rye flour to stir up an interesting texture. It is ground from the entire grain.

Rye flakes, like oat flakes, add chewiness to breads if added in small portions. They can also be scattered on top of the unbaked loaves.

SOY FLOUR: Whole dried soybeans are ground into a fine-milled flour, which should always be stored in the refrigerator. Soy is loaded for the vitamin-hungry: highly concentrated proteins (but not gluten and starch), calcium and iron. It has fat, so shortening in recipes can be decreased. One word of advice: Soy has a strong taste; use with discretion until you feel you have a good balance. It also causes heavy browning of crust, so you may have to reduce oven heat. Yeast breads made with soy are light in texture (unless you use too much!) and we recommend adding two tablespoons (30 ml) as substitutions in one cup (250 ml) wheat flours. To avoid lumping, mix soy flour with other flours before adding to dough or batter.

TRITICALE: A hybrid of wheat (*triticum*) and rye (*secale*) developed in recent years and hailed as having a great future. It is a major taste improvement, favoring the rye family, with a slight sweet edge, and boasting an even higher protein content than either (a third more than wheat). It is still available only at natural-foods stores or by mail from specialty mills. The minor hangup is that you will have to bake any bread made with triticale longer. The flour is perishable; keep it refrigerated or frozen. Substitute one-third cup (75 ml) for one-third cup (75 ml) unbleached white flour in each cup (250 ml).

FRESH IS PRECIOUS

If there's anything we have learned as bread people, it's that *freshness* is a prime ingredient of successful baking.

There is no way to know how long that flour you are buying has stood on a shelf. There are no laws requiring manufacturers to date it, and your only assurance is that the turnover of stock is faster in a big store than a small. For instance, each day on a shelf for whole-wheat flour means a lessening of its food value *and* the nearer it is to oxidation when oils become rancid. This is not said to frighten you or turn you off from making bread. What we are saying is this: Take extra effort to look for and find flour that is as fresh as possible. Ask questions. You owe it to your pleasure as a breadmaker. (Store personnel will often put the oldest stock in front to sell it first and the new is at the back, much as with milk and cheese products.)

Many home bakers have turned to natural-foods and health-food stores, particularly for the whole grains and the less common flours, and as you will notice, we constantly suggest them as sources in this book. Scores of bins are filled with rice flour, wheat germ, garbanzo flour, bulk yeast, but are they fresh? You have no way of being sure. Certainly millions of loaves of whole-wheat bread are baked in home kitchens every day and we have baked our share, without dire results. It's just that they *could* be better if the ingredients were fresh.

Paprika and cayenne have short shelf life—buy smallest quantity.

17

We *did* find the answer by acquiring a kitchen mill that grinds just the amount needed for a recipe—and fresher you can't get! Owning a mill may just give you more sweet sounds than a new stereo. Think about it.

STORING

Unbleached white and all-purpose flours are less susceptible to time and ask only to be stored in a dry, dark place away from excessive heat. Whole-wheat and whole-grain flours, wheat germ and flakes should be stored in the refrigerator or freezer (remember to bring to room temperature before using). Fresh wheat germ is sweet. It starts to get bitter as it ages unless refrigerated. Metal, glass, ceramic or plastic containers are fine for storing white flours. Use a crock or glass or enameled box with loose lid for wheat (meal needs to breathe, even in the refrigerator), but keep tightly closed in the freezer. Some plastics may impart their chemical composition. Check by sniffing before you use. If the flour bag is torn, put it in a plastic food bag. White flour will store for up to two years if protected from pests and mice, and unbleached will become whiter with age.

PESTS

Worms and moths and those tiny meal bugs are the uninvited and frustrating nuisance. If their eggs are in one package on a shelf, the bugs will spread through the cupboard. Once new packages are opened, slip them immediately into plastic food bags and close tightly, or transfer contents to glass jars with tightly fitting lids.

Bugs don't like cold, so the refrigerator is ideal. However, most of us do not have that much space to share, so whatever space you can give, leave it for the whole-wheat products and keep the others in a dry, well-ventilated, cool place.

If you see a tiny gray moth flitting around the kitchen, check the rolled oats or any walnuts sitting in a bowl. These are likely homes and a fat, happy little worm may have been eating up the profits right there. They don't carry disease—they just bug you. Here are some offbeat suggestions for combating these pests: Heating grain products and nuts in a 150°F (65°C) oven for half an hour will kill any interlopers. Dry ice is a deterrent. Using gloves, lay a few pieces of it in a large picnic storage box and place plastic-covered packages or bags on the ice for a few hours,

A bay leaf stashed in container of flour or cereals will ward off pests.

18

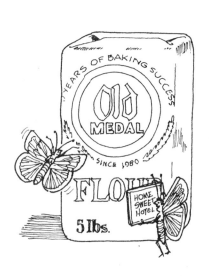

covered, to cool the heels. Keep bags or cans off the floor; date containers and use the older batch first. Buy the unusual flours in small quantities. Try stowing a bay leaf in each package.

And if you see the moth again, you know what to do to *him*.

LEAVENERS: THE BREAD ALSO RISES

YEAST

The air around us, the ground, the fruits and leaves of plants are the growing arena of a living organism called *yeast*. Wild yeasts are unstable, and although the use of fermentation has been going on for thousands of years, it wasn't until a Hungarian named Fleischmann invented a process of drying yeast that was reliable, and modern baking was assured. (There are several excellent yeasts besides Fleischmann's brand, such as El Molino and Red Star High-Potency Nutritional.) Under his name, contemporary scientists have isolated a tough, durable and predictable yeast and standardized it. Now it is possible to find yeast in two practical forms, *cake* and *active dry*.

Cake yeast has been the favorite for many generations, but its weaknesses are exasperating. It does not keep well (it lives on itself and when that is ended, it dies). Because it is fragile, you won't know whether there is life in it until it is proofed. A little brown on its edges will not hurt. Most critical is the date on the package: Do not use it if that date has passed.

Active dry yeast is a relatively new addition to the scene, and we have chosen to use it because it removes one of the major uncertainties of baking. It is dormant and will last for months if kept tightly covered and refrigerated. You'll find it in airtight packages, or in bulk in natural-foods stores.

The mission of yeast is to transform oxygen and sugars into carbon dioxide gases and alcohol, which then find homes in the cell walls of dough that has been strengthened by gluten. This will cause the dough to lift up until it faces heat in the oven of about 140°F (60°C), then the yeast dies. Yeast dough can stand cold like a penguin. It can be frozen, and begins to rejuvenate at about 50°F (10°C). Its best working temperatures are 78° to 85°F (23° to 29°C). These temperatures, and the amount of food available for yeast to feed on, are critical factors in the life of a yeast.

Plastic wrap is ideal for the first risings of yeast bread —it keeps the moisture in; use a tea towel for the final rising.

19

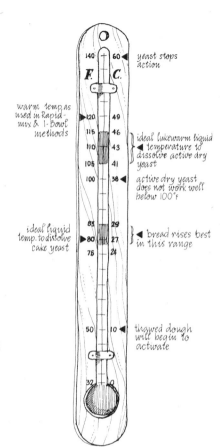

warm temp. as used in Rapid-mix & 1-Bowl methods ▶120 49

ideal lukewarm liquid ◀ temperature to dissolve active dry yeast

ideal liquid temp. to dissolve cake yeast ▶80

140 — 60 ◀ yeast stops action

F. *C.*

115 46
110 43
105 41
100 — 38 ◀ active dry yeast does not work well below 100°F

85 29
80 27 ◀ bread rises best in this range
75 24

50 10 ◀ thawed dough will begin to activate

32

The temperature of the liquid (water, fruit juices, milk, broth) in which the yeast is dissolved is in that same critical factor group. Ignore the rules and you'll end up burying the yeast under a rock. To dissolve cake yeast, liquid should be 80°F (32°C); packaged and bulk active dry yeast need warmth between 105° and 115°F (42° and 46°C). If the liquid is less than 100°F (38°C), yeast will be a slowpoke; over 115°F (46°C) and it begins to whirl itself into a dead dervish.

The safest way to measure temperature is to use an instant thermometer (see Sources, page 232); you can also use a standard meat thermometer, though it is slower to record. Old hands depend on the wrist method: Run warm tap water over your wrist, and if it feels pleasantly warm but not hot, it should be in range. Warming the mixing bowl before starting will keep the liquid at its sassy best.

THOUGHTS WHICH MAY RAISE YOUR CONFIDENCE
● Compressed cake yeast and active dry yeast can be inter-changed: one package dry yeast equals .6 ounce (16 g) cake yeast; one package dry yeast equals one scant tablespoon (13 ml) active dry yeast.
● Note that packaged dry yeast carries the statement that yeast will not grow without sugar and flour; bulk active dry yeast does not have this disclaimer, though it will proof faster with the addition of a sweetener.
● Yeast should dissolve completely and be foamy in 15 minutes.
● Sugar and honey can be used interchangeably in activating yeasts (we prefer honey), but too much sugar inhibits yeast.
● For speedier rising, a little extra yeast may be used, but this affects flavor and gives a porous look.
● Salt also inhibits yeast and should not be added until after yeast has foamed. In very hot weather, a pinch of salt will slow too-rapid fermentation.
● Doughs made by the new quick methods may indicate higher temperature of liquid when yeast is incorporated in dry ingredients. Check recipes carefully.
● Dough punched down too many times can "tire" the yeast and it may decide not to get up again.
● Too much rising "suffocates" yeast and your only hope of reviving it is to punch it down to release gaseous by-products and freshen its air.

Did you remember to date your bulk yeast when you bought it at the natural-foods store?

- Yeast will be livelier if a pinch of ground ginger is added to dough before rising.
- If you want to cut a recipe in half and it calls for a tablespoon (15 ml) of yeast, use the whole amount and the whole amount of water it is dissolved in; if it calls for two tablespoons (30 ml), reduce to one (15 ml); but do not reduce water. Doubling a recipe with two tablespoons (30 ml)? Use only three tablespoons (45 ml) and double the amount of water.
- Starting the baking process in a cold oven instead of a preheated one gives the dough another extra boost until the yeast is killed by heat.

BREWER'S YEAST: There are two kinds available (see Bread Language, page 229). The one that is a leavening agent is very difficult to find, is used only commercially. Our recommendation: Stick to active dry yeast.

OTHER LEAVENERS

MALT: The long-time fellow traveler of beer is also a little-known good friend of bread. European bakers find it mellows and softens gluten and adds a nutty flavor. It is sold in natural-foods stores as malt extract and may be either a thick syrup or a powder. Look for the powder, which is easier to handle but must be kept airtight and moisture free or it will change its character and be difficult to handle. Malt will make a dough more sticky.

The real importance of malt is that it is a food for yeast to feed on, and an able assistant in converting starch into another form that ferments readily. Malt comes from barley, and is made from sprouted grain that has been dried at a low temperature. To use, add one-half teaspoon (2.5 ml) to a two-loaf batch. Powdered malt sold for drinks can be substituted; store airtight.

BAKING POWDER: The backbone of quick breads, muffins, cakes and coffee cakes, baking powder is a gas-forming agent, a mixture of acid and alkali that reacts chemically when mixed with liquid. It produces a texture more like cake and rarely one like yeast bread, even though they both operate on the same gas.

There are two kinds, single and double-acting. Check labels for this difference when you shop. Double-acting baking powder offers more help by releasing a small amount of gas created by the interaction of baking powder with moisture, while ingredients are being put together. The main booster rockets take off when the dough meets oven heat; baking powder biscuits are a fine example of the extremes.

As with any chemical combination (baking powder is made up, among other things, of bicarbonate of soda and cream of tartar), it does not live to a ripe old age. *Check the date on the bottom of the can* when you buy. If not there, date it the day you buy. If there is any question whether baking powder has gone over the hill, add one teaspoon (5 ml) to one-third cup (75 ml) hot water. It is okay if it bubbles like detergent. Note: Do not use more than one teaspoon (5 ml) for each cup (250 ml) of flour in any recipe. For high-altitude adjustments, see page 55.

● Speed is of the essence in working with baking powder or baking soda. Always preheat oven and grease pans before you start to make quick breads.

● Measurements given in recipes are carefully adjusted; do not use more than indicated as this will antagonize the action. Overuse increases loss of thiamin by alkalinity, and vitamin B is susceptible to overreaction.

● Breads made with baking powder will dry out faster than yeast breads, but they are superb freshly baked and probably will be eaten faster. They are even better the second day.

BAKING SODA: Baking soda is the friend of buttermilk, yoghurt, sour milk and sour cream, fruit juices and the family of sourdough starters. It is the oldest chemical leavener, a neutralizer of acids that all of these have. The resultant gases work immediately, causing breads to expand so they must be rushed from scratch to oven in marathon time. For the most effective preparation, proceed as for baking powder or as recipe indicates. Formula for measuring soda: Use one-half teaspoon (2.5 ml) to one cup (250 ml) buttermilk, etc. Do *not* add extra for "good measure."

Soda is sometimes used with sourdoughs, but it tends to make them bland and the sour taste is dissipated.

SOURDOUGH STARTERS: See the section on Sourdough, beginning on page 143.

Caught without baking powder? Blend 1/4 teaspoon (1.2 ml) baking soda with 5/8 teaspoon (3.2 ml) cream of tartar, mix well and substitute for 1 teaspoon (5 ml) double-acting baking powder.

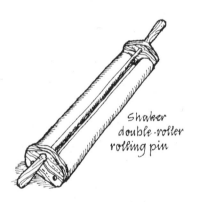

Shaker
double-roller
rolling pin

LIQUID ASSETS

BEER: Always use at room temperature, and open the bottle just before using. Light beers have fewer calories and blander flavor. To give whole-grain bread an airy texture, substitute beer for one cup (250 ml) of the water or milk.

BROTH: Clear vegetable, chicken or beef broth adds a special dimension to whole-wheat and herb breads, and can be substituted for the water. If the broth has been salted, reduce amount of salt indicated in recipe.

EGGS: Egg yolks furnish enrichment and color to bread doughs, and the whites give a lift and proteins. Quick breads sometimes indicate separating yolks and whites and beating separately. Be very careful in separating that no yolk gets into the white, as yolks contain fat and fats keep whites from forming air pockets. Incidentally, beating whites first means you don't have to wash the beaters before tackling the yolks. Whites should be beaten until stiff but not dry. As with all ingredients, eggs should be at room temperature when used. If you have forgotten to remove eggs from the refrigerator, place them in a bowl of hot water for five minutes.

In all our recipes, we have used grade A large eggs unless otherwise specified to adjust for metric measure. Eggs vary in size: large size should measure about one-fourth cup (60 ml). To be sure eggs are fresh, place in a bowl of cool water and if they are fresh, they will sink. If they are medium-fresh, one end will stick up, and if they are bad, they will float.

JUICES: They add flavor and sweetness. Fruit juices need baking soda to neutralize acids if used in quick breads. Orange juice often can be substituted for water in yeast breads; the yeast likes fruit sugar.

MILK, FRESH: Fresh whole, low-fat or skim milk contributes to a richer, more tender-crumb bread, and the bread does not stale as quickly as if made with water. If you're counting calories, use either low fat or skim. Fresh unpasteurized milk must be scalded and cooled; it has a high content of undesirable wild yeasts and enzymes that must be eliminated. Today's milks are almost all pasteurized, so the choice is yours as to whether to scald or not.

The color of an egg shell is not important. It's what is inside that counts.

23

Add extra leftover egg whites to French bread to make airy, crunchy loaves.

We find scalding a good way to melt butter and dissolve sweeteners that go into bread.

Milk also gives a brown crust when used in the dough, and a soft crust if brushed on the outside before baking. To make milk or cream sour, add the juice of one-half lemon or one teaspoon (5 ml) cider vinegar to one cup (250 ml) of fresh.

BUTTERMILK AND YOGHURT: These two have been snubbed more times than almost any food—except perhaps parsnips and turnips. Anyway, they are both rewarding additions to the bread-maker's palette. Buttermilk has acids that aid the absorption of iron into blood.

Originally buttermilk was the leftover from the butter churn, but today it is made from pasteurized skim milk with a culture added to produce a heavier consistency and increase the amount of lactic acid. It is more quickly digested than skim milk. Butter particles are added; shake well before pouring.

Yoghurt has been the mainstay of Middle Eastern countries since biblical times, and starts from the milk of goats, reindeer, mare and ewe, as well as Bessie the cow.

Cultured buttermilk and yoghurt perform with baking soda to give delicious quick breads—and you'll never know what's in the bread. Note: Check dates on both before measuring.

MILK, NON-INSTANT DRY: The type we prefer for baking because it has more nutrients. It must be sifted with part of the flour as it forms lumps in liquid alone. Non-instant dry milk is skim that has been spray-dried at low heat so that much of its goodness is still intact after processing. Keep tightly covered and refrigerated. It is available at natural-foods stores.

MILK, INSTANT NON-FAT DRY: Available at supermarkets and is usually reconstituted for drinking or cooking. It is dried by a high-heat process, leaving less vitamin and mineral content than the non-instant variety. To use in recipes that call for non-instant, add five teaspoons (25 ml) for each tablespoon (15 ml) indicated.

Non-instant dry milk is powdery, instant is granular. Always store in an airtight container in a cool place because moisture and humidity will destroy some of the amino acids.

24

MILK, EVAPORATED: Has 16 percent less water than whole milk, but more protein and milk sugar. It makes a richer loaf.

POTATO WATER: This is the water potatoes have been boiled in; it adds characteristic flavor, moisture, gives more volume and produces a faster-rising dough. Texture of bread seems coarser than usual.

WATER: All water is not the same, so don't start out thinking you can use it from the tap until you know whereof it begins. Hard water is alkaline, diminishing the gas-retaining properties of gluten and making a smaller loaf. One way to neutralize it is to add a few drops of vinegar. Soft water is slightly acid and needs less yeast to do the same job; very soft water will make a soggy, sticky bread.

    Water gives a crisper loaf, and in the case of French bread is all important in making a hard crust. Bread made with water will dry out faster unless fat is added. If dough seems too stiff during kneading, water can be added by misting or sprinkling a little at a time and working it in.

ABOUT LIQUIDS IN GENERAL

Too much liquid makes a slack dough; too much flour will make it heavy. You will note in the metric measurements that sometimes the amounts suggested may differ, one from another, for the same spoon or cup measure. This is done deliberately to maintain the right proportions. (See Metrics, page 44.)

    Hot weather: Ice may be placed around the bowl of rising dough to slow action; it may make a "holey" loaf.

hard water is alkaline, makes a smaller loaf; soft water is slightly acid & very soft water makes soggy, sticky yeast breads

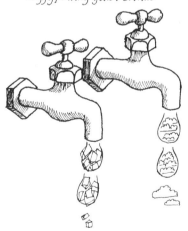

SWEETEN LOW

SUGAR, GRANULATED: The American diet is heavily into sugars, so we have limited additions. If you want to add more to make a "sweeter" loaf, consider using honey. It's better for you.

Yeast needs sweetening like sugar, honey or molasses to create the gas that breads rise to. Sugar also helps brown the crust and adds flavor (if it browns too rapidly, cover the bread with foil), but has little other value aside from calories and a short spurt to energy.

To add color, sugar can be caramelized over low heat in a heavy pan. Add a pinch of cream of tartar to prevent crystalizing. Molasses adds deep color. Use only honey or sugar in white breads to preserve non-color.

BROWN SUGAR: Imparts a special taste and is often used with molasses in darker breads. Measuring can be tricky if the sugar is lumpy: Dry it out in a flat pan in a lukewarm oven for a few minutes, then roll it between two sheets of waxed paper with a rolling pin. To measure, always pack firmly into cup or spoon.

POWDERED SUGAR: If it is old and has formed lumps, sift, or press through a fine sieve, using the back of a teaspoon. If your cupboard is bare, you can make powdered sugar out of granulated by putting it in a blender for two minutes or more.

SUGAR SUBSTITUTES: When sugar is indicated, we suggest you use it unless there is a medical reason. Do *not* try to bake with saccharin; it casts a bitter spell. Cyclamates change the texture.

HONEY: Wild or tame, it is the best sweetener (although wild can get a demerit if it is too strong). It has fewer calories than sugar, but does have potassium, more flavor, and will keep breads from drying out too fast. When it is unfiltered, unblended and uncooked, it retains important enzymes. Try different flavors: avocado, buckwheat, tupulo, orange, sage or choice fancy. Honey is predigested by the bee and so is more digestible for humans. Don't refrigerate as it may "sugar." If this happens, set the container in a pan of hot water over low heat until it is liquid once more. To measure honey, oil spoon or cup first for easy emptying.

26

Brush a loaf with melted butter to get a fine, evenly browned crust (also a softer one).

before measuring honey or molasses, oil spoon so they won't stick to it

CORN SYRUP: A thick, sticky liquid prepared from corn starches. Dark corn syrup has a stronger flavor than light.

MALT SYRUP: Sprouted barley and ground corn steeped in pure water, filtered and evaporated to a syrup form. It is 80 percent as sweet as honey, provides for a healthy yeast growth and gives crust a golden boost.

MOLASSES: This is made during the refining of sugar, when the cane is crushed and heated up and cooled three times. The heavier particles, with minerals, sink to the bottom of the boiling-down pot. The top layer becomes sugar, the bottom layer blackstrap molasses, very high in thiamin and niacin, calcium and potassium and is sold as crude-undiluted. It has a bitter, insistent taste that can upset the flavor of bread. There is a layer above the bottom that is a light molasses, and although still dark, the flavor is milder, sweeter. "Unsulphured" is a purer product.

Molasses gives wheat, rye and oatmeal breads their attractive deep color. Both honey and molasses have more moisture than sugar. To measure, oil spoon or cup first for easy emptying.

wooden molds from Sweden & England: pretty butter patties compliment a bread

27

FATS AND LEAN

BUTTER: Fats in general help dough or batter stretch more, encourage yeast to develop faster. They make bread tender, keep it soft with a cakier crumb.

We have chosen to use butter over margarine in this book for the simple reason that it is a natural food. Not much is used and it isn't tampered with. Margarine has the advantage of being made with polyunsaturated oils, infinitely better for our hearts, but if you read the long list of chemicals and dyes needed to make a look-alike taste-alike, perhaps you'll end up agreeing with us. If your choice is still margarine, it is interchangeable in amount with butter. We do, however, think butter gives bread a better flavor.

To measure solid fats, practice with water and a cup. For instance, to measure one-fourth cup (60 ml), fill the cup three-fourths full, then add fat until water reaches the brim of the cup. Pour off the water and fat is easily removed.

Party butter pats: Pack butter in tiny shortbread or chocolate molds, freeze; to remove, dip quickly in hot tap water and ease out with fork onto chilled plate.

LARD: It can be made at home from pork fatback, and stored in small containers in the freezer; then use as needed.

OILS: Safflower oil is almost tasteless, of light viscosity, has more polyunsaturates than soy, corn or cottonseed oils and is recommended for deep-fat frying. Peanut oil is heavier than safflower and is also recommended for deep-fat frying. Raw oils get cloudy, are heavy and smell of home (theirs); processed oils keep better but are not as good for us. Avoid rancid oils. Your nose will tell you when to grease the wheel instead of bread with it. Olive oil is too heavy for breads, except when used in Italian bread, or on pizza (which is already floating in odors).

Oiling or Greasing Pans: Thanks to a friend, we have found one great answer to the problem of breads and cakes which stubbornly refuse to leave the pan: It is the addition of lecithin (see below). We mixed a quantity and stored it in a plastic squeeze bottle so that oiling pans is a breeze and bread comes out happily and in one piece. Use one-third lecithin to two-thirds oil, or more oil if you prefer.

Clarify butter? Melt slowly, pour off clear yellow liquid and discard white residue.

28

LECITHIN (les´-a-thin) A unique fatlike substance that forms an emulsion with oil. It is used medically to lower cholesterol and to enhance absorption of vitamins A and D. It can be added to any yeast loaf: one to two teaspoons (5 to 10 ml) will give the bread a boost. It is sold as a liquid and in granular form.

SOLID VEGETABLE SHORTENING: In some instances, solid shortening is recommended for greasing casseroles and heavy pans. Otherwise, use the mixture above.

SALT

Unfortunately we all need to halt the intake of salt, but bread without it is frankly insipid and flat, so we have compromised and have used only what we thought would not deprive flavor. Too much will keep the yeast from fermenting, while omitting salt will result in a sticky rather than elastic dough, which will give a poor shape and small volume. Salt slows the proofing of yeast and must not be added until after the proofing; salt strengthens the gluten action.

Plain or iodized salt can be used interchangeably. Unrefined sea salt is a coarse grind, but with the natural iodine and minerals left in, and it has a slightly saltier taste. If it is too coarse, put it in the blender for a few seconds. We recommend that you use sea salt in your baking if possible. It is also ideal for sprinkling on top of bagels or pretzels.

SOME OF BREADS BEST FRIENDS ARE . . .

This is an invitation to breadmakers to test the stretch of their imagination. We have given ground rules for making breads, but, to use an overused phrase, "It's your choice." Add a little herb here, change the cheese there, toast the nuts. Add your personal signature to your baking, and when you hold up a beautiful loaf and announce "I made it!", you will have it made. That's the nice part about *real* bread. Blind instinct and a playfulness will develop an ongoing and passionate attachment to this simple art.

Here are some suggestions. Make your own list, *but* don't go overboard. Any addition that will affect the flavor or the texture must tease the palate, not strangle it.

CAROB: Given the choice, we use carob in place of chocolate because it has a lower fat content. It is available in powder form, in chunks, bits, granules and syrup. Three tablespoons (45 ml) powder plus two tablespoons (30 ml) milk or water are equivalent to a one-ounce square (28 g) of chocolate. Carob scorches easily. You may have to lower oven temperatures.

CEREALS AND RICE: When cooked, they add moisture and texture. Substitute for one-half cup (125 ml) of the unbleached white or whole-wheat flour in the recipe. Try crushed shredded wheat in place of wheat germ.

CHEESE: The Swiss Gruyere and Emmenthaler and the Italian Parmesan appear in our breads, but look around for others, like white sharp cheddar, feta, Muenster, etc. Grate old cheeses and store in the refrigerator; don't freeze because they will lose flavor.

CHOCOLATE: You'll find it used in dark yeast breads, and in chunks with dough wrapped around. But try a little grated into poppy-seed coffee cake or banana bread. To melt, chop solid choco-

Granulated kelp (dried seaweed) will furnish minor salt taste but also give a helping of calcium and iodine.

29

When grating cheese, be sure it is refrigerator cold.

herbs, fresh or
dried, sprinkled on dumplings
before simmering, introduce a
surprise lift

30

*Herbs are the flavored leaves
of the plant; spices are
obtained from seeds, roots,
buds, blossoms or bark.*

*Dry herbs will give out
more flavor if crushed or
rubbed between fingers or
in the palm of the hand.*

late into chunks, place in small pot and sit it in a pan of water on low heat (never melt chocolate over direct heat). Cocoa may be substituted for chocolate. Use one-fourth cup (60 ml) plus two tablespoons (30 ml) butter for each ounce (28 g) of chocolate; carob makes an even better substitute.

HERBS: There are many herbs waiting in line to give their all for bread: sage, fennel, dill, thyme, oregano, savory, chives, and parsley. However, to warn you again, *don't* overuse. Subtlety is the trick with herbs. If you're using fresh, an extra tablespoon (15 ml) will give better recognition; dry herbs are concentrated so use only one third as much as you would fresh. Also, use *less* of ground than crumbled dry.

DRIED FRUITS: Most foods shrink in baking, but dried fruits expand. Dried figs, apricots, prunes, raisins, peaches, pears and apples may double in bulk. Warm them slightly before adding to yeast doughs so they won't slow fermentation (add *after* first rising). Remember that in adding, they count as dry ingredients, and you may have to adjust the liquid quantity so bread will not be dry. Also, they can be dredged in a little of the flour before being added to quick breads to keep fruit from sinking to the bottom. They should be stored in a dark place in tightly covered containers. Dried fruits normally turn dark with age; some are treated with sulphur to hold back darkening.

Simplest way to cut fruits is with kitchen shears. Heating the blades or dipping cutting edges in warm water will take care of stickiness. Dates are 80 percent sugar; raisins are high in iron count. Golden raisins are used in white-flour dough to keep a pale look, and currants give a more elegant touch to batters. Soaking in warm water will plump raisins to more tenderness; they should be dried and floured before adding to dough. Raisins plumped in boiling water become very soft, and the soaking water can be used as part of the bread's liquid measure for more flavor.

Candied fruits, like ginger, cherries, pineapple and citron, are high in sugar, and corresponding amounts of sweetening can be adjusted down, except in the yeast coffee-cake recipes.

FRESH FRUITS: Berries—cranberries (high in ascorbic acid and vitamin C), blueberries and wild berries—all have moisture and are slightly acid, so you may need a little baking soda to neutralize. Apples are fickle in the taste department. Doctor as you go with fresh lemon juice and/or peel, cinnamon, nutmeg and butter. Some lemons are more tart than others; ornamental bush Meyer are very mild, so check to be sure of right balance. If you want just a few drops of lemon, pierce fruit with a fork and squeeze.

NUTS: Nuts are particularly compatible with quick breads and coffee cakes, both inside and outside as a topping. Walnuts, almonds, pecans and filberts are favorites, but look for some of the unusual, like pine and pistachio. Nuts in yeast breads slow the rising action, so should be added as last dry ingredient. To chop, use a nut grinder or the old wooden bowl and chopping knife; if you use a blender, add one tablespoon (15 ml) of the sugar indicated in recipe to the nuts and they won't jam in the knife blades (you do have to blend carefully or they will end up looking like bread crumbs, lose crunchiness and release oils). Once nuts are shelled they should be kept in the freezer or refrigerator to prevent oils from turning rancid. Salted peanuts can be used in breads, but decrease salt in recipe. Amusing idea: Add a pinch of curry to walnuts to pep up their flavor.

PEELS: Citrus peels are the seductive friends of bread. They capture the best in rye bread; they make loving overtures to the fillings of sweet wreathes and braids. Dried peels available in spice selections are insipid; use fresh. Grate the morning orange before you peel it, store the peel in a jar and freeze; you can continue to add and have a goodly amount in no time. We use a little tool, a citrus peeler, for removing zest in shreds that then can be quickly chopped into bits with a sharp knife.

POTATOES: Baking potatoes deliver moisture and a taste to bread that is earthy, particularly if you leave the scrubbed peel in the blended batch. New potatoes can be used, too.

SEEDS: Poppy seeds are among the oldest seasonings used in baking. Sesame is another; however, unless the sesame seeds are chopped (try the blender) the nutrients are not released. Buy untoasted and if you want that "toast flavor," do it yourself. But don't toast too much or the nutrients suffer. Sesame ground into a paste is called tahini and is available in natural-foods stores. Caraway, dill, hulled sunflower, anise, chia and flax (linseed) are

Garlic: Sprinkle salt indicated in recipe over garlic when chopping—bits will not stick to knife.

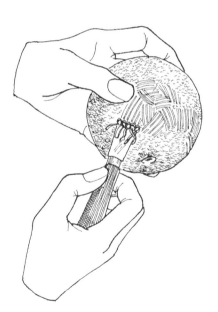

all ace-high with bread, but by pounding them or crushing with a mortar and pestle (add a cube of sugar to make the job easier), the real flavor shows up.

SPICES AND FLAVORINGS: Ground cinnamon and nutmeg are runaway winners with bread, but try an injection of ground cardamom, anise, cloves, ginger or mace for contenders. Spices age noticeably in one year, even if covered and held in dark storage. When using vanilla, look for pure vanilla extract, or use scrapings from vanilla bean: one-sixteenth teaspoon (.3 ml) equals one-fourth to one-half teaspoon (1.2 to 2.5 ml) liquid.

VEGETABLES: If you have a garden, unload the freshest, youngest carrots, zucchini and green onions into quick breads. They share flavor, color and conversation. When using zucchini, do not grate until the very last minute before blending into other ingredients because it is very high in water content. Dill and fennel are handsome plants and do well in a city garden—save some for winter breads and muffins.

Dried onion and garlic flakes can be found in supermarkets and should be on your shelf. You can sun-dry your own, or dehydrate in a convection oven.

Fresh corn is a special ingredient—high in sweetness and moisture. To remove from the ear, slit each row down the center with a sharp knife to open the kernels, then cut off the rows, working as shown in sketch. Finally, with back of knife, scrape down each cut to "milk" it.

DIETARY FIBER: One important additive needed in our lives. It is totally lacking in nutritional value and does not supply calories, but it adds bulk, or "roughage" to the diet. Bran, the hull of grains, is the best source of fiber and you'll find we use it often, in modest amounts. Some fresh foods have fiber, like pumpkin and squash; filberts (hazelnuts) have more than other nuts. Blackberries, kumquats and guava hold the honors for fruit.

Hominy grits are a form of corn invented by the Indians (hominy meant "corn without skin").

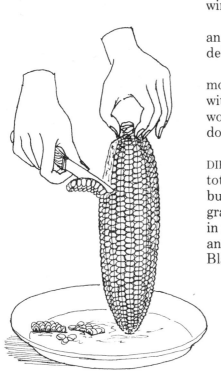

Equipment: Tools of the Trade

It does not take a dream kitchen to make a good loaf. In fact, a much-worn wooden counter, a stone bowl and wooden spoon, and a cup to measure, plus a great old wood stove to bake in spawned a bread that won first prize for an ex-Life photographer at a northwest state fair not too many years ago. Breadmaking is a simple affair. There are gadgets that make the job easier, but you can decide if they are necessary. Our lists may seem long, but they probably include things already in your kitchen.

First, particularly for yeast breads, you need a place to work. Locate a counter spot in the kitchen where there's a clear space about 24 inches (61 cm) square; 24 by 30 inches (61 by 76 cm) would be even better, so that there will be room for working, for ingredients and utensils. The other critical measurement is the height of the counter: It should be a good working height for kneading, about 34 inches (85 cm) is right for a five-foot, six-inch person, 36 to 38 inches (90 to 95 cm) for a six-footer. Mixing, beating and kneading will be strenuous efforts and you should be as comfortable as possible, not bending awkwardly or having to lift your arms chest high to stir (we like sitting on a stool with the bowl in our lap while we give a sponge what-for).

Next, a good working board. Some kitchens have a pull-out bread board. But the best investment you can make is to buy a

line up all the ingredients & tools before starting; if counter is too low, add cleats on the bottom of kneading board to raise

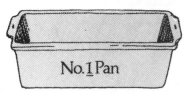

No. 1 Pan

9" x 5" x 3" (23 x 13 x 8 cm)
2 lbs. dough

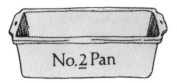

No. 2 Pan

8½" x 4½" x 2½" (21.5 x 11.5 x 6.5 cm)
1½ lbs. dough

No. 3 Pan

7½" x 3½" x 2¼" (19 x 9 x 5.7 cm)
1 lb. dough

No. 4 Pan

5½" x 3" x 2" (14 x 8 x 5 cm)
½ lb. dough

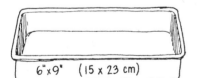

6" x 9"   (15 x 23 cm)

hardwood baker's board 20 to 24 inches (50 to 60 cm) square, one you may oil but never wash (a thorough scraping with steel scraper will clean wood acceptably). Store it when you don't need it. Wood will not chill yeast doughs as marble and tile do; the latter are essential for croissants and brioche.

Find an old pottery jar, an old cookie jar without lid or even a decorative tall tin to keep wooden spoons, spatulas, whisks, ruler, etc. at hand so you don't have to open drawers constantly with floury fingers.

That's about all you need to put together. Below are three lists: Things That Make The Job Easier; Things It Would Be Nice to Have; and the extra-lenses-for-the-camera baker, The Indulgences. Just for fun, take an inventory of your kitchen and compare. If you are missing a key item, be inventive until you want to indulge: a wine bottle makes a sturdy rolling pin; chopsticks make good fingers if there are no tongs; and a broiler wire rack becomes a good place to cool a hot loaf.

THINGS THAT MAKE THE JOB EASIER

Baking sheet
Bowl: a small one for
 proofing
Bowls for mixing (2)
Biscuit cutter
Casserole
Cheese grater
Coverings, towels
Egg beater (hand or electric)
Flour sifter
Foil/plastic wrap
Griddle
Knife, serrated edged
Mister/atomizer
Measuring cups (2 sets, one
 for wet, one for dry)

Measuring spoons
Muffin pan
Pans, 2 sizes for bread:
 #2 and #4
Pie plate, 9 inch (23 cm)
Plastic dough scraper
Potholders (hot pads)
Razor blade
Ruler
Rubber spatulas
Sieve
Square cake pan, 8 or 9
 inch (20 or 23 cm)
Squeeze bottle for oil
Timer
Wire racks
Wooden mixing spoons

THINGS IT WOULD BE NICE TO HAVE

- Baker's steel dough scraper
- Blender
- Bundt pan
- Cast-iron muffin or popover pan
- Feather applicator to add washes to dough
- French-bread pans
- Grain mill
- Heavy plaque or baking pan
- Heavy-duty mixer
- Hot tray (to keep food warm)
- Kettle for deep-frying
- Kitchen shears
- Nutmeg grater
- Pans, 4 sizes: #1, #3, 6 by 9 inch (15 by 23 cm), 9 by 13 inch (23 by 33 cm)
- Pastry blender
- Pastry brush
- Plastic book holder
- Rolling pin
- Steel or plastic graduated mixing-bowl set
- Thermometer, instant
- Thermometer, for room temp
- Thermometer, oven
- Waffle iron
- Wall scale
- Wall clock with big face

wall clock with big face

instant thermometer

goose feather pastry brush

pastry brush

rolling pin

wall scale

steel bakers scraper

kitchen shears

bundt pan

brioche pan

heavy-duty mixer

hot tray

heavy plaque or baking pan

French bread pans

35

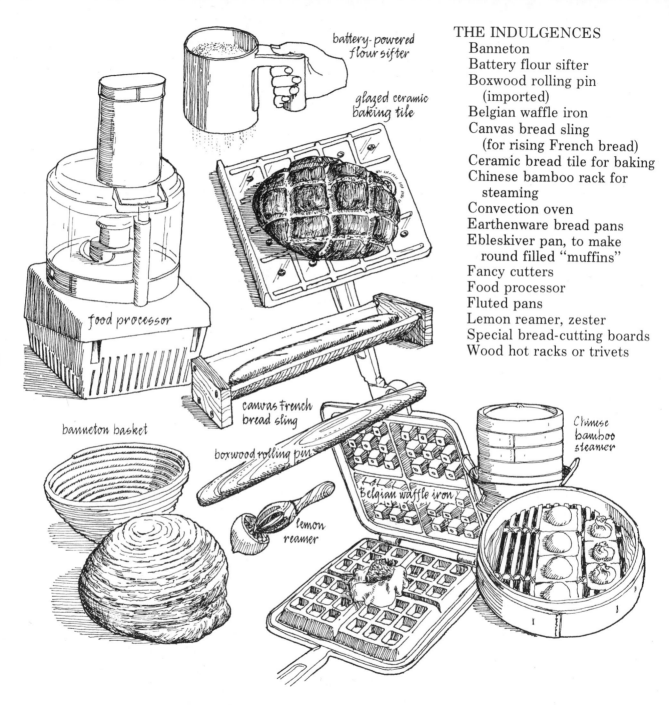

battery-powered
flour sifter

glazed ceramic
baking tile

food processor

banneton basket

canvas french
bread sling

boxwood rolling pin

lemon
reamer

Belgian waffle iron

Chinese
bamboo
steamer

MORE ABOUT THE KITCHEN ESSENTIALS

HEAVY BOWLS that retain heat are better than lightweight for making yeast breads; heating bowl with warm water before dissolving yeast speeds up action. Plastic and metal bowls do just fine for quick breads.

BREAD PANS with a medium to dark finish make a darker, firmer crust than shiny aluminum; dull metal bakes better than shiny also. A Teflon-coated pan eliminates sticking; glass pyrex pans should be used in an oven set 25°F (12.5°C) lower. Brick-oven bread pans, like cured clay flower pots, bake a crusty bread.

LARGE FLAT BAKING SHEET or cookie sheet will handle big round loaves or long ones, but a 450°F (230°C) temperature may make it buckle. If you are addicted to breads that are baked at high heat, buy an extra-heavy aluminum plaque, or cake sheet with low rolled edges (not more than 1 inch [3 cm] high).

BAKER'S SCRAPERS are ingenious third hands. The rectangular steel ones with wood handles are invaluable when you start to knead soft dough, for lifting the dough free of the board so you can sprinkle more flour under, and also for scraping "used" flour aside. Inexpensive plastic scrapers are curved to clean dough out of bowls.

ELECTRIC HAND MIXERS work well for liquids, but are not up to heavy doughs. They'll heat up after a short period if you persist, perhaps even blow a motor.

ELECTRIC BLENDERS: The blender was a post-World War II baby, designed to puree, chop, grate, mix, grind, blend, liquefy and more, in limited amounts. The sophisticated food processors are descendants of blenders and have taken over many of their jobs. But, for modest quantities, for reconstituting dry milk solids, for making bread crumbs, grinding cereals or sprouted grain, they are still invaluable. Shop carefully—there are many choices—for one which will grind millet, grate coconut or chop nuts satisfactorily.

old wood lemon reamers

Bread pans do not need to be washed after each baking. Simply wipe the tin or use a stiff, non-wire brush and soapless water. Dry in a warm oven and oil before storing.

37

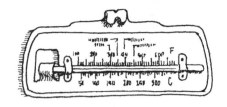

THERMOMETERS are definitely an asset in baking. The instant type, made by Taylor, tells temperature of liquids immediately so you don't cook the yeast; an oven thermometer lets you verify accuracy of controls (you have no idea how erratically stoves may operate); a room thermometer gives clues for the best place to let doughs rise.

BREAD KNIFE: The most important post-operating tool . . . you don't want to hack away at a beautiful loaf, so buy a long sharp one with serrated edge—*only* to be used for bread—and always cut against a wood board. The knife should last a lifetime.

THE BIG THREE

Large equipment, large investment, but they could make a crucial difference in *real* breadmaking and baking. . . .

electric hand mixer

electric blender

electric heavy-duty mixer

HOME GRIST MILLS OR KITCHEN MILLS: Unless you've sampled breads and cereals vitalized from freshly ground grains, your taste buds have been miserably deprived! The difference in flavor, like comparing caviar to tuna, is impossible to describe. Most of us never dream of making flour or cereals, but in the past two or three years, several compact and revolutionary electric mills have appeared, and what they do is quite enough to convert a regular breadbaker. They grind wheat, which is the hardest berry, as fine or as coarse as you want, at speeds of up to a pound a minute. They process all grains: corn, barley, soybeans, rye, millet, oats. They are compact, practical, self-cleaning *and* they preserve all the original ingredients intact—the whole bran, the germ—at cool temperatures so that vitamins are not lost, and that gluten elasticity is protected. We highly recommend Magic Mill; All-Grain is another outstanding kitchen mill. (See Sources, page 232).

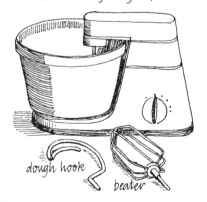

dough hook

beater

HEAVY-DUTY MIXERS: Beating and kneading yeast doughs by hand is like getting the brass ring on the analyst's couch: All your not-so-merry-go-round frustrations vanish into the dough. We highly recommend this therapy, but with a reservation: There is a critical moment of compromise when it's time to call in the heavy-duty reserves, to surrender arms to a dough hook. Mixers, such as KitchenAid, Braun, Kenwood, General Electric, Mixmaster, Oster, Rival and Bosch (the last-named is our candidate for the most efficient) are equipped with powerful motors to take over when you can't get enough steam up to beat dough the required time (and beating makes the bread, remember?). One quirk of the mixers: Too large a batch will cause the dough to "creep" up the hook. Switch to "off" and use a rubber spatula to force it down. Before you buy, check (1) size of bowl (it should take the makings of up to four loaves at a time), (2) and that there is a spatter cover, (3) a non-splash funnel for pouring liquids, and (4) a kneading hook, as well as whips for delicate action. Most mixers are designed with ingenious attachments to keep skilled trenchermen happy: shredders, slicers, juicers, grinders, pasta makers, etc.

The food processors are right in there, too, as breadmakers, but they are limited in size: Cuisinart, Sunbeam, Rival and Farberware have eager, lemming-like followers and say "Leave the beating to us." So, to repeat, look—and listen—before you invest. Ask to see the action. Is the motor quiet or noisy? Which one processes best? Is it durable? Can it be easily serviced? Is it easy to wash?

OVENS: The last major hurdle for breads to jump through. Before you start baking bread, check to see that the temperature stays just where the control indicates. This is necessary even for new ovens, for gas, electric, propane and toaster types; buy or borrow a Taylor thermometer, available at hardware stores. (See section on Baking, page 50, about using ovens.) One of the more interesting developments is the small portable *convection* oven, with built-in fan which swirls the heat evenly around food, cooking or baking uniformly on all sides. These ovens will certainly encourage more people to bake because the units take less energy than a normal oven, they bake in a shorter period at a lower temperature, they are "cool bakers" in summer and for the most part are self-cleaning. Convection ovens are designed as workmanlike counter-toppers, use ordinary house current and are

portable convection ovens… speed up baking, save energy; self-cleaning; they also broil, roast, slow-cook and dehydrate foods

39

Don't be afraid to change the temperature of an oven if the bread is getting too brown or is too pale. Some ovens can be temperamental.

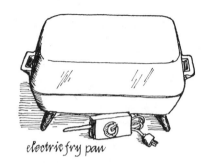

electric fry pan

single burner
hot plate

oven substitutes require experimentation to bake successfully;
always use heavy pan & cover with
steam vent, or foil pierced with fork

about one half the cost of microwave ovens (which do *not* make an acceptable loaf, although they do almost everything else except wash the dog). Convection baking has been a standard part of commercial baking for many years. Now these offspring are available for home use, a giant step for home bakers. For families with only one oven, this could mean a much more flexible entertaining schedule, too. Ovens are available at all major department stores and most kitchenware shops. Farberware's Turbo-Oven roasts, bakes and broils, is also self-cleaning and parts are dishwasherproof. The Maxim has three baking shelves, six levels for dehydrating fruits and vegetables, and an oven-ready indicator. Rival and Toastmaster also make efficient models.

No oven at all? It is possible to bake bread on top of the stove in an iron pot, a pressure cooker, a high-dome electric frying pan (follow manufacturer's directions). You can bake in a Romertopf clay casserole, according to manufacturer's instructions. You can steam bread (a crockpot will do this as well as a steaming kettle on stove top); you can make bread dough into English muffins, baking them on a griddle or over open campfire. And you can deep fry many different kinds of yeast and quick breads.

The *how* of putting a bread together, particularly if your genii is on sabbatical, is what scares the urge out of a procrastinating breadmaker facing that unnerving specter of making a botch instead of a batch.

There are several no-fail methods to bail out your hesitation, including three new ones, developed in the past 20 years, to speed up production, to meet time schedules of working bread-winners. Most recipes can be adapted to any of them. There's the Rapid-Mix plan, where the undissolved yeast is added to the dry ingredients; liquids and fats are warmed and poured over, with electric mixing doing beating. The One-Bowl method is similar, except butter or margarine is placed on top of dry ingredients and very warm tap water is added. CoolRise is a copyrighted method in which dough is mixed, kneaded and shaped in a single operation that takes about 45 minutes; loaves in pans are refrigerated up to 24 hours, and baking is done when convenient. It differs from conventional refrigerator doughs, which are chilled before shaping, then must be allowed to rise.

These shortcuts will produce a good loaf, but somehow rushing through just to get something done doesn't make sense, compared to the sensory rewards of breadmaking by the familiar

Getting Started

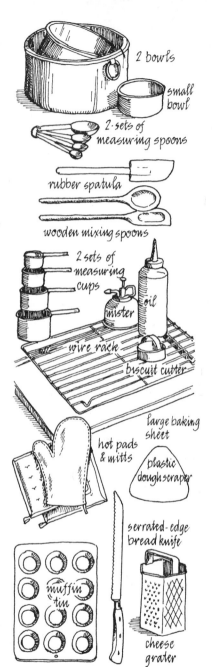

2 bowls

small bowl

2 sets of measuring spoons

rubber spatula

wooden mixing spoons

2 sets of measuring cups

mister

oil

wire rack

biscuit cutter

large baking sheet

hot pads & mitts

plastic dough scraper

serrated-edge bread knife

muffin tin

cheese grater

method. So although a few recipes in this book use them, there is no need to go into more detail here. Fleischmann's Yeast offers informational booklets (see Sources, page 232).

The sponge method, described in this section, allows you to start a sponge at night, refrigerate it and finish baking the next day. Sourdough starters are quite another way to change a bread's beginnings (see page 142). Batter breads (see page 95) are beaten, not kneaded, and make excellent quick casserole breads. And finally, there is the familiar way, which we use in most of the yeast breads in this book: Yeast is dissolved in a small quantity of lukewarm water until foamy, added to the other liquids, and then flour is beaten in.

We have tried them all, and bags and bags of flour later, we chose the method for each recipe that fits best—the simplest, safest. (We tested batches several ways, sometimes with results even a genii couldn't love.) Here are a few basics which will insure a good start.

- Reread the recipe and gather all the ingredients (room temperature) at your work area.
- Temperature of the liquid is all important. Ignore the directions and you'll end up with suffocated yeast or hardtack.
- Yeast is activated at about 50°F (10°C) and begins to die around 120°F (48°C); hot tap water is between 120° and 135°F (48° and 57°C), so be sure you use *lukewarm* if the recipe calls for water.
- We recommend active dry yeast over cake yeast; freshness is essential for any yeast, so check dates.
- Dry yeast comes to life faster if a little sweetening is added; yeast normally dissolves in 5 minutes but can stand 15.
- The first beating is the most important. Don't cut corners; continue as long as directions indicate.
- Salt inhibits yeast's first action; add it after the first vigorous beating.

THE FEARLESS WAY TO MAKE BREAD

A friend writes: "I just pulled the most elegant scones out of the oven. Charles and I had one (they're huge) with tea and there was raving from C. And would you believe, I did everything wrong. I never read recipes all the way through. I just leap. . . ."

Therein lies the anachronism of making bread. You may be a leaper, too, and things may turn out just fine. That's *real* fearless baking. But what this book offers is a bread life-insurance policy. Read and reread the directions and you can be *sure* of success every time, and you can even borrow on the policy, and share with others, whether you're a beginner or have a permanently floured thumb.

MOBILIZE INGREDIENTS   Develop a very important habit as you bake bread: Line up all the ingredients and tools you'll use. You will save steps, drawer handles won't be butter-smeared. Taking out flour and eggs that have been hibernating in the refrigerator will remind you they must be warmed to room temperature. Or heat flour in an oven at 150°F (65°C) for ten minutes or on a baking sheet set on top of a hot tray. Eggs can be bathed in hot water for five minutes to raise their temperature. Lastly, keep a sheet of plastic wrap near the phone so you can wrap it around the receiver for that inevitable call at the wrong moment.

Organize all *ingredients before starting* and *re-read the recipe so that you won't miss a step.*

43

PANS AND OVEN AT THE READY   If you're baking quick breads, oil or grease pans, cans or casseroles and set aside. Baking powder and soda breads must spurt through mixing without a moment to lose to get bread into the oven before the gases lose their ardor. Start preheating the oven before you mix anything; 15 minutes is a good average figure, to be sure the maximum temperature has been reached.

Yeast breads have a more relaxed time schedule, so you have more time to oil pans, start the oven. Unleavened and deep-fried or steamed breads have their own peculiarities, so check individual recipes.

WEIGHTS AND MEASURE   One of the better investments is to own *two* sets of measuring cups and spoons—one for dry things, one for the wet, sticky or oily ingredients (you save wash-up time, and you won't have the flour or dill sticking to a wet spoon). When

measure dry ingredients by spooning into cup & leveling with a flat edge

A cup is a volume measure, regardless of how much the contents weigh; so is a teaspoon or a tablespoon.

balance
scale

44

measuring dry ingredients, place a paper towel under the bag or container to catch overflows; dip cup or spoon into bag, level top of measure with small spatula or back of a knife. If the flour has compacted, before measuring stir with a fork to loosen particles.

When to sift flour? Only if the recipe indicates, otherwise don't, particularly with home-ground grain when you want to include all the bran and germ. (When you do sift, tilt the sifter so that leftover kernels will fall into flour mixture.)

There is a whole array of non-measurements. A *pinch* is as much as you can hold between thumb and forefinger; a *bit more* is adding enough to increase taste or enhance texture, but be careful not to add *too much.* Let your taste buds and your eye be the guide. *To taste* is adding or subtracting things like sweets and sours. *Moderation* means if one teaspoon (5 ml) of dill will barely enhance a loaf, add one and a half to two (7.5 to 10 ml) the next time, but beware of three (15 ml) if you seek a subtle fragrance.

METRIC   Turn up your nose if you will at the metric system, but it's just around the corner and inevitably must be integrated, just as we accepted change from horse-and-buggy and you'll-never-get-me-up-in-one-of-those-things thinking.

Manufacturers have flooded the kitchenware market with measuring containers for milligrams and liters; thermometers and rulers carry both kinds of measurements. The recipes in this book are carefully programmed both ways, so you may use your cups and spoons merrily from bowl to oven, but won't be caught off guard when metric is spoken. This book will still be your fearless guide to baking.

If you have an eye much sharpened by recipe reading, you'll catch some metric eccentricities. A quantity given for the same standard measurement will differ from another in the metric count. This is to adjust more critically the relationships of dry ingredients to liquid, particularly in the quick breads. For instance, three-fourths cup may be 200 ml or it may be 175 ml (actual metric is 177 ml). For yeast breads, the quantities may be more casual; for quick breads, the quantities have been very carefully computed.

Measuring in spoons and cups, translate into milliliters (ml) and liters (L)

Measuring in weights, ounces and pounds, translate into grams (g) and kilograms (kg)

Measuring in inches and feet, translate to millimeters (mm) and centimeters (cm)

Measuring in Fahrenheit temperature; translate to Celsius (C)

STIRRING UP A STORM *Stirring* is a horizontal motion, when the spoon is guided around and around the bowl. *Mixing* is almost the same, except that the spoon cuts into the batter to incorporate the ingredients. *Beating* is a combination of both, with faster action, and a little aggression-letting to get up steam. It's a great place to even scores, to think up the smart remarks you couldn't say when you wanted them. (Adrenalin adds at least five minutes to your beating arm; theory, not fact.)

When to add ingredients? One recipe may suggest that the liquids get dumped into the dry, another puts the dry into the liquid. Answer: Follow the recipe and stop worrying. Mixing a large amount of dry into wet at one time will bring on the "lump syndrome" and it's harder to get a smooth consistency. Add only the recommended amount, like one-half or one cup (125 to 250 ml) at a time. Adding liquid to dry: Make a hole in the center of the dry, pour liquid into hole and slowly stir from center to the outside, edging the flour into the liquid.

The heavier the yeast batter, the harder it is to do the necessary beating. Try stabbing the dough with the sturdy wooden spoon, lifting it up, turning it over and repeating . . . over and over. If there is no heavy-duty mixer, beat in as much flour as long as you can, then depend on kneading to do the rest.

CREAMING IT When butter and sugar are to be *creamed,* make sure the sugar is placed in the bowl first, then add the softened butter (cold butter is about as cooperative as a two-year-old boy). Use a wooden spoon with slots and blend by pressing butter into sugar against sides of bowl, turning and pressing until neither has identity and the result is a smooth, puttylike, pale-yellow mixture.

FOLDING IN *Folding* is a vertical circular motion, oh so slow as not to break any bubbles that might be in the added ingredient, like beaten egg white. The spoon or rubber spatula cuts down through the batter, pulling up on the side close to you to fold over the center.

WE KNEAD YOU This is almost the very best part of making yeast breads. It's the moment when you and your dough work

To get the last dough out of the bowl as you turn it out to knead, sprinkle some of the flour into the bowl, and with your hand, rub out the bowl clean—right into the dough to be kneaded.

45

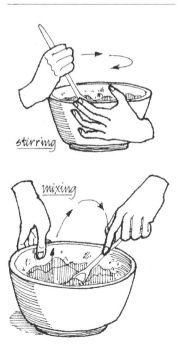

stirring

mixing

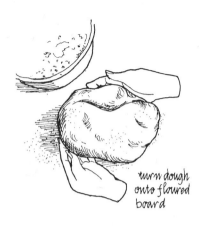

turn dough
onto floured
board

fold dough forward & push back
with heel of hands, turning dough a
quarter rotation each time repeated

several times during kneading
rub palms of hands together to
remove layers of accumulated dough
-- it can be kneaded right back in

together—your arms and hands and back tame the gluten—and then suddenly, the dough becomes smooth and elastic. The stickiness disappears and the moment of truth arrives when it is just right.

Before you start kneading, oil a bowl and have it ready to receive the kneaded dough.

The mystery of kneading is simply to strengthen the gluten in the flour. It lets the cells stretch to form a kind of honeycomb that will hold the gas and that makes a lighter bread. When the bread rises, the gas expands, and the stronger the gluten, the finer the loaf. Kneading is relaxing. Let the kids try; make it a family celebration. Motions may be jerky until everyone gets the hang of it, but by the end you'll all be wanting to start another batch, right now. Rhythm is what you strive for.

The height of the work area is critical to endurance. A good guide is that the counter be level with your wrist as you stand next to it. If it's too high or too low, you're not going to get that mind-emptying feeling of warmth and an even pattern of movement that makes kneading therapeutic.

When the dough is turned onto the board that has been dredged, or strewn, with flour, dip both hands into flour; keep a small bowl handy nearby for adding "as needed." That's a phrase you'll read over and over in yeast recipes. It depends on the stickiness of the dough, on humidity, on the amount of moisture in the flour used, the weather outside, and maybe your own annoyance at the high price of lobster. The stickier the dough, the more flour it seems to need. If the dough flattens slightly when you stop kneading, it probably needs more, but if you find yourself fighting to get the dough to fold over as you knead, it has too much, a common problem with beginners. Try misting with an atomizer filled with lukewarm water and slowly knead in more water.

If the dough is very soft when turned onto the floured board, a baker's scraper is the tool to have at hand. Use it to scrape under the dough to add more flour, and to knead it in until you can take over with fingers. The scraper is pulled up and cuts into the soft dough, turning it also. Use this handy gadget if dough sticks to the board during kneading to free it and add more flour underneath. Also, it scrapes away flour when you don't want to incorporate any more.

During this kneading, even with flour on your hands, the dough will sometimes begin to build layers on the heel of the hand. Stop and rub hands together. Little rolls of dough will fall on top of the dough mass and can be kneaded right back in.

The Motion of Kneading: Each baker has a personal style of kneading, but it is basically a pushing-shoving-folding-turning action, as shown in the sketches, repeated over and over like a mantra. If loose flour seems to drift all over, ignore it. We all go through that in the beginning. Even experienced bakers throw a little flour around! With a heavy-duty mixer, the turning-shoving, etc. is done with the dough hook, which slaps the dough against the side of the bowl.

use steel baker's scraper to work more flour into soft doughs; scrape up & into center of dough

There is another action from which the dough benefits: During kneading, if you must stop to rest a complaining shoulder or elbow, take a few deep breaths. Then, pick up the dough, lift it 8 to 12 inches (20 to 30 cm) above the board and slam it down hard. Do this two or three times. It helps redistribute the gas cells. Then, back to the rhythm again.

If you are interrupted by the telephone or by the door bell, place a towel or the oiled bowl over the dough until you can get back to it. A five-minute break won't hurt. In fact, the dough seems easier to manage when it has had a rest period.

place ball of dough in oiled bowl; turn over & cover with plastic wrap & a clean tea towel

Finally, knowing the moment of *enough* kneading is elusive, and like learning to ride a bike the first time, filled with bumps and uncertainties. The more you bake, the surer you'll be. The dough should be smooth, still slightly pliable and as soft as a baby's bottom. It will bounce back when you push into it; in white bread little blisters will appear just under the skin and sometimes you can hear a little squeak of bubbles letting go. One more test: If you can slap the dough with your hand, hold it there for a few seconds and have it come up clean, the job is done. Then it's ready to rise up. The first action of yeast and liquid is called "proofing" (the English "prove" their yeast); the first rising comes after the kneading, or for batter breads, after the heavy beating. Sponges have a first rising after the addition of about half of the flour.

47

The dough should be formed into a ball and then placed smooth side down to oil it (the bowl was oiled and ready, remember?); then the dough is turned smooth side up. This oiling prevents a "skin" of hardened dough from forming on top that would keep the dough from expanding.

test risen dough by pressing 2 fingers into it; if depressions stay it is ready to be punched down

Cover the bowl with plastic wrap to keep the moisture in the bowl, then cover with a clean tea towel and set the dough in a warm place, 70° to 85°F (21° to 29°C). Be sure the dough is out of

punching down

pull dough from edges to center after punching down

48

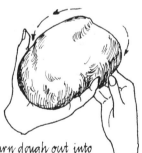

turn dough out into your hand & continue folding under with fingers of other hand; pinch the bottom to seal & place directly into oiled pan, or form as shown in following sketches

drafts, a prime enemy. Too much warmth will force yeast, or even kill it. Usual room-temperature rising takes much longer, one and a half to two hours; rising overnight in the refrigerator will take eight to twelve hours.

WARMTH Where is there a warm place? Check the kitchen with a thermometer. You may find the pilot light of a gas oven will furnish adequate temperature. Preheating an electric oven for five minutes at lowest temperature will keep it warm for a long time. Check with oven thermometer to be sure it isn't too warm. Remember, each time you open the oven door to check you lose heat. A large cake pan filled with very hot water and set on the bottom of a cold oven will give warmth and moisture. If you have a hot tray or warming tray, set a cake pan upside down on the tray, place a folded hand or bath towel on top, then the dough bowl, leaving the tray heat on low. Or fill a sink half full of hot water and rest the dough on a wire rack set across the sink top.

The next hour is yours—to catch up on old magazines, change the canary's reading material or brush the dog.

The dough must rise until it is about double its original bulk. One test is to press two fingers into the dough, and if the depressions stay, it is ready. Over-rising can cause bread to fall later in the oven, or make it coarse and dry. If you've had an emergency and the dough has risen too high, take it back to the floured board and knead it again for three to five minutes, then repeat the rising process.

There is no exact time for rising, nor for kneading, so don't let the timing worry you. A little one side or the other won't ruin a loaf.

PUNCH DUTY Now for the fun: Take your fist and punch down the center of the dough as if you meant it—like sticking a pin in an obstreperous kid's balloon! Pull the dough from the edges over toward the center, and turn the dough out into your hand, continuing to fold it under with your fingers. There are some bakers who advocate slamming the dough down onto the board again at this point to achieve more "punching down," and if it makes you feel good, try it. For breads that rise again before shaping, do this slamming before the second rising. Just a good punching down and brief kneading and back into the oiled bowl to repeat the first rising. This second rising will be faster.

SHAPING UP   After punching down, divide the dough with floured knife or baker's scraper into the number of loaves or shapes you are making. If two, divide evenly in half, and let rest, covered with a bowl or tea towel, for ten minutes. The resting period will make the dough easier to form.

While you are waiting, oil the bread pans. Check the recipe to be sure the amount of dough fits the pans. This is the moment when a good weighing scale comes in handy: Weigh the amount of dough in the piece, and check with the information on page 34 for the pan size. The formed loaf should fill the pan about two thirds full. Less will make a flat loaf; too much dough and it may rise too high in the oven, spread over the sides and collapse in the center. If the unrisen loaf fills more than two thirds of the pan, find a larger size.

Breadmakers have as many ways of forming loaves as there are breads. The simplest is to first form one of the pieces into a ball. Some flatten the ball with a rolling pin, others pat it with the flat part of the hand until it is a rough rectangle slightly longer than the length of the pan. Starting with the long edge farthest from you, roll forward into a sausage, and seal the edge by pinching it the full length. Then tuck the ends under and pinch them to seal. Use as little flour as possible when doing this. Place the roll in the pan, smooth side up. Don't worry if seams show on baked bread as long as they are on the bottom.

Another method for forming loaves is to roll and stretch the dough until it is twice as long as the pan and fold as shown in the sketch. The pinched edges must always be on the bottom.

Forming a loaf or rolls that will be baked on a flat sheet or plaque is done in the same way. You can end up with a round, an oval or a skinny baguette, depending on how your hands manage the dough. A symmetrical loaf is more appealing than one with bulges, squeezed hour-glass middle or double chins, so use care in shaping. If you are feeling playful and want to make an alligator or a braided wreath, this is the moment. See the sketches on ideas for bread shapes throughout the book.

Don't play with bread too long. The yeast may get tired or the dough chilled. (The first time we tried braiding five ropes we ended up 20 minutes later with something a little fatter and about as acceptable as a manila hawser!) Three-rope braided

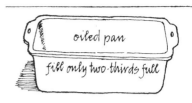

oiled pan

fill only two-thirds full

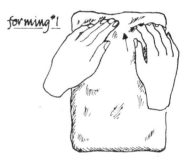

forming #1

press dough into a rectangle about 1" thick and slightly wider than pan

49

roll firmly, pressing down with hands, to force out air pockets & streaks

pinch seam to close roll & tuck under ends & pinch, place in oiled pan, seam side down

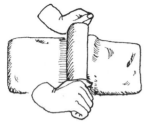

forming #2

roll until twice as long as pan

fold over from each end to the middle; roll tightly as before

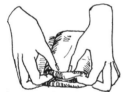

pinch seams & tuck ends under

egg wash

50

breads (see how-to sketch, page 134) are pretty, not difficult and particularly adaptable to egg breads. A braid made of wheat and white doughs, or one made with ropes that have been filled, puts the bread in a party mood. If the loaf is to have cornmeal on the bottom, sprinkle or sift it over the pan before placing the bread on it. Once the forming is done, cover with tea towel (no plastic) and let rise again in a warm place until almost double in size, or if bread is in a pan, until the center of the loaf is about a half inch (1.5 cm) above the lip of pan.

TOPPINGS   Some breads are brushed with a wash before the final rising, others just before they are about to go into the oven. Check each recipe for instructions. Slashing with a razor or sharp knife, or nicking with the tips of scissors, may also be done before or after the last rising. Slashing has a purpose: It allows expansion, which is what sometimes causes breads to crack on the sides.

While the final rising is doing its thing, preheat the oven for at least 15 minutes before the baking starts.

Once the dough has risen, it's time to add topping (or repeat wash if done earlier). An egg wash will make the bread brown faster and it will also act as an adhesive to hold seeds or grain flakes. An egg white wash gives a shine, milk gives a softer crust, and water makes it harder, chewier. If you don't want to bother with a "wash," it won't hurt the bread. We like to think of it as a last-minute makeup to give the loaf a company "look."

BAKE OFF   The bread can go right in the preheated oven, on the center rack. However, we've done considerable experimenting with starting bread in a cold oven, which gives it an added period of rising until the temperature reaches 140°F (60°C) when the yeast is killed, and found it most practical. One warning: If your electric oven is an older model and preheating is accomplished with *both* bottom and top elements, this won't work.

Resist the temptation to be an oven voyeur in the first 15 minutes. Every time you open the door, it loses heat. After that, the bread will have stopped rising. If your nose tells you it is browning too fast, cover the loaves with a sheet of foil. (A brushing of butter later will soften a hard, brown crust.)

TESTING AND COOLING When is a yeast loaf done? (Convection ovens bake in a shorter period than that indicated in the recipe, so check manufacturers' instructions.) The classic test is to knock your knuckles or snap your middle finger against the hot crust, and if it sounds hollow, it can be removed from the oven. Turn the loaf out onto your hand (protected with oven mitt or towel) and tap the bottom; if it doesn't have the same hollow sound, place the loaf back in the oven without pan for another five to seven minutes. If you have baked in a baguette or flat pan, do the same thing.

When the loaf is finally done, place it right side up on a wire rack to cool. This is the moment to brush with melted butter for a softer crust, or a glaze to make it pretty. Covering with a cloth will also soften crusts, so do not cover if you want a crispy one.

Quick breads and coffee cakes are tested with a cake tester or toothpick. If it comes out clean, the bread is done. Also, the bread will pull away from the sides of the pan when it is done. These breads are better left in their pans for 10 to 15 minutes before being turned out and set right side up on the wire rack to cool.

"IS IT READY?" Yeast breads must wait longer than quick ones to cut, even if it is pure torture to wait, to withstand the fragrance. The texture will be better when breads have cooled at least two hours. But we *have* cut—with a very sharp, serrated knife—within 20 minutes. Testing, you know. . . .

THE SPONGE METHOD

"I can never bake bread—I work full time!" Could we make a suggestion? *Sponge* may be the time stretcher you've overlooked. This method may never make you a million as a bakery franchiser, but it certainly puts breadmaking on your regular list. It will fit into almost anyone's time because the bread goes together in stages. None of its needs are screaming at you. A few moments lost here and there won't ruin a batch. And a sponge can be a short method, ready in as little as 30 minutes, or it can wait all night for you. (One exception to the overnight rising: heavy breads with multigrains.)

For instance you start a sponge at night, before the late news. Next morning, it will be doubled in bulk and foamy. You

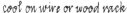
testing

tap with knuckles against crust: if it sounds hollow it can come out of the pan

turn loaf onto oven mitt or towel to protect hand; if bottom does not sound hollow, continue baking, without pan, for 5-7 min. longer

cool on wire or wood rack

51

quick-bread testing

On a clear, windless day, set the yeast bread out in the sunshine to rise; place it on a stool or chair, out of reach of small four-footed visitors.

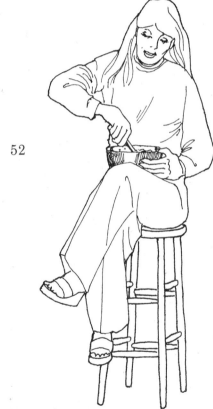

the success of the sponge depends on the thorough first 3 minute beating

add the other ingredients and the rest of the flour before breakfast while the coffee is slowly going through the filter; cover the dough and finish eating. Remove the cloth, dump the dough onto a floured board and knead 8 to 10 minutes; shape into loaves, put in pans, oil the top, cover with damp cloth and slip back into the refrigerator. When you finish your workday, bring the loaves out to warmth to finish rising, at least 15 minutes. Start them in a cold oven set for temperature suggested (they'll do some more rising while the oven warms) and your bread is a-borning.

If loaves have been formed at night and refrigerated, they can be baked before you leave in the morning. Sometimes bread will be sneaky and rise too high: Remove from pans, punch down the dough, reshape and let rise again. Too much rising will cause large holes and the bread may be crumbly when cut. It may even collapse.

MAKING A SPONGE The sponge method was the only safe way to make breads in the old days because yeasts were erratic. If nothing happened during proofing, it was tossed out. Flour was too precious to take a chance. Milk, scalded to eliminate vagrant bacteria, was the prime liquid because it made a richer bread than water. (Today's milks have been heat-treated so scalding is not necessary. If you feel you want to do it, go right ahead; warming gives you a quick way to melt butter and sugar.) Bread baked the sponge method is lighter textured and has a coarser grain than the familiar way.

The formula for making a sponge is usually one measure of liquid (105° to 115°F or 42° to 46°C) plus yeast (one tablespoon or 15 ml active dry yeast for each two loaves) and two measures of flour. First, the yeast is dissolved in the total amount of liquid, with all of the sweetening, like honey, for the yeast to feed on. Then part of the flour is added to make a soft, batterlike dough Now comes the important beating. The success of a sponge dough depends on thorough beating for at least three minutes, or 250 to 300 strokes by hand, to get the bubbling started. Then the bowl is covered and the sponge is allowed to ferment. If you are going to use it immediately, set it in a warm place to develop for at least 15 to 30 minutes. Refrigerating overnight allows it more time to work slowly. The sponge will be spongy (you guessed!), and about double in bulk; the longer it waits, the more you add to flavor and texture. Gluten is formed when the sponge stretches, so you don't have to knead as long, and flour mixes in more easily.

Do not stir or beat the sponge vigorously at this stage, or cut through it with a spoon, since a cutting motion disturbs elasticity. Press down in the center, and with a rubber spatula, work from the sides, pulling the dough up and into the center. Add the rest of the ingredients except flour, and continue upward folding. Sprinkle remaining flour over the top a cup (250 ml) at a time, continuing to turn wet mixture over dry and rotating the bowl with your free hand. When dough is heavy and leaves sides of bowl, it's ready for kneading, and from that point proceed as with all yeast breads.

always date & label breads that are to be frozen

OPERATION DEEP REFRIGERATOR

The refrigerator is The-Friend-by-the-Side-of-the-Road to yeast, to flour, to unbaked and baked breads, to bread crumbs, nuts and cheese. Baked yeast breads can store in the freezer for up to six months; quick breads store well, but for shorter periods because of the added fruits and nuts.

Freezing in glass can be dangerous—you must leave one-inch (2.5 cm) head space between food and top to allow for expansion.

53

We don't recommend freezing unbaked breads, just because it seems a shame to spoil the pleasant, orderly process of finishing what you start. But there are times when an emergency surfaces in the middle of a baking session and there is no other answer but to save the dough by freezing. If you can finish the kneading, you've passed the critical point.

UNBAKED BREAD DOUGH made of white, whole-wheat or dark flours should be well oiled and then placed in a freezer bag and sealed. It will keep up to four months; if it is enriched with eggs or fat, use it within two months. To thaw, take from the freezer and leave at room temperature for six to seven hours; remove to an oiled bowl, let rise, shape and let rise again. The yeast loses some of its effect the longer it is frozen. If you are deliberately planning to freeze the dough, add 50 percent more yeast when you start, to compensate.

gadget for slicing two thin slices from one

Dough can be frozen right after forming the loaves and bedding them down in their pans, too. They will start to rise slightly, so cover with plastic wrap and quick-freeze. Then remove them from the freezer and rewrap tightly in heavy freezer foil and return to the freezer immediately. If you are going to bake free forms, place the dough on sheets, again cover with plastic wrap and quick-freeze. Repeat the above, but take the breads off the sheets, wrap each separately in foil and dash them back into the freezer.

When you are ready to bake formed doughs, allow six to seven hours at room temperature for thawing (place them on oiled sheets or in forms when removing from the freezer and removing wrappers). Allow to rise until almost double in size, then bake as directed. For small rolls, allow two and a half hours from freezer to oven time.

Wrapping for freezing: Heavy foil or airtight freezer bags are best. Eliminate as much air as possible.

Special note: Always date and label breads going cold so you'll know what recipe you used.

BAKED BREAD, with thin crust, will freeze for up to six months when wrapped and sealed; allow four hours thawing time at room temperature.

CRUSTY BREADS, like French, should be eaten within 48 hours from the oven or they will dry out. It is possible to keep them in the freezer up to a week, but the crust will then begin to flake off.

SOFT YEAST ROLLS, baked, will freeze up to four months, can be thawed at room temperature and reheated. Crisp rolls do not freeze as well.

RICH YEAST COFFEE CAKES AND PIZZA, baked, will freeze up to three months. Do not put icings or glazes on coffee cakes before freezing; add after thawing.

FLAT AND UNLEAVENED BREADS, baked, can be frozen in plastic bags for easy access (take out one or a few at a time) and will keep up to three months.

QUICK BREADS AND COFFEE CAKES, baked and wrapped in freezer foil, will keep up to six months, and take about three hours to thaw at room temperature.

One of the neat advantages of the freezer is for the single person who cannot use a whole loaf of bread or package of muffins before they stale. Slice bread before freezing so that one

In hot weather, freeze sliced breads or rolls and muffins to avoid mold; wrap in foil or plastic so air cannot reach.

54

Heavy-weight aluminum foil is best for wrapping bread for freezing; either shiny or dull side out is fine.

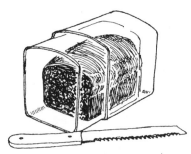

acrylic bread box expands from 7½" to 12¼"

or two slices can be taken out at a time and thawed in the toaster.

Using the refrigerator (not freezer) for overnight rising of sponges is explained in The Sponge Method section.

YOUR ALTITUDE
HAS A LOT TO DO WITH BAKING

If you live in Denver (5,280 feet), Santa Fe (6,947 feet), Monument (7,400 feet) or even Salt Lake City (4,354 feet), baking bread can present problems. Flour may be drier and doughs may require more liquid to reach the proper relationship. Some cakelike breads need very little adjustment—reduce the sugar content by three tablespoons (45 ml) per cup—but most quick breads with modest sugar will need a slight increase in liquid so they will not be dry. You will need to experiment to discover what are the best adjustments for you and your altitude.

The quirk of nature you deal with is the lower atmospheric pressure due to the thinner blanket of air above. That decreased pressure is the number one problem. It affects the baking because the leavening gases expand more, and the climate of high-altitude areas is drier.

With yeast breads, the fermentation is faster and breads may rise too fast, so they must be closely watched. Experts recommend letting them rise a second time to help develop better flavor rather than changing the yeast content. Baking-powder biscuits bake without problems, but an additional tablespoon (15 ml) of flour for each cup (250 ml) indicated seems to improve their texture.

ABOUT FLOUR: At elevations of 3,500 feet, increase flour by 1 tablespoon (15 ml) for each cup (250 ml); 5,000 to 6,000 feet, increase by 2 tablespoons (30 ml); 6,500 to 8,000 feet, increase by 3 tablespoons (45 ml). Fluff up flour with a fork before measuring.

ABOUT BAKING POWDER AND SODA: At elevations of 3,000 feet, reduce by 1/8 teaspoon (.8 ml) for each teaspoon (5 ml); at 5,000 feet, reduce by 1/8 to 1/4 teaspoon (.8 ml to 1.2 ml); at 7,000 to 8,000 feet, reduce by 1/4 teaspoon (1.2 ml). Measure *carefully*.

Sourdough breads bake just as well at high altitudes as at sea level.

55

Make potholders out of old soft terry towels; use a double thickness and bind edges with bias tape. Make big ones!

ABOUT SUGAR: At elevations of 3,000 feet, reduce by 1 tablespoon (15 ml) for each cup (250 ml); at 5,000 feet, reduce by 2 tablespoons (30 ml); for 7,000 to 8,000 feet, reduce 1 to 3 tablespoons (15 to 45 ml).

ABOUT LIQUIDS: At elevations of 3,000 feet, increase liquids by 1 to 2 tablespoons (15 to 30 ml) for each cup (250 ml); at 5,000 feet, increase 2 to 4 tablespoons (30 to 60 ml); at 7,000 to 8,000 feet, increase 3 to 4 tablespoons (45 to 60 ml).

ABOUT BAKING: Oven temperatures must be increased by 25°F (12.5°C) because the baking action will speed up the rising and cells will be "set" faster to keep the bread from rising too much in the oven.

ABOUT SOURDOUGH BREADS: Use the same changes suggested for yeast breadmaking and baking.

SPROUTING IS GOOD INFLATION

When does one tablespoon (15 ml) equal one quart (1 L)? When you put grains or seeds and moisture together in a quart jar and add a few days. You'll end up with a jar *filled* with crisp, fresh, living sprouts! The sprouted results will also give an extra bonus: up to ten times the amount of vitamins (A, B, C and E), and proteins as the dry seed.

First, buy the grains or seeds. They're available in natural-foods stores in cities and at farm-supply stores in small towns. Ask for fresh lots, and when you get them home, store them in tightly sealed glass containers. The glass containers are attractive, you can see what you have, and this is a good way to keep the bugs out. A quarter pound (125 g) of each grain or seed is a good way to start.

Hard-wheat kernels sprout better than soft, in two to four days. Rye is tough and should be taken from the jar before the leaves form. Lentils, sunflower and soy sprout well (raw soy sprouts taste like young peas, but when cooked have a nutty flavor). Start with four to six tablespoons (60 to 90 ml) grain, or one tablespoon (15 ml) of small seeds.

There is a sprouting jar made by the Appleseed people in Colorado (see Sources, page 232), or you can make your own by

sprouting: keep jar on its side

rinse with fresh water 3-4 times daily; drain off water thoroughly & place on side again taking a clean canning jar and fitting the mouth with a square of cheesecloth held in place by the ring.

The theory is to soften the seeds or grains by soaking them, then keeping them moist. The kernels should be rinsed, then soaked overnight in two cups (500 ml) of water. Then the water is poured off and the jar is drained by inverting. The contents must be rinsed with fresh water three or four times a day to stave off mold, and drained thoroughly each time so they are lightly moist but not wet. The cheesecloth lets in air; a tightly closed jar left too long will burst the glass, so mind your Cs, Bs, As, and Es.

Keep the jar in the dark for the first two days, then bring it into the light to encourage greening of the tiny sprouts, but not direct sunlight until the last two hours. The sprouting time depends on the grain or seed and the temperature. As soon as the kernels have burst and little greenies start popping out you know they're ready.

"WHAT DID I DO WRONG?"

There's bound to be a day (we've *all* had them), particularly in the beginning when you are feeling your way through the flours, that disaster strikes and the sad, handicapped loaf cooling on its wire rack definitely is not a sleeping beauty. "What did I do wrong?" Maybe you did not do something right, but also, it may not be your fault at all. One thing is sure: There will always be a hungry kid who loves homemade bread and could care less that it isn't "purty."

Don't let one bread infirmity cool your spirit. The next batch could be a winner. If your anguish is doubled because you promised to give the loaf for a special occasion, whip up a quick bread—you can do it in less than 90 minutes—and no one will know the difference, unless you let the catastrophe out of the bag.

Look over our list of the kinds of things that can upset a yeast bread. Keep these in mind and you may skirt disaster—indefinitely.

Poor insulation in an oven can make bread bake unevenly; rotate loaves during baking to gain even browning.

58

Using unbleached white flour when shaping yeast loaves means the crust will be smooth and not gritty.

YEAST BREAD PROBLEMS

● *Why didn't the dough rise?* The yeast may be too old, and the other ingredients too cold. Was there a window open nearby to cause a draft?

● *Your pan is not the size recommended?* Don't overload a small pan but make more loaves, remembering not to fill any pan more than two thirds full. A loaf can be baked in a free form on a sheet, but will expand sideways as well as up.

● *Is the crust too pale?* The temperature in the oven was too low, or the pan was not placed in the middle of the oven so the heat could circulate. Maybe there wasn't enough sugar for the yeast to feed on in the beginning (sugar makes crusts golden brown).

● *Do slices break up and is the bread crumbly?* Too much liquid for the amount of flour or insufficient kneading.

● *Big holes in the loaf?* Too much yeast, inadequate punching down between risings or needs more salt. Holes are an asset in French bread, so don't complain.

● *Thick crust with air space underneath?* Moisture was trapped under the crust and turned crust hard when loaf cooled, leaving space. Or the dough did not rise enough.

● *The loaf is smaller than I expected.* Flour may have been too soft; too much salt was added; not enough rising time; oven not warm enough or pan too large. Heavy whole grains do not make big fluffy loaves.

● *Is the loaf higher on one side than the other?* That's the oven's fault. Next time rotate the pan during baking.

● *Did the loaf crack on one side?* Don't let it bother you. The bread has to expand, and once the crust is formed, this is the only outlet for expansion. It does not harm the bread. Slashing top before baking with a razor or knife allows even expansion.

● *Are the bottom and sides of the loaf pale?* Put the loaf back in the oven, without its pan, for another five to ten minutes.

● *Is the loaf denser at the bottom?* Oven was probably too hot on the bottom and it baked too quickly (Don't throw the loaf away; just cut a longitudinal slice off the bottom.)

● *Free-form loaves flatten out too much?* Not enough flour.

● *Does a slice of the bread sag, is it soggy?* Too much liquid, not enough kneading, or needs more baking time. Whole grains take longer baking than unbleached white breads.

● *Strong, yeasty flavor?* Too much yeast for the amount of flour or you let the dough rise too long.

● *Lumps in the dough?* Not enough mixing or kneading; too much flour, or ingredients like dry milk added without blending with flour.

● *Emergencies?* If you only have time to let the bread rise once, it will bake okay, but with coarser texture. The more times the dough rises, the finer the bread (though *too* much rising will tire the yeast).

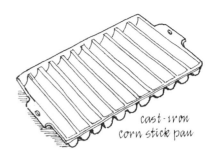

cast-iron corn stick pan

QUICK BREAD PROBLEMS

● *Does high altitude affect baking of quick coffee cake?* Yes, use less baking powder or soda.

● *Do I always have to bake in a loaf pan?* No, try fruit-juice cans but check the baking time. Use a cake tester to be sure they're done before removing from the oven.

● *Why does my bread always crack?* This is a characteristic of quick breads—a way for the gases and steam to escape as the crust bakes rapidly.

● *Why are the muffins tough?* Too much beating. This also is the reason for tunnels in muffins.

● *What makes muffins uneven?* A small peak in the center is the result of an oven that is too slow; non-symmetrical tops are caused by too much heat.

● *Biscuits do not have a perfect round shape?* Always dust the cutter with flour and do not twist it or you will distort the shape.

● *Lumps in the dough?* Not properly mixed.

Dark pans bake a darker bread; however, they should be used only in moderate ovens to avoid burning bottom.

59

Yeast Breads

WHITE BREADS
WHOLE-WHEAT BREADS
RYE BREADS
OTHER YEAST BREADS
BATTER BREADS
ROLLS & SMALL BREADS
CROISSANTS & BRIOCHE
FILLED BREADS
SWEET BREADS

Good guys wear white hats. Everyone knows that. Now, you take bread. All through the history of baking, from early days in Rome and Egypt, white was the bread voted most likely to succeed. It was a sign of social standing because machinery to grind grain was still a gleam in Socrates' eye, and what little grain was available was pounded by slave hands and sifted through fine linen. Only the rich could have that bread and eat it, too. In the Middle Ages, the boys up in the big castle demanded white, and millers mixed chalk dust and alum into the flour to keep them happy. Rogue bakers profited by adulterating with bean meal, slaked lime and bone ash (!), often to the detriment of their heads.

Measured by the fine mess of impurities in the name of white bread, perhaps the enrichments added now to a bought loaf are not so half-baked. Commercial and packaged flours are usually processed by bleaching to turn on the bright white and thereby robbed of all the goodies. Chemists load back essential vitamins and minerals, the "enrichments" on the package, plus additives that will artificially keep bread alive longer. White bread today is status quo for the poor as well as for the well bred.

61

French banneton, a coiled reed basket, used in final rising; beehive impression remains when dough is turned onto buttered & floured sheet & baked; holds 1½ pounds of dough

62

When measuring flour, do not tap the cup to settle the flour. It tends to distort and compress.

Even good guys stumble, however. With all of today's know-how, the packaged loaf on your grocer's shelf, the squeezin' soft white bread, wins hands up over all other breads, yet its spineless texture leaks jelly, and it is a damp sponge minutes after mayonnaise makes contact. Given two slices and pot roast in between, and the thumb-pressure prints let you read right through to the mustard. And as to flavor—*what* flavor?

Clearly, it's time to leave the squeezing to others and start making breads that any good guy will head back to the ranch for—or take over the kitchen and make by himself. These are breads with firm but tender body, breads so good they never last long enough to need preservative, delivering fragrance to sigh over. Have *you* ever tasted bread made with potato, skin and all, in it? That's flavor and fragrance which can be addictive. Who said: "They don't make traditions like they used to?"

And how do you achieve this beautiful nose-tickling loaf? You start by using *unbleached* white flour, by trusting a simple, straightforward recipe, and by practice. And patience. There's nothing to be afraid of, really. Each of these recipes was tested at least three times, one, five times. Even old hands have off days. Breads can vary from batch to batch, depending on the temperature, the humidity, even one's attitude. Our challenge is to make breadbaking comfortable, like Mother making cocoa on a cold night, or propping your elbows on the table.

Bread is only flour, water and yeast, and a little other stuff—all the freshest you can buy—and time. Of course, there are those rules that are in the Getting Started section. Read them through again if this is The First Time. Just remember: Everything at room temperature to start, every ingredient lined up next to your bread board (so you don't leave out the salt or have to send across the street for a clean measuring cup). When the bowl is at the ready, read the recipe once more before starting.

Relax. Everyone says it once: "Oh, I had flour everywhere!" The first batch may not be what you expect, but don't apologize. Just say "I made it this morning," and bask in the squeals of rapture over that first slice.

WHITE BREAD
WITH VARIATIONS

Makes One Large Loaf

1 tablespoon (15 ml) active dry
   yeast
1/3 cup (75 ml) lukewarm water
3 tablespoons (45 ml) honey
3 tablespoons (45 ml) butter, cut
   in bits
1/2 cup (125 ml) milk, scalded
1/2 cup (125 ml) cold water
1/3 cup (75 ml) non-instant
   nonfat dry milk
2 tablespoons (30 ml) soy flour
3-1/4 cups (750 ml) unbleached
   white flour, or as needed
2 teaspoons (10 ml) salt

Sprinkle yeast over lukewarm
water, stir to dissolve and let
stand until foamy. Stir honey and
butter into milk until dissolved
and melted. Stir in cold water
and cool to lukewarm. Add
proofed yeast. Sift dry milk and
soy flour with 1-1/2 cups (350
ml) of the unbleached white
flour. Stir into yeast mixture
and beat vigorously about 3
minutes until air bubbles form.
Gradually beat in remaining
flour and salt to form a stiff
dough. Turn out onto floured
board and knead, adding additional flour as needed, 5 minutes or until smooth and pliable.
Form into smooth ball, place in
oiled bowl, turn to coat all
surfaces, cover with tea towel
and let rise in warm place 1
hour and 15 minutes or until
double in bulk. Punch down,
turn out onto board and knead
briefly.

Form into loaf and place in
oiled #1 loaf pan, cover with
tea towel and let rise in warm
place 1 hour, or until almost
double in size. Bake in oven
preheated to 350°F (180°C) 35
minutes or until bread tests
done. Turn out onto wire rack,
turn right side up and cool.

CORNMEAL-PARSLEY Add with
salt 2/3 cup (150 ml) yellow
cornmeal and 3 tablespoons
(45 ml) finely minced fresh parsley.
Reduce flour measure by 2/3 cup
(150 ml). Allow extra time for
rising.

SAGE-ONION Add with salt 6
tablespoons (90 ml) finely minced
onion and 2 teaspoons (10 ml)
crumbled dried sage. Allow extra
time for rising.

WHEAT GERM Add with salt 6
tablespoons (90 ml) untoasted
wheat germ.

OATMEAL Bring the 1/2 cup
(125 ml) cold water to boil and
pour over 2/3 cup (150 ml)
unprocessed rolled oats. Decrease
flour in 3-minute beating by 1/2
cup (125 ml). After 5-minute
kneading, lightly oil board and
hands and continue kneading, 3
minutes more. Allow extra time
for rising.

*If you are kneading a sticky
dough, use one hand. Keep
the other one free for adding flour or answering the
phone.*

oiled pan
fill only two-thirds full

roll firmly, pressing down with
hands, to force out air pockets
& streaks

POTATO WHITE BREAD

Here's a happy bread with "an attachment a la Plato for a bashful potato," as Mr. Sullivan's friend Sir Gilbert explained. Toast a slice and you'll hum all morning and wish you'd opted for two. This is good earthy bread, full of nourishing comfort. Try it for sandwiches. It makes the dull one-bread habit easy to break.

Makes Two Medium Loaves
12 to 14 ounces (450 to 500 g)
   baking potatoes
3 tablespoons (45 ml) firmly
   packed brown sugar
1 tablespoon (15 ml) active dry
   yeast
4-1/2 cups (1 L) unbleached
   white flour, or as needed
3 tablespoons (45 ml) butter,
   melted and cooled
2 teaspoons salt
1/4 teaspoon (1.2 ml) ground
   ginger (optional)

Scrub potatoes, slice and boil in water to cover until soft. Place the potatoes and cooking water in blender container and add water to bring measure to 3 cups (700 ml); puree and transfer to large bowl. Stir in brown sugar and cool to lukewarm. Sprinkle yeast over, stir to dissolve and let rest at room temperature 45 minutes. Stir in 1-1/2 cups (350 ml) of the flour and beat vigorously about 3 minutes until air bubbles form. Stir in butter and salt, beat well and gradually add 1-1/2 cups (350 ml) of the remaining flour. Let rest at room temperature 45 minutes. Mound remaining flour on board, turn dough out and, using a steel baker's scraper, knead in the flour until dough is stiff enough to knead by hand. Adding additional flour as needed to prevent sticking, knead 3 to 5 minutes. Dough will be soft and slightly sticky. Divide into 2 equal portions, knead briefly, form into 2 loaves and place in 2 oiled #2 loaf pans. Cover with tea towel and let rise in a warm place 45 minutes or until almost double in size. Place in oven, turn heat to 350°F (180°C) and bake 45

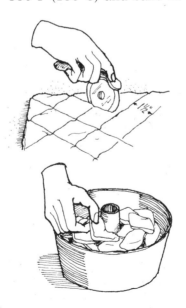

minutes or until bread tests done. Turn out onto wire rack, turn right side up and cool.

POTATO EGG BREAD After first 45-minute rest, stir in 1 or 2 lightly beaten, room-temperature eggs. Increase flour measure as needed. Shape half the dough into a loaf and shape the remaining half into rolls. Let the rolls rise only 20 to 25 minutes and bake according to recipe directions.

SESAME OR POPPY-SEED POTATO BREAD Beat in with butter and salt 1/2 cup (125 ml) sesame or poppy seeds, or to taste.

DRIED CURRANT-POTATO BREAD Beat in with butter and salt 2/3 cup (150 ml) dried currants.

MONKEY OR PULL-APART BREAD After kneading, form into smooth ball, place in bowl, cover with plastic wrap and chill 30 minutes. Pat and roll out into a rectangle approximately 3/4 inch (2 cm) thick. Cut into diamonds 3 inches (8 cm) long, dip each diamond in melted butter and arrange in overlapping pattern in buttered Bundt or other large ring pan. Let rise 45 minutes and bake 55 minutes. To test for doneness, carefully turn upside down onto a large plate as you would a mold. Tap bottom, and if not baked enough, return to pan to bake longer.

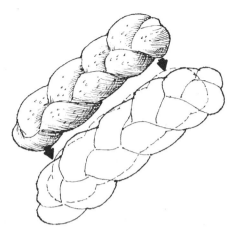

EGG BREAD

Historically, the braid is symbolic of a ladder to heaven, and *challah,* the mellow yellow bread of the Jewish Sabbath, is always braided. (A pinch of saffron will give this *challah*like egg bread a deeper yellow.) Bakers for centuries have made these huge, soft loaves with intricate twistings—four, five, even six strands of dough woven expertly. Braiding four strands, let alone more, is like sorting wires in a telephone junction box, so we suggest a simple three-rope. You can also impress with a spectacular braid-on-braid loaf (see sketch) and add ten to fifteen minutes extra baking time. This magnificent loaf will be heavenly tender with a shiny dark brown crown.

Makes One or Two Loaves

2 tablespoons (30 ml) active dry yeast
1/2 cup (125 ml) lukewarm water
1 tablespoon (15 ml) granulated sugar
6 tablespoons (90 ml) butter, cut in bits
1 cup (250 ml) milk, scalded
3 eggs, at room temperature
1 teaspoon (5 ml) milk
4-1/4 cups (1 L) unbleached white flour, or as needed
1/2 tablespoon (7.5 ml) salt
1 teaspoon (5 ml) malt powder (optional)
2 tablespoons (30 ml) sesame seeds

Sprinkle yeast over water, stir in sugar and let stand until foamy. Stir butter into 1 cup (250 ml) scalded milk to melt and cool to lukewarm. In large bowl, beat eggs lightly; remove 1 tablespoon (15 ml), beat with the 1 teaspoon (5 ml) milk and set aside. To remaining eggs, add proofed yeast and milk mixture. Blend well and stir in 2 cups (500 ml) of the flour. Beat vigorously about 3 minutes until air bubbles form. Sprinkle salt and malt powder over, blend well and gradually beat in 1-1/2 cups (350 ml) of remaining flour. Sprinkle board with 1/4 cup (60 ml) flour and knead, adding additional flour only as needed to prevent sticking, 10 minutes or until smooth

and pliable. Form into smooth ball, place in oiled bowl, turn to coat all surfaces, cover with tea towel and let rise in warm place 1 hour and 10 minutes, or until double in bulk. Punch down, knead briefly and divide into 2 equal portions. Cover with tea towel and let rest 10 minutes. Working with 1 portion at a time and keeping other portion covered with the towel, divide into 3 equal portions. With hands, roll each portion into a smooth, even rope approximately 13 inches (33 cm) long. Butter a large baking sheet and make a three-strand braid on half of the sheet, pinching ends of braid together and tucking them in. (See braid instructions on page 134.) Repeat with second portion of dough. Cover with waxed paper and lightly dampened tea towel and let rise in warm place 35 to 45 minutes or until half again as large. Beat reserved egg and milk again and carefully and evenly brush over braids. With paper toweling, remove any excess glaze from baking sheet so bread will not stick. Sprinkle braids evenly with sesame seeds and bake in oven preheated to 375°F (190°C) 35 minutes or until bread tests done. Braids will be quite brown on top. Transfer to wire rack and cool.

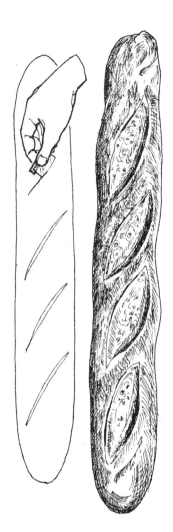

Spread thin baguette slices with mixture of butter, Parmesan and Bovril; dry in oven and store for serving with soups.

FRENCH BREAD

It's maddening, but *real* French bread eludes home bakers. Americans don't have the same flour, the same yeast, the wood-fired brick ovens. After many false starts, we've found a superb imposter that promises a craggy crust, a pungent crumb that blend into a thoroughly seductive scent. We found, too, that the secret ingredient is beating. So, rev up your tennis muscles (or latch on to a left-end tackle), because you'll have to give ten minutes of your most active beating to the dough, and eight to ten minutes of enthusiastic kneading. The first beating is important to provide airy texture, so don't cut corners. The long rising lets it expand lazily, so don't hurry it; the slower the rising, the finer the texture. The steam in the oven while baking is the other "must," because it insures "French crust."

If you bake free-form loaves, they need more flour to hold their shape and not flatten out. When baking is completed, remove the bread from the pans or sheet and return it to the oven for five to ten minutes more to strengthen and brown the bottom crust.

Another don't: Don't let the six hours it takes from scratch to success scare you from trying (you can get in a set of tennis while it's rising). Also, it's possible to bake bread in stages over 24 hours; check the section on making a sponge, page 51. This will produce a more typical loaf with holes.

P.S. French wives don't bake. They leave it all to the *boulanger.* You can leave the work to the electric mixer in case your beating arm is in distraction; we've included the easy directions.

Never seal French bread in plastic or anything that inhibits air movement. A brown bag is best, and to reheat, sprinkle bag or bread with water, and place in a 400°F (210°C) oven for 10 minutes.

Makes Two Large Loaves
2 tablespoons (30 ml) active
  dry yeast
2-1/2 cups (600 ml) lukewarm
  water
6 cups (1.4 L) unbleached
  white flour, or as needed
2 teaspoons (10 ml) salt
Yellow cornmeal
Egg White Wash, page 222

In bowl of heavy-duty mixer with dough hook or in a large mixing bowl, sprinkle yeast over water, stir to dissolve and let stand until foamy.

MACHINE METHOD Stir 3 cups (700 ml) of the flour into proofed yeast. Beat on dough hook setting 10 minutes. Sprinkle in salt, beat in, and then gradually add as much of the remaining flour as needed for dough to clean sides of bowl. Continue beating 5 minutes, turn out onto board, knead by hand briefly and form into a smooth ball.

HAND METHOD Stir 3 cups (700 ml) of the flour into proofed yeast. Beat until smooth and continue beating vigorously a full 10 minutes. Beat in salt and as much of the remaining flour as possible. Turn out onto board and, adding additional flour only as needed to prevent sticking, knead 8 to 10 minutes, occasionally throwing dough onto board (see general instructions for kneading). Form into smooth ball.

RISING Place ball in large lightly oiled or floured bowl. Sprinkle top lightly with flour, cover with plastic wrap and let rise at room temperature at least 2 hours or until treble in bulk. Punch down, knead 3 to 5 minutes, cover with plastic wrap and let rise at room temperature 1-1/2 to 2 hours or until treble in bulk. Punch down, knead briefly and divide into 2 equal portions. Cover with tea towel and let rest 5 to 10 minutes. Grease 1 very large baking pan or 2 medium pans and sprinkle evenly with cornmeal. Form each dough portion into shape of choice, place on baking sheet or sheets, cover with tea towel and let rise at room temperature 45 minutes or until double in size.

BAKING Twenty minutes before baking, place a large shallow pan on lowest shelf of oven; turn oven heat to 450°F (230°C) for 15 minutes. Pour 1 to 2 cups (250 to 500 ml) cool water into heated pan to produce steam. With razor, make slashes on risen bread according to shape and carefully and evenly brush bread with Egg White Wash. When oven has heated for 20 minutes, place bread on second from bottom rack in oven and bake 15 minutes without opening oven door. Then remove shallow pan from oven and mist loaves with water. Bake, misting several times, another 20 minutes or until top is brown. Remove from pans or sheet and return to oven until bottom has browned. Transfer to wire rack and cool.

67

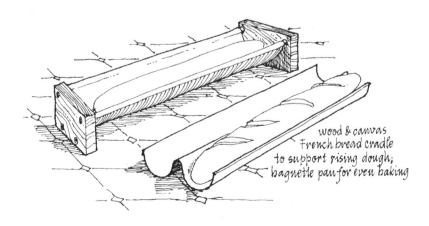

wood & canvas
French bread cradle
to support rising dough;
baguette pan for even baking

As we said earlier, white bread once stood for social distinction, snobbery and scalawags who profited by adulterating the flour and producing bread that looked like it had many uses, not including being eaten as food. Now, it's a matter of nutrition and the roles are reversing. Whole-wheat flour, *real* stone-ground or micronized flour, has all the germ (rich in Vitamin E, fat and enzymes), bran (the shell or husk that furnishes Vitamin B_1, roughage, to keep you regular) and proteins. The bread made from it is honest and rough hewn, and no one can stop at the first warm slice. It has flavor never found in a loaf of white and as mother says, it's *good* for you.

There are a few things to put into your computer before you work with whole wheat. Because it should be stored in the refrigerator or freezer, always warm the flour to room temperature before using. Stone-ground flour has natural oils that tend to turn rancid in a warm storage spot. Package it in glass or plastic containers, not metal. Don't sift before measuring—just stir with a fork; flour at the bottom of a container tends to pack. You'll find in kneading tweedy whole-wheat dough that it's slightly abrasive and more resistant than white flour. There will be times when you use more or less flour than the directions indicate: relax and do what comes naturally. Breadmaking success depends on time of year, temperature, temperament of the baker, even the altitude of your kitchen . . . and it depends on a healthy curiosity.

Whole Wheat Breads

68

roll up dough into tight cylinder, pressing down to keep out air pockets. Moisten ends & pinch closed; tuck in ends

BASIC WHOLE-WHEAT BREAD

This is the loaf that always goes first at the church bake sale, or flies a blue ribbon at the county fair. It is a beginner's no-fail bread with a lot going for it: four delectable flavors (maybe you can invent another), including the framework whole-wheat loaf and one with millet, one with cinnamon and, a tempting currant. The early beating required for some breads is not part of this recipe, just the kneading. You'll find that the wheat dough will be more resistant and elastic than white. It's that gluten at work. But once you get in the swing of using your body as well as your arms, the kneading part becomes the best therapy for frayed-at-the-edges days; you'll feel good and the bread will be superior.

Makes Two Large Loaves

3 cups (700 ml) whole-wheat flour
3-1/2 cups (825 ml) unbleached white flour, or as needed
1/3 cup (75 ml) honey
5 tablespoons (75 ml) butter, cut in bits
2 teaspoons (10 ml) liquid lecithin (optional)
2 tablespoons (30 ml) active dry yeast
1/2 tablespoon (7.5 ml) salt
2-1/2 cups (600 ml) hot water (120°F (48°C))

In large bowl, combine and stir together whole-wheat flour, 3 cups (700 ml) of the unbleached flour, honey, butter, lecithin, yeast and salt. Blend well. Gradually stir in hot water until dough is uniformly mixed. The butter will have melted and dough will be slightly sticky. Turn out on board floured with 1/2 cup (125 ml) unbleached white flour and knead 5 to 10 minutes, adding additional unbleached flour as needed to prevent sticking. Dough will be pliable and smooth and when formed into a ball will relax on the board. Form into smooth ball. Place in oiled bowl, turn to coat all surfaces, cover with tea towel and let rise in warm place 1 hour or until double in bulk. Punch down and knead on lightly floured board 5 minutes using approximately 2 more tablespoons (30 ml) un-

bleached flour. Dough will be almost the same consistency it was before rising. Form into 2 loaves and place in 2 buttered or oiled #1 loaf pans. Cover with tea towel and let rise in warm place 45 minutes or until almost double in size. Bake in oven preheated to 350°F (180°C) 30 minutes or until bread tests done. Turn out onto rack, turn right side up and cool.

MILLET WHOLE-WHEAT BREAD
Add to flour mixture before adding water 1/2 to 3/4 cup (125 to 175 ml) millet. Dough may take a little longer to rise.

CINNAMON WHOLE-WHEAT BREAD
Prepare dough as directed in basic recipe through first rising, then form as shown in sketch. Brush with honey, sprinkle with brown sugar, ground cinnamon, ground nutmeg and freshly grated orange peel. Roll up as shown in sketch, place in loaf pans and let rise until almost double in size. (Loaves may take longer to rise in pans.) Bake as directed in basic recipe.

CURRANT WHOLE-WHEAT BREAD
Roll out as directed in Cinnamon-Whole-Wheat Bread, above. Brush with honey, sprinkle with brown sugar and ground cardamom, strew dried currants over and roll up. Proceed as directed above.

QUICK WHOLE-WHEAT BREAD

Throughout this book, we've advocated the hand-mix, hand-knead methods because they give you a true feeling of making bread. This basic whole wheat is a rare—and important—exception. It's mixed entirely in a heavy-duty mixer, using whole-wheat flour that we ground fresh in a home milling machine (this aids the one-rising process). It's a quick yeast bread and it's adaptable: Try adding two tablespoons (30 ml) sunflower seeds, flax seeds, sesame seeds or untoasted wheat germ. The dough hook does all the work; you rest your arm this time.

Makes Two Medium Loaves
1-1/2 tablespoons (22.5 ml) active dry yeast
1/2 cup (125 ml) lukewarm water
2-1/4 cups (525 ml) hot water (120°F or 48°C)
1/2 cup (125 ml) unprocessed rolled oats or unprocessed bran
1/4 cup (60 ml) safflower oil
1/4 cup (60 ml) malt syrup, honey or molasses
6-1/2 cups (1.5 L) freshly ground whole-wheat flour, or as needed
2 tablespoons (30 ml) non-instant nonfat dry milk
2 tablespoons (30 ml) sesame seeds
1/2 cup (125 ml) pure gluten flour
1 tablespoon (15 ml) salt
2 teaspoons (10 ml) liquid lecithin (optional)

Sprinkle yeast over lukewarm water, stir to dissolve and let stand until foamy. Measure hot water into large mixing bowl of heavy-duty mixer and stir in oats. Add oil, malt syrup, 3 cups (700 ml) of the whole-wheat flour, dry milk, sesame seeds, gluten flour, salt and lecithin and proofed yeast. Mix with dough hook until blended and gradually add remaining whole-wheat flour until dough cleans sides of bowl. Beat 10 minutes, remove to lightly oiled board and form into a smooth ball. Divide into 2 equal portions and form into loaves. Place in 2 oiled #2 loaf pans. Cover and let rise in a warm place 30 minutes or until almost double in size. Turn oven heat to 350°F (180°C) and bake 40 minutes or until bread tests done. Turn out onto rack, turn right side up and cool.

NOTE Gluten flour may be omitted, but loaves will not rise as high; add additional whole-wheat flour to compensate.

SUNFLOWER WHOLE-WHEAT BREAD

Don't have time to bake? Get out your pocket computer and let's see how much time it takes to make a really superior bread: Mix the first ingredients, then go do something for 45 minutes (set the timer). Come back, add more flour, salt and oil, and finish what you went off and started in the next 30 minutes. Add the rest of the flour, knead 3 minutes, cover and let rise for 40 minutes. That adds up to almost two hours of *not* making bread, but spending time changing beds, clipping recipes out of old issues of *Gourmet* or washing the dog. The 45 minutes when it's baking, make a cup of tea, prop your feet up and abandon yourself to that oven fragrance. *Of course* you can find time to bake.

Makes Two Large Loaves
2 tablespoons (30 ml) active
   dry yeast
1/2 cup (125 ml) lukewarm
   water
1/3 cup (75 ml) molasses
1 can (5.33 ounces or 158 ml)
   evaporated milk
2 eggs, at room temperature
6 cups (1.4 L) whole-wheat
   flour, or as needed
1/3 cup (75 ml) safflower oil
2 teaspoons (10 ml) salt
1/2 cup (125 ml) sunflower
   seeds

In large bowl, sprinkle yeast over lukewarm water, stir to dissolve and let stand until foamy. With whisk, beat in molasses. Add water to evaporated milk to measure 1-3/4 cups (425 ml) and stir into yeast mixture with eggs; whisk until frothy. Beat in 2 cups (500 ml) of the flour and let stand at room temperature 45 minutes. Add oil, salt and 3 more cups (700 ml) of the flour. Beat well and let rest 30 minutes. Stir in sunflower seeds. Mound remaining flour on board, turn dough out and knead flour in. Knead, adding additional flour only as needed to prevent sticking, 3 minutes. Form into 2 loaves and place in 2 oiled #1 loaf pans. Cover with tea towel and let rise in warm place 40 minutes or until almost double in size. Place in oven, turn oven heat to 350°F (180°C)

and bake 45 minutes or until bread tests done. Turn out onto wire rack, turn right side up and cool.

WHOLE-WHEAT POTATO BREAD

Toast a dark slice and spread with unsweetened pleasure. You'll never find this one in any bakery, and it's a boon for the groggy dawn patrol in the kitchen looking for hearty sandwich makings for school boxes. The procedure for making departs from the usual: First, the dough gets two 45-minute rest periods; then, just before kneading, the last cup of flour is dumped on the board, a well is made in the center and the dough is set in it. With baker's scraper, the flour is folded into the dough, over and over, until stickiness lessens. This again illustrates that there are many ways to handle yeast and baking free-hand is never boring.

Makes Two Large Loaves
1 medium baking potato
1/4 cup (60 ml) molasses or
   malt syrup
1 tablespoon (15 ml) active
   dry yeast
2 teaspoons (10 ml) salt
1 tablespoon (15 ml) olive oil
2 teaspoons (10 ml) liquid
   lecithin (optional)
1 cup (250 ml) unbleached
   white flour
5 cups (1.2 L) whole-wheat
   flour, or as needed

Scrub potato, slice and boil in water to cover until soft. Place the potato and cooking liquid in blender container and add water to measure 3 cups (700 ml); puree and transfer to large bowl. Cool to lukewarm and stir in molasses and yeast. Let rest at room temperature 45 minutes. Add salt, oil, lecithin, unbleached white flour and 4 cups (1 L) of the whole-wheat flour. Beat well and let rest 45 minutes. Mound remaining whole-wheat flour on board and turn dough out. Knead in flour and, adding additional flour to prevent sticking, knead 3 more minutes. Divide into 2 equal portions, form into 2 loaves and place in 2 oiled #1 loaf pans. Cover with tea towel and let rise in warm place 45 minutes or until almost double in size. Place in oven, turn heat to 350°F (180°C) and bake 45 minutes or until bread tests done. Turn out onto wire rack, turn right side up and cool.

dividing dough

FARM POTATO BREAD

Potatoes (skin and all), honey, bacon, garlic, caraway, oregano, wheat germ and stone-ground whole wheat—*much* too good to be hidden down on the farm! This bread will leave a permanent impression on city folk. Try it for a block party, a picnic before the game starts, or take a loaf, some sweet butter, hot bouillon and a basket of fruit the next time you spend a lazy afternoon floating over the countryside in a balloon.

Makes One Large Loaf
1/2 pound (225 g) baking
  potatoes
2/3 cup (150 ml) water
1 tablespoon (15 ml) active dry
  yeast
1 tablespoon (15 ml) honey
Evaporated milk
2 tablespoons (30 ml) butter,
  cut in bits

1 cup (250 ml) whole-wheat
  flour
1 egg, at room temperature
10 to 12 slices bacon, crisply
  cooked and crumbled
1 small onion, minced
1 garlic clove, minced
1/2 tablespoon (7.5 ml)
  caraway seeds
1/4 to 1/2 teaspoon (1.2 to
  2.5 ml) salt
1/2 teaspoon (2.5 ml) crumbled
  dried oregano
3 tablespoons (45 ml) un-
  toasted wheat germ
2 cups (500 ml) unbleached
  white flour, or as needed

Scrub potatoes, slice, and boil in the water until soft. Measure 1/4 cup (60 ml) of the potato water, reserving remainder, into a large bowl. Cool to lukewarm, sprinkle yeast over, stir in honey and let stand until foamy. Transfer potato and remaining water to blender, add evaporated milk to measure 1-3/4 cups (400 ml), add butter and puree. Cool to lukewarm and stir into proofed yeast with whole-wheat flour. Beat vigorously about 3 minutes until air bubbles form. Cover with tea towel and let rest at room temperature 30 minutes. Beat egg lightly and stir into sponge with bacon, onion, garlic, caraway seeds, salt, oregano, wheat germ and 1-1/2 cups (350 ml) of the unbleached white flour. Mix well and turn out onto board floured with remaining white flour. Knead flour in and, adding additional flour as needed to prevent excessive sticking, knead 5 minutes. Onions will make dough slightly sticky. Form into smooth ball, place in oiled bowl, turn to coat all surfaces, cover with tea towel and let rise in warm place 45 minutes or until double in bulk. Punch down, turn out onto floured board and knead briefly.

Form into smooth, slightly flattened ball and place in 2-quart (2 L) souffle dish or other straight-sided baking dish that has been greased with bacon drippings and/or butter. Place in oven, turn heat to 350°F (180°C) and bake 45 to 50 minutes or until bread tests done. If top is browning too fast, loosely cover with foil. Turn out onto wire rack, turn right side up and cool.

WHEAT BERRY BREAD

Trying to decide which wheat bread to put together first is like ordering Chinese food for six, family style. If you're the daring type, try wheat berry with raisins, a forthright dark loaf with crunchiness, good body and long life, just like the fortune cookie said. The berry, or seed, is the wholest wheat there is, a hard kernel to crack, but with all the vitamins waiting to be shared. Look to your natural-foods or grain store for a supply.

Makes Two Medium Loaves
1/2 cup (125 ml) wheat berries
3/4 cup (175 ml) boiling water
1/2 cup (125 ml) raisins
1/2 cup (125 ml) milk, scalded
2 tablespoons (30 ml) active
   dry yeast
1/3 cup (75 ml) malt syrup
3 tablespoons (45 ml) safflower
   or corn oil
1/2 tablespoon (7.5 ml) salt
1/2 tablespoon (7.5 ml) liquid
   lecithin (optional)
1/2 cup (125 ml) barley flour,
   lightly toasted
1/3 cup (75 ml) untoasted
   wheat germ
2 cups (500 ml) whole-wheat
   flour
2 cups (500 ml) unbleached
   white flour, or as needed

Soak wheat berries in cold water to cover overnight. Bring to boil, lower heat and cook, covered, adding more water as needed, 1-1/2 to 2 hours or until berries are soft but still firm. Remove lid and let water boil away; cool to lukewarm and set aside. Pour boiling water over raisins and let stand 10 minutes. Drain, set raisins aside and measure raisin water to make 1/2 cup (125 ml). Add to milk, cool to lukewarm and sprinkle yeast over. Stir to dissolve and let stand until foamy. In large bowl, combine proofed yeast, malt syrup, oil, salt and lecithin. Mix well and stir in barley flour, wheat germ and whole-wheat flour. Beat vigorously about 3 minutes until air bubbles form. Stir in berries and unbleached white flour; if dough is too difficult to stir, knead in the flour. Dough will be heavy. Turn out onto floured board and knead 8 minutes, adding additional flour as needed to prevent sticking and scraping

board often. Lightly oil hands and board; continue kneading 3 more minutes. Form into a smooth ball, place in oiled bowl, turn to coat all surfaces, cover with tea towel and let rise in warm place 2 hours or until almost double in bulk. Punch down, turn out onto floured board and knead 3 to 4 minutes. Form into 2 loaves and place in 2 oiled #2 loaf pans. Cover with tea towel and let rise 1-1/2 to 2 hours or until almost double in size. Bake in oven preheated to 350°F (180°C) 35 minutes or until bread tests done. Turn out onto wire rack, turn right side up and cool.

73

Bread is not *fattening when part of a well-balanced diet.*

VOLLKORNEN BREAD

A chewy coarse bread, made with the best protein parts of the wheat and yet chastened by the addition of cottage cheese, so that it makes delicious cinnamon toast for tea break as well as being the perfect accomplice for cheese, sliced onions and beer. It can be sliced very thin and keeps for days in the refrigerator if wrapped in plastic.

Makes Three Small Loaves
2 cups (500 ml) strong beef broth
1/3 cup (75 ml) wheat berries
2 tablespoons (30 ml) active dry yeast
1/2 tablespoon (7.5 ml) salt
1 tablespoon (15 ml) safflower oil
1 cup (250 ml) low-fat, small-curd cottage cheese, at room temperature
2/3 cup (150 ml) instant nonfat dry milk
4 cups (1 L) stone-ground whole-wheat flour
1 cup (250 ml) unbleached white flour, or as needed

Heat broth to simmer, remove from heat and stir in wheat berries. Cover and let stand overnight or at least 12 hours. Next day, drain berries, reserving liquid, and set aside. Warm the broth to lukewarm, sprinkle yeast over it, stir to dissolve and let stand until foamy. Place in warmed large ceramic or glass mixing bowl; add salt, oil, cheese, dry milk, 3 cups (700 ml) of the whole-wheat flour and reserved wheat berries. Beat well and add remaining whole-wheat flour and enough unbleached white flour to make a firm dough. Turn out onto floured board and knead, adding additional unbleached flour only as needed to prevent sticking, 8 minutes. If dough is still sticky after 5 minutes, lightly oil board and hands and finish kneading. Dough should be smooth and pliable. Form into smooth ball, place in oiled bowl, turn to coat all surfaces, cover with tea towel and let rise in warm place 1 hour or until double in bulk. Punch down and let rise another hour or until double in bulk. Punch down, divide into 3 equal portions, cover with tea towel and let rest 10 minutes. Form each portion into a loaf and place in 3 well-greased #3 loaf pans. Cover with tea towel and let rise in warm place 1 hour or until almost double in size. Bake in oven preheated to 375°F (190°C) 40 minutes or until bread tests done. Turn out onto wire rack, turn right side up and cool.

Heating a sharp knife before cutting very fresh bread will make it work better.

CARROT-POPPY SEED WHEAT BREAD

Carrots add a whole new dimension to bread. They impart moisture and color you don't expect, and married up with the wheat, a new taste sensation. The poppy seeds and raisins change the texture from that of basic whole-wheat bread, and their flavor is more evident when you make toast out of this healthy loaf.

If you decide the vigorous three-minute beating is more than your muscles bargained for and you opt for the food processor, add the carrot-raisin-poppy seed mixture just before you turn the dough onto the board to knead. The blades tend to pulverize those three, and will rob the slices of their identity.

Makes Two Large Loaves

1 cup (250 ml) hot water (120°F or 48°C)
1 cup (250 ml) grated carrots
2/3 cup (150 ml) raisins or pitted dates, coarsely chopped
2/3 cup (150 ml) poppy seeds
1-1/2 tablespoons (22.5 ml) active dry yeast
1/3 cup (75 ml) lukewarm water
5 tablespoons (75 ml) butter, cut in bits
1 cup (250 ml) milk, scalded
1/2 cup (125 ml) honey
5-1/2 cups (1.3 L) whole-wheat flour
2 teaspoons (10 ml) salt
1/2 cup (125 ml) unbleached white flour, or as needed

Pour hot water over carrots, raisins and poppy seeds. Stir and let stand 10 minutes. In large bowl, sprinkle yeast over lukewarm water, stir to dissolve and let stand until foamy. Stir butter into milk to melt; cool to lukewarm. Add to proofed yeast with honey and 3 cups (700 ml) of the whole-wheat flour. Beat vigorously about 3 minutes until air bubbles form. Stir in salt, carrot mixture and remaining whole-wheat flour. Mound unbleached white flour on board, turn dough out and knead in flour. Adding additional unbleached flour as needed to prevent excessive sticking, knead 3 minutes. Lightly oil hands and board and continue kneading 3 minutes. Cover with tea towel and let rest 10 to 15 minutes. Knead briefly, form into smooth ball, place in oiled bowl, turn to coat all surfaces, cover with tea towel and let rise in warm place 1 hour and 20 minutes or until double in bulk. Punch down, knead briefly and divide into 2 equal portions. Form each portion into a loaf, place in 2 oiled #1 loaf pans, cover with tea towel and let rise in warm place 50 minutes or until almost double in size. Place in oven, turn heat to 350°F (180°C) and bake 45 minutes or until bread tests done. Turn out onto wire rack, turn right side up and cool.

CHIA-CARROT WHEAT BREAD

Chia seeds are cousins once removed from the herb sage, and are available at natural-foods stores. They do nice things to bread, and like pumpkin seeds, have a goodly amount of Vitamin B_1 (thiamin) to share. Add carrots, buttermilk and whole-wheat flour and you have a loaf that smells heavenly and makes promises to taste divine.

Makes One Large Loaf
1 tablespoon (15 ml) active
    dry yeast
1/4 cup (60 ml) lukewarm
    water
1 cup (250 ml) buttermilk
2 tablespoons (30 ml) butter,
    cut in bits
1/3 cup (75 ml) molasses
2 cups (500 ml) whole-wheat
    flour
2 tablespoons (30 ml) chia
    seeds
1 teaspoon (5 ml) salt
2/3 cup (175 ml) grated carrrots
1/4 cup (60 ml) unsalted
    pumpkin seeds
1-1/4 cups (275 ml) unbleached
    white flour, or as needed

In large bowl, sprinkle yeast over water, stir to dissolve and let stand until foamy. Heat together buttermilk and butter, stirring to melt butter. Add molasses, cool to lukewarm and stir into proofed yeast with whole-wheat flour. Beat vigorously about 3 minutes until air bubbles form. Stir in chia seeds, salt, carrot, pumpkin seeds and 1 cup (250 ml) of the unbleached white flour. Mound remaining unbleached flour on board, turn dough out and knead in flour. Adding additional unbleached flour as needed to prevent sticking, knead 3 minutes. Lightly oil hands and board and continue kneading 3 minutes. Dough will be smooth but still slightly sticky. Form into smooth ball, place in oiled bowl, turn to coat all surfaces, cover with tea towel and let rise in warm place 1 hour or until double in bulk. Punch down, knead briefly and form into a loaf. Place in an oiled #1 loaf pan, cover with tea towel and let rise in warm place 45 minutes or until almost double in size. Place in oven, turn heat to 350°F (180°C) and bake 40 minutes or until bread tests done. Turn out onto wire rack, turn right side up and cool.

for the live-alone baker: shape dough into 2 balls & place side by side in pan. Eat one, freeze the other half

BRAN BREAD

In England during the Middle Ages there were White Bakers and Brown Bakers. The latter made black loaves for the poor, mainly of bran, which is the shell, or husk, of the wheat berry (the white part went to the White Bakers). Bran cannot be digested alone (but it *did* strengthen the teeth and develope digestive tracts of cast iron). We've taken bran, mixed it with whole-wheat and white flours, and enhanced it with nuts and flecks of orange peel.

Makes One Large Loaf
1-1/2 cups (350 ml) unpro-
    cessed bran
1-3/4 cups (400 ml) whole-
    wheat flour
1-1/2 cups (350 ml) unbleached
    white flour, or as needed
1 teaspoon (5 ml) salt
1/2 teaspoon (2.5 ml) ground
    ginger (optional)
2 teaspoons (10 ml) freshly
    grated orange peel
4 tablespoons (60 ml) butter,
    cut in bits
2 tablespoons (30 ml) honey
3/4 cup (175 ml) milk, scalded
1/2 cup (125 ml) hot water
    (120°F or 48°C)
1 tablespoon (15 ml) active
    dry yeast
1 egg, at room temperature
    and lightly beaten

2/3 cup (150 ml) chopped
  walnuts, pecans or filberts
  (optional)

In large bowl, combine bran,
1/2 cup (125 ml) each whole-
wheat and unbleached flours,
salt, ginger and orange peel; set
aside. Add butter and honey to
milk, stir until butter melts and
honey dissolves; add water;
cool to lukewarm. Sprinkle yeast
over, stir to dissolve; let stand
until foamy. Stir milk and egg
into bran mixture, beating vigorously about 3 minutes until air
bubbles form. Gradually beat
in remaining whole-wheat flour
and enough of the unbleached
white flour to make a stiff
dough. Turn out onto lightly
floured board and knead 5 to
10 minutes or until dough is
smooth and pliable, adding
additional unbleached flour to
prevent sticking. Form into
smooth ball, place in oiled bowl
and turn to coat all surfaces.
Cover with tea towel and let
rise in warm place 1 hour and
15 minutes or until double in
bulk. Punch down, turn out
onto floured board and knead 1
to 2 minutes. Form into loaf
and place in oiled #1 loaf pan.
Cover and let rise in warm
place 50 minutes or until double
in size. Bake in oven preheated
to 350°F (180°C) 35 minutes or
until bread tests done. Turn
out onto wire rack, turn right
side up and cool.

BUTTERMILK-WHEAT GERM BREAD

Say "buttermilk" and many
people say "eeech!," without
ever really having tried a tall,
cold glass. Perhaps in their
revulsion there's a connection
with sour milk, which has a
strong, unattractive smell. Buttermilk has none of this. It is
the residue of cream left in the
churn after the butter is ex-
tracted, and it does eloquent
things for the flavor of the loaf
when you bake with it. This
bread is pungent, with subtle
overtones of brown sugar and a
sturdy texture fortified with
wheat germ. Mark it worth a
Saturday's baking.

Makes Two Medium Loaves
2 tablespoons (30 ml) active
  dry yeast
1/2 cup (125 ml) lukewarm
  water
1-1/2 cups (350 ml) buttermilk
3 tablespoons (45 ml) butter,
  cut in bits
1/4 cup (60 ml) firmly packed
  brown sugar
2 eggs, at room temperature
  and lightly beaten
2 cups (500 ml) whole-wheat
  flour
1/2 cup (125 ml) untoasted
  wheat germ
2 teaspoons (10 ml) salt
3 cups (700 ml) unbleached
  white flour, or as needed

In large bowl, sprinkle yeast
over lukewarm water, stir to
dissolve and let stand until
foamy. Heat together buttermilk
and butter and stir to melt
butter; cool to lukewarm. Stir
into proofed yeast with the
sugar, eggs and whole-wheat
flour. Beat vigorously about 3
minutes until air bubbles form.
Stir in wheat germ and salt;
gradually add unbleached white
flour. Turn out onto floured
board and knead, adding additional unbleached flour only as
needed to prevent sticking, 5
minutes or until smooth and
pliable. Form into smooth ball,
place in oiled bowl, turn to coat
all surfaces, cover with tea
towel and let rise in warm
place 1 hour and 10 minutes or
until double in bulk. Punch
down, knead briefly and divide
into 2 equal portions. Form
into 2 loaves, place in 2 oiled
#2 loaf pans, cover with tea
towel and let rise in warm
place 45 minutes or until almost
double in size. Place in oven,
turn heat to 350°F (180°C) and
bake 45 minutes or until bread
tests done. Turn out onto wire
rack, turn right side up and
cool.

FLAX SEED-OAT BREAD

Flax seed is protein rich. The ancient Greeks, recognizing their worth, salvaged the seeds as they pounded and worried the fibers of the flax stalks into linen to weave fine cloth. This flax-oat combination will weave a good spell for you. It has solid, pleasing bite, a moist, compact texture and an aroma sweeter than the perfume of spring. It is a bread no computer technology can dream up. You can offer it as a custom-baked loaf—bread to enjoy sitting properly at a table instead of eating a leaky sandwich over the sink.

Makes Two Medium Loaves
1 cup (250 ml) milk
1 cup (250 ml) water
1/2 cup (125 ml) flax seed
1/2 cup (125 ml) steel-cut oats
2 tablespoons (30 ml) active dry yeast
1/2 cup (125 ml) lukewarm water
1/4 cup (60 ml) honey or molasses
1 teaspoon (5 ml) liquid lecithin (optional)
3 tablespoons (45 ml) safflower or corn oil
1/2 tablespoon (7.5 ml) malt powder (optional)
4 cups (1 L) whole-wheat flour
1/2 tablespoon (7.5 ml) salt
1 cup (250 ml) unbleached white flour, or as needed

Bring milk and water to boil, pour over flax seed and oats, stir and let stand until lukewarm. In large bowl, sprinkle yeast over lukewarm water, stir to dissolve and let stand until foamy. Stir in flax seed-oat mixture, honey, lecithin, oil, malt powder and 2-1/2 cups (600 ml) of the whole-wheat flour. Beat vigorously about 3 minutes until air bubbles form. Stir in salt, remaining whole-wheat flour and 3/4 cup (175 ml) of the unbleached white flour. Turn out onto board floured with remaining unbleached flour and knead in

flour. Knead, adding additional flour as needed to prevent sticking, 8 minutes. Lightly oil hands and board and continue kneading 3 minutes. Dough should be smooth and pliable but still slightly sticky. Form into smooth ball, place in oiled bowl, turn to coat all surfaces, cover with tea towel and let rise in warm place 1 hour or until double in bulk. Punch down, knead briefly, form into 2 loaves and place in 2 oiled #2 loaf pans. Cover with tea towel and let rise in warm place 45 minutes or until almost double in size. Place in oven, turn heat to 350°F (180°C) and bake 40 minutes or until bread tests done. Turn out onto wire rack, turn right side up and cool.

Seeds? Use dill, chia, caraway, celery, fennel, poppy, whole or cracked; grate or grind allspice, cardamom, cloves, coriander and nutmeg.

Sliced bread placed in containers with hard cookies will soften them.

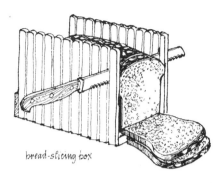

bread-slicing box

OATMEAL-WHEAT GERM BREAD

Wheat germ gives color and has a softening effect on the protein in flour. It is rich in vitamins E and B, iron, the amino acid lysine and polyunsaturated fats. And if that isn't enough, anyone who knows about such dry things will be impressed that you baked these light delectable loaves incorporating it. Of course, the munchy rolled oats and bulghur add their bit to the success, as well as your developing beating-kneading prowess.

Makes Two Large Loaves

1-1/2 tablespoons (22.5 ml) active dry yeast
2-2/3 cups (650 ml) lukewarm water
1/4 cup (60 ml) molasses or malt syrup
2/3 cup (150 ml) non-instant nonfat dry milk
2-1/2 cups (600 ml) unbleached white flour, or as needed
3-1/2 cups (825 ml) whole-wheat flour
3 tablespoons (45 ml) corn oil
2 teaspoons (10 ml) salt
2/3 cup (150 ml) untoasted wheat germ
2/3 cup (150 ml) unprocessed rolled oats
6 tablespoons (90 ml) fine- or medium-grind bulghur (cracked wheat)
Unhulled sesame seeds (optional)

In large bowl, sprinkle yeast over water, stir to dissolve and let stand until foamy. Stir in molasses. Sift together dry milk and 1 cup (250 ml) of the unbleached white flour, combine with 1 cup (250 ml) of the whole-wheat flour and stir into yeast mixture. Beat vigorously about 3 minutes until air bubbles form. Cover with tea towel and let rest in warm place 20 to 30 minutes. Stir in oil, salt, wheat germ, oats, bulghur and remaining whole-wheat flour. Beat vigorously about 3 minutes until air bubbles form. Gradually beat in 1 cup (250 ml) of the unbleached flour, mound remaining unbleached flour on board and turn dough out onto board. Knead in flour and, adding additional flour only as needed to prevent sticking, knead 3 minutes. Lightly oil hands and board and continue kneading 5 minutes. Dough will be slightly sticky. Form into smooth ball, place in oiled bowl, turn to coat all surfaces, cover with dampened tea towel and let rise in warm place 1 hour or until double in bulk. Punch down, knead briefly and form into 2 loaves. Place in 2 oiled #1 loaf pans, cover with tea towel and let rise in warm place 45 minutes or until almost double in size. Place in oven, turn heat to 350°F (180°C) and bake 45 minutes or until bread tests done. Turn out onto wire rack, turn right side up and cool.

Rye Breads

Think "rye," and Swedish *limpa* or Finnish rye comes to mind. The Scandinavians have raised rye bread to an art. The grain grows well in their cool climate and they have made the most of it. Rye breads respond to their culture: The fine dark texture, its aromatic hint of seeds and spices are happy companions to the many faces of herring, to the smorgasbord, to open-face sandwiches. It has an affinity for cheeses and for beer, which gives it an edge over wheat breads at buffets and picnics.

Rye is the only grain other than wheat that embraces gluten, but only mildly. Rye dough has to work hard to hold the fermenting gases, and unless it is blended with whole-wheat or white flour, bread made from it will be rubber-boot heavy and nothing to brag about. Rye flour does ferment faster than wheat, and it needs a careful nose to determine the amount of sourness. The longer the sponge time, the more sour it will be.

The flour is ground in grades: light, medium and dark. The dark, which is difficult to find, has more bran particles, which are sharp and will murder the nice little gas cells, so loaves made with it are usually small, long and narrow. Rye meal has a fine-sand feel and can be used for replacement of part of the rye flour in a recipe to give more texture to the bread.

Rye bread crust is usually soft and chewy. Slashing the top of a loaf with a razor or sharp knife lets the loaf expand without cracking, thereby also giving it more personality. Slashing is also a cure for a common rye problem: loaves baked in pans often break on the sides. The expansion is solved that simply.

Suggestion: Triticale flour may be substituted for the rye indicated in recipe (it is a hybrid of wheat and rye) for an interesting taste variation. It is a different consistency and may require more kneading. The most satisfactory formula is one part triticale to three parts unbleached white flour, as triticale, like rye, is low in gluten, and needs a friend. Allow an extra five to ten minutes baking if you make this substitution.

A one-pound loaf (450 to 500 g) should cut into 15 slices.

LIGHT RYE BREAD

Rye is shy in the gluten department, so it won't take any prizes used alone. Wheat flour is always added to get a well-risen loaf. This happy alliance makes a fine-textured, moist, dense bread, which slices nicely and becomes an immediate magnet for finger-food addicts. When you shop for rye flour, look for stone ground (it comes in bulk in natural-foods shops), because the intensity of flavor is abundant in this kind. If there's none available, you'll find most grocery chains carry a very acceptable boxed rye.

Makes Two Round Loaves

5 cups (1.2 L) unbleached white flour
2 cups (500 ml) rye flour
6 tablespoons (90 ml) non-instant nonfat dry milk
2 tablespoons (30 ml) active dry yeast
1 tablespoon (15 ml) salt
1 tablespoon (15 ml) caraway seeds
1 tablespoon (15 ml) butter, cut in bits
1/4 cup (60 ml) molasses or malt syrup
1 teaspoon (5 ml) liquid lecithin (optional)
2-1/2 cups (600 ml) hot water (120°F or 48°C)
Egg Wash, page 222

Mix flours together. In large bowl, combine 2-1/2 cups (600 ml) of flour mixture with dry milk, yeast, salt, caraway seeds, butter, molasses and lecithin. Stir well and gradually add water, beating constantly. Beat vigorously about 3 minutes until air bubbles form. Stir in 3 cups (700 ml) of remaining flour mixture to form a stiff but pliable dough. Turn out onto board floured with 1/4 cup (60 ml) of remaining flour mixture. Knead, adding additional flour mixture as needed to prevent sticking, 2 minutes. Dough should be very firm. Form into smooth ball, place in oiled bowl, turn to coat all surfaces, cover with tea towel and let rise in warm place 45 to 60 minutes or until double in bulk. Punch down, knead briefly and divide into 2 equal portions. Form each into a round loaf and place on oiled or greased baking sheet. Brush with Egg Wash, cover with tea towel and let rise in warm place 45 minutes or until double in size. Bake in oven preheated to 375°F (190°C) 25 minutes or until bread tests done. Transfer to wire rack and cool.

81

to slice a round, cut it in half, turn cut side of one half down & slice as for a standard loaf -- on its side

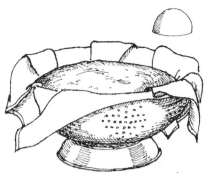

line a deep bowl or colander with cloth; dough will be dome-shaped

ONION RYE BREAD

Looking for something irresistible to take to a picnic, or to build your ego after you've made a magazine-recipe casserole that tastes like a TV dinner labeled "strictly gourmet"? Bring on this beautiful pungent loaf studded with onion and crisply cooked bacon bits to wow the crowd. It won't have that dominating sour character that comes from a long sponge period, because rising time is limited and the white flour makes up a major part of the recipe. But the husky, dusky loaves cut like a deck of cards and the fragrance is simply too much for dieters to resist. To get a truly symmetrical loaf, let the dough rise in a cloth-lined deep mixing bowl and then carefully invert it onto a baking sheet.

Makes Two Round Loaves

5 cups (1.2 L) unbleached white flour
2 cups (500 ml) rye flour
2 tablespoons (30 ml) active dry yeast
1 tablespoon (15 ml) salt
1-1/2 tablespoons (22.5 ml) caraway seeds
1 tablespoon (15 ml) butter, cut in bits
1/4 cup (60 ml) molasses
1 teaspoon (5 ml) liquid lecithin (optional)
3/4 cup (175 ml) minced onion
1/2 cup (125 ml) crumbled crisply cooked bacon (optional)
1-1/4 cups (300 ml) hot water (120°F or 48°C)
1-1/4 cups (300 ml) milk, scalded and cooled to 120°F or 48°C
Egg Wash, page 222

Proceed as with Light Rye Bread, page 81, adding the onion and bacon with the dry ingredients and combining the water and milk.

SWEDISH LIMPA RYE BREAD

Spicy *limpa* is the daily steady of most Swedes. It has a flavor that never dulls sharp conversation, and it will keep for days if well wrapped and stashed in a cool corner. It is baked in pans grandmothers use, and in households where "store bought"

is a dirty word. It can also come out of new pans in your kitchen and endear itself to your family.

Keep in mind that dark pans give a firmer, darker crust; if they're not in your pan inventory now, start filling a sugar-bowl with spare nickels and dimes so that one day you can splurge on the very best.

Makes Two Round Loaves

5 cups (1.2 L) unbleached white flour
2 cups (500 ml) rye flour
2 tablespoons (30 ml) active dry yeast
1 tablespoon (15 ml) salt
1 tablespoon (15 ml) butter, cut in bits
1/4 cup (60 ml) molasses
1/4 cup (60 ml) firmly packed brown sugar
1 teaspoon (5 ml) liquid lecithin (optional)
2 teaspoons (10 ml) anise seeds, lightly crushed
2 to 3 tablespoons (30 to 45 ml) freshly grated orange peel
1-1/4 cups (300 ml) hot water (120°F or 48°C)
1-1/4 cups (300 ml) milk, scalded and cooled to 120°F or 48°C

Proceed as with Light Rye Bread, page 81, adding the anise seeds and orange peel with the dry ingredients and combining the water and milk.

ORANGE-CARAWAY RYE BREAD

Make a note that this is a fast, one-rise bread with aromatic overtones, and simply scrumptious. It has rye flakes (made from the grain, like oatmeal) for good volume, and molasses, orange peel and caraway for good tempting. The dough has two "rest" periods of 30 minutes each when you can make half a dozen phone calls while waiting (set the timer—it will give you good reason to hang up quickly on your mother-in-law). Give the dough 40 minutes to rise, 45 to bake and an hour to cool. If you time it right, guests will just be arriving, the house will be filled with that aroma, and everything will get off to a great start.

Makes Two Large Loaves
1 cup (250 ml) rye flakes
1-3/4 cups (425 ml) boiling
    water
2 cups (500 ml) cold water
1/4 cup (60 ml) molasses
1 tablespoon (15 ml) active
    dry yeast
3 tablespoons (45 ml) safflower
    oil
1-1/2 cups (350 ml) unbleached
    white flour
1 tablespoon (15 ml) freshly
    grated orange peel
1 tablespoon (15 ml) caraway
    seeds
2 teaspoons (10 ml) salt
6 cups (1.4 L) whole-wheat
    flour, or as needed

Stir rye flakes into boiling water and boil slowly, uncovered, approximately 10 minutes or until flakes have absorbed all the water. Transfer to large bowl and add cold water, molasses and yeast, stir well and let rest 30 minutes. Add oil, unbleached white flour, orange peel, caraway seeds and salt. Let rest an additional 30 minutes. Stir in 5 cups (1.2 L) of the whole-wheat flour. Mound remaining whole-wheat flour on board and turn dough out onto board. Knead in flour and, adding additional whole-wheat flour only as needed to prevent sticking, knead 3 minutes. Divide into 2 equal portions and form into loaves. Transfer to 2 oiled #1 loaf pans or oiled 2-pound (1 kg) high-sided baking pans or casseroles. Cover with tea towel and let rise in warm place 40 minutes or until half again as large. Place in oven, set heat to 350°F (180°C) and bake 45 minutes or until bread tests done. Turn out onto wire rack, turn right side up and cool.

Freeze thin strips of orange and lemon peel, then process in blender a half cup (125 ml) at a time—easier than grating.

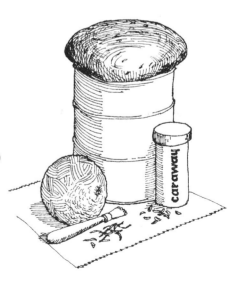

PUMPERNICKEL BREAD

A robust, peasanty, dark loaf, the kind held close to the chest of the fat bartender and sliced with a big knife in the old days of the five-cent beer and free lunch. This bread, "one you can't phony," to use a young baker's expression, is dense and slightly sour. Potato, skin and all, carob powder and molasses give the batch its tall, dark, handsome appeal. The bran brings just the right chewiness, and caraway gives pumpernickel its famous flavor, which lasts longer in memory than taste.

Makes Two Large Loaves

2 large baking potatoes (approximately 1 pound or 450 g)
3-1/2 cups (850 ml) water
3 tablespoons (45 ml) active dry yeast
2 tablespoons (30 ml) butter, cut in bits
3 tablespoons (45 ml) malt syrup or molasses
2-1/2 cups (600 ml) rye flour
3 cups (700 ml) unbleached white flour, or as needed
1 tablespoon (15 ml) carob powder, dissolved in 1 tablespoon (15 ml) water
1 tablespoon (15 ml) caraway seeds
2 teaspoons (10 ml) salt
1/4 cup (60 ml) whole-grain bread crumbs, lightly toasted
1/2 cup (125 ml) nondegerminated cornmeal
2/3 cup (150 ml) unprocessed bran
Egg White Wash, page 222

Scrub potatoes, cut into thick slices and boil in the water until soft; drain, reserving potatoes and measuring 3 cups (700 ml) of the potato water into large bowl. Cool water to lukewarm, sprinkle yeast over, stir to dissolve and let stand until foamy. While yeast is proofing, put potatoes through ricer (skins will remain in ricer) and gently pack into measuring cup to make 1-1/2 cups (350 ml). Stir butter into potatoes to melt and cool to lukewarm. Stir malt syrup into proofed yeast with 1 cup (250 ml) of the rye flour and 2 cups (500 ml) of the unbleached white flour. Beat vigorously about 3 minutes until air bubbles form. Stir in potato mixture, carob-water mixture, caraway seeds, salt, bread crumbs, cornmeal and bran. Blend well and gradually add remaining flours to form a stiff dough. Turn out onto floured board and knead, adding additional unbleached flour as needed to prevent sticking, 8 minutes. Lightly oil board and hands and continue kneading 3 more minutes. Dough will still be slightly sticky. Form into ball, cover with tea towel and let rest 10 to 15 minutes. Knead briefly, adding a little flour only if excessively sticky, form into ball, place in oiled bowl, turn to coat all surfaces, cover with tea towel and let rise in warm place 50 minutes or until double in bulk. Punch down, cover and let rise 35 minutes or until double in bulk. Punch down, knead briefly and form into 2 smooth balls. Place in 2 oiled 9-inch (23 cm) round baking pans and flatten slightly. Cover with tea towel and let rise in warm place 40 minutes or until almost double in size. Brush with Egg White Wash and bake in oven preheated to 350°F (180°C) 50 minutes or until bread tests done. Transfer to wire rack and cool.

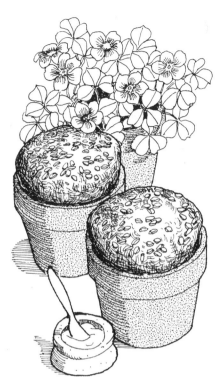

new 6" flower pots can substitute for 8" pans; coat with oil and place in fairly hot oven for 20 minutes. Repeat, cool and grease well before adding dough

SPROUTED RYE BREAD

Sprouts are Mother Nature's best act. Put some dry rye berries and moisture together in a glass jar and presto! In two or three days tiny green sprouts appear on the seeds. Her trick is that when seeds germinate,

time and moisture release gold mines of vitamins C, B_2, A and E, increasing amounts hundreds of times over those in the dry seeds, all of which makes this bread a mint of vitamins for the energy conscious. Once the sprouting is checked off (see details on page 56), the making is easy. The result is a light colored loaf with strong rye flavor, a bread to make you pause in mid-munch and contemplate the good things in life.

Makes Two Medium Loaves
2 cups (500 ml) sprouted rye berries
1 tablespoon (15 ml) active dry yeast
2/3 cup (150 ml) lukewarm water
2 tablespoons (30 ml) honey
1-1/4 cups (300 ml) whole-wheat flour, or as needed
1-1/2 tablespoons (22.5 ml) corn or safflower oil
3/4 teaspoon (3.6 ml) salt
1 tablespoon (15 ml) liquid lecithin (optional)
2 tablespoons (30 ml) soy flour
1/4 cup (50 ml) pure gluten flour

Grind sprouted rye berries in meat grinder and set aside. (If you do not have a meat grinder,

use a blender or food processor.) In large bowl, sprinkle yeast over water, stir to dissolve and let stand until foamy. Stir in honey, ground rye berry sprouts and whole-wheat flour. Beat vigorously about 3 minutes until air bubbles form. Stir in oil, salt, lecithin, soy flour and the gluten flour. Turn out onto floured board and, adding additional flour only as needed to prevent sticking, knead 4 minutes. Lightly oil hands and board and continue kneading 4 more minutes. Dough will be pliable but still slightly sticky. Form into smooth ball, place in oiled bowl, turn to coat all surfaces, cover with dampened tea towel and let rise in warm place 1-1/2 hours or until double in bulk. Punch down, knead briefly and form into 2 loaves. Place in 2 oiled #2 loaf pans, cover with tea towel and let rise in warm place 1 hour or until almost double in size. Place in oven, set heat to 350°F (180°C) and bake 45 minutes or until bread tests done. Turn out onto wire rack, turn right side up and cool.

SPROUTED TRITICALE OR WHEAT BREAD Substitute 2 cups (500 ml) sprouted triticale or wheat berries for the sprouted rye.

SMORGASBORD RYE

If you're planning a big bash, this is the bread to earmark for high marks: when it is baked in long, slim baguette loaves, you can count on at least 150 three-eighth-inch (1 cm) slices, or more if you orchestrate a sharp knife. It's slightly sweet, with a dark handsome manner to entice herring, ham, hot pastrami and a host of cheeses, as well as providing a worthy base for open-face sandwiches. Bake it ahead and freeze; it will recover like freshly baked.

Makes Three Large Loaves
2 cups (500 ml) rye flour
2 teaspoons (10 ml) salt
2 tablespoons (30 ml) caraway
   seeds
1-1/2 cups (375 ml) boiling
   water
2 tablespoons (30 ml) active
   dry yeast
1 cup (250 ml) lukewarm water
1/4 cup (60 ml) firmly packed
   brown sugar
3/4 cup (175 ml) molasses
1/2 cup (125 ml) melted and
   cooled bacon drippings or lard
4-3/4 cups (1.1 L) unbleached
   white flour, or as needed
Molasses Wash, page 222

In large bowl, combine rye flour, salt and caraway seeds. Blend well and pour boiling water over mixture, stir and cool to lukewarm. Sprinkle yeast over lukewarm water, stir to dissolve and let stand until foamy. Add to cooled rye mixture together with brown sugar and beat vigorously for 2 minutes; cover with tea towel and let rise in warm place 1 hour or until double in bulk. Stir down and beat in molasses and bacon drippings. Gradually add unbleached white flour 1 cup (250 ml) at a time, until 4 cups have been added. Mound 1/2 cup (125 ml) of remaining flour on board, turn out dough onto board, and using a baker's scraper, work in more flour until dough can be kneaded by hand. Knead for 10 minutes, adding more flour as needed.

Dough will still be slightly sticky. Form into smooth ball, place in oiled bowl, turn to coat all surfaces, cover with tea towel and let rise again in warm place until double in bulk. Punch down, knead briefly and form into 3 loaves. Place in 3 oiled #1 pans or shape into long loaves and place in oiled baguette pans. Cover with tea towel and let rise in warm place 35 to 45 minutes or until almost double in size. With razor, make slashes on risen bread and evenly brush with Molasses Wash. Bake in oven preheated to 350°F (180°C) 1 hour and 10 minutes or until bread tests done. Repeat Molasses Wash twice during baking, at 20 minutes and at 40 minutes. Turn out onto wire rack, turn right side up and cool.

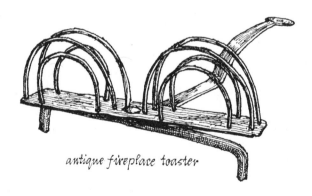

antique fireplace toaster

86

No rack to cool bread? Use extra oven shelf or plastic dish drainer.

BLACK BREAD

While it smacks of a good solid rye, this black bread has a distinct personality. Its makeup is colored by instant coffee, a whisper of minced onion and vinegar, by both caraway and fennel, by carob and unprocessed bran. In fact, it is a superb hearth loaf, round and shiny, of unequaled rye flavor, a perfect buffet complement to a tray of imported cheeses. The only way it could be improved would be to bake it in an old brick oven fired with apple wood. Of course, that's hardly possible, but a preheated heavy plaque or ceramic stone baking sheet would make passable substitute to produce that fine crust.

Makes Two Round Loaves

3 tablespoons (45 ml) active dry yeast
1/2 cup (125 ml) lukewarm water
4 tablespoons (60 ml) butter, cut in bits
2 cups (500 ml) hot water (120°F or 48°C)
1/4 cup (60 ml) dark molassses
4 cups (1 L) rye flour
2 cups (500 ml) unprocessed bran
2 tablespoons (30 ml) caraway seeds, lightly crushed
1 to 2 teaspoons (5 to 10 ml) fennel seeds, lightly crushed
2 teaspoons (10 ml) instant coffee powder or granules
2 teaspoons (10 ml) salt
2 to 3 tablespoons (30 to 45 ml) finely minced onion
3 tablespoons (45 ml) carob powder, dissolved in 2 tablespoons (30 ml) water
1/4 cup (60 ml) distilled white vinegar
2-1/2 cups (600 ml) unbleached white flour, or as needed
Cornstarch Glaze, page 222 (optional)

Sprinkle yeast over lukewarm water, stir to dissolve and let stand until foamy. In large bowl, stir butter into hot water until melted. Stir in molasses, cool to lukewarm and mix in proofed yeast. Gradually stir in rye flour, beating vigorously 5 minutes. Cover with tea towel and let rest up to 30 minutes.

Toss together bran, caraway and fennel seeds, coffee powder, salt and onion. Combine dissolved carob powder and vinegar; blend into yeast mixture. Stir in bran mixture until well mixed. Gradually add 1-1/2 cups (350 ml) of the unbleached flour, beating well to make a stiff dough. Turn out onto board floured with 1/2 cup (125 ml) of remaining unbleached flour. Knead, adding additional flour as needed to prevent sticking, 10 minutes. Lightly oil board and hands and continue kneading the rather sticky dough 5 more minutes. Form into smooth ball, place in oiled bowl, turn to coat all surfaces, cover with tea towel and let rise in warm place 1 hour and 10 minutes or until double in bulk. Punch down, divide in 2 equal portions, knead 1 to 2 minutes and shape each portion into a ball approximately 4-1/2 inches (11 cm) in diameter. Place each ball in center of buttered or oiled 8-inch (20 cm) round cake pan. Cover with tea towel and let rise in warm place 1 hour or until almost double in size. Bake in oven preheated to 350°F (180°C) 45 minutes or until bread tests done. If softer crust is preferred, brush with Cornstarch Glaze and return to oven for 2 to 3 minutes. Turn out onto wire rack, turn right side up and cool.

DARK RYE BREAD

To set your taste buds quivering, just bake a couple fat round loaves of this nutty, moist rye. It's assertive, but yields to hungry crowds with infinite charm. Dark rye flour and molasses will insure the proper depth of color, but if you can't find dark rye, settle for the medium. A shiny glaze on top, made with a little molasses and water, will make it seem darker.

Note: Like all ryes, this one will seem sticky for a long time as you knead and you'll wonder if it will ever change. Then suddenly, it stops, and you know you've won. If there's danger of getting too much flour into the dough, scrape the board clean of flour and oil the board and your hands lightly.

Makes Two Round Loaves

1 tablespoon (15 ml) active dry yeast
1/4 cup (60 ml) lukewarm water
1-1/2 cups (350 ml) hot water
2 tablespoons (30 ml) butter, cut in bits
1/4 cup (60 ml) firmly packed brown sugar
1/4 cup (60 ml) light molasses
2-1/2 cups (600 ml) rye flour
2-3/4 cups (650 ml) unbleached white flour, or as needed
1 tablespoon (15 ml) salt
2 teaspoons (10 ml) freshly grated orange peel
1/2 teaspoon (2.5 ml) fennel or anise seeds (optional), or
1 to 2 teaspoons (5 to 10 ml) caraway seeds (optional)
Molasses Wash, page 222

Sprinkle yeast over lukewarm water, stir to dissolve and let stand until foamy. In large bowl, combine hot water, butter, sugar and molasses. Stir to melt butter and dissolve sugar and cool to lukewarm. Add proofed yeast, rye flour and 1/2 cup (125 ml) of the unbleached flour. Beat vigorously about 3 minutes until air bubbles form. Stir in salt, orange peel and seeds of choice; gradually beat in remaining unbleached white flour to form stiff dough. Turn out onto floured board and knead, adding additional flour as needed to prevent sticking, 8 minutes until smooth, pliable and firm. Form into smooth ball, place in oiled bowl, turn to coat all surfaces, cover with dampened tea towel and let rise in warm place 1 hour and 40 minutes or until double in bulk. Punch down, knead briefly and divide into 2 equal portions. Form each into a round loaf, place on oiled baking sheet, cover with lightly dampened tea towel and let rise in warm place 1 hour and 40 minutes or until almost double in size. Brush with Molasses Wash and bake in oven preheated to 350°F (180°C) 40 minutes or until bread tests done. Transfer to wire rack and cool.

88

BREADS LIKE MOTHER NEVER BAKED

Here are a few whimsical breads that are devilishly good, yet don't quite fit the family patterns of other breads, so we've corraled them under this prejudiced heading. Each is a gem. If you like banana quick bread, you'll betray mother for the last slice of this whole-wheat yeast loaf. The Yam Bread is a grand adventure and makes unbeatable toast. Triticale (tritacay'lee) is a new experience for most bakers. It is a hybrid of wheat and rye with a nice taste improvement over both, and as the title of our recipe indicates, it's a winner for sandwiches. Anadama bread has as many tales of origin as it has variables of "authentic" recipes. We like this one because it's simple and downright New England.

Why not share these with mother? She may even have some bread recipes from *her* mother that you didn't know existed.

ANADAMA BREAD

A New Englander's version of cornmeal bread, but with yeast. The perpetrator who was supposed to have resented a lifetime of breakfasts of cornmeal porridge and molasses, took the bowl by the horns, tossed in yeast and white flour, and came up with a good brown loaf. According to the tale, he showed it to his wife: "Anna, dammit, *this* is what I want!" In his day, blackstrap molasses was the poor man's sweetener. It's suggested in this recipe, but if the strong flavor is not to your taste, substitute the light, New Orleans type. Also, a half cup of golden raisins stirred in before the last flour is added will give a little iron for other Annas.

Makes Two Medium Loaves
1 tablespoon (15 ml) active
   dry yeast
1/4 cup (50 ml) lukewarm
   water
4 tablespoons (60 ml) butter,
   cut in bits
1-3/4 cups (450 ml) hot water
   (120°F or 48°C)
1/2 cup (125 ml) dark molasses
1 cup (250 ml) nondegerminated
   yellow cornmeal
2 teaspoons (10 ml) salt
5-1/2 cups (1.3 L) unbleached
   white flour, or as needed

Sprinkle yeast over lukewarm water, stir to dissolve and let stand until foamy. In large bowl, stir butter into hot water until melted. Stir in molasses, cornmeal and salt and let cool to lukewarm. Mix in proofed yeast and gradually add 3 cups (700 ml) of the flour. Beat well and then beat in remaining flour to make stiff dough. Turn out onto floured board and knead, adding additional flour to prevent sticking, 5 minutes. Form into smooth ball, place in oiled bowl, turn to coat all surfaces, cover with tea towel and let rise in warm place 1 hour and 35 minutes or until double in bulk. Punch down, knead briefly on floured board, form into 2 loaves and place in 2 oiled #2 loaf pans. Cover and let rise 1 hour and 15 minutes or until double in size. Bake in oven preheated to 350°F (180°C) 40 minutes or until bread tests done. Turn out onto wire rack, turn right side up and cool.

There are five families of corn: flint *corn,* flour *or* soft *corn favored by the Indians,* dent *(the main commercial variety),* sweet *(eating) and* popcorn.

NINE-GRAIN BREAD

Never let it be said too many grains do a flaky bread make. Today's most respected diet and health authorities tout long lists of cereals for the nutrition and the fiber content, and so multigrains proliferate. Trouble is, they're outrageously expensive. So we've put together our idea of a grain load of good stuff, keeping in mind the loaf must not be dry or drab. You will be delighted with its taste and texture. It's based on a nine-grain cereal available in natural-foods stores, and it has cracked wheat, oats, rye, barley, corn, soya, brown rice, millet, triticale, plus flax seed— all finely ground to produce a farinalike texture.

Makes Three Small Loaves
1-1/2 tablespoons (22.5 ml)
   active dry yeast
2 tablespoons (30 ml) non-
   instant nonfat dry milk
1-3/4 cups (425 ml) nine-grain
   cereal
1 cup (250 ml) pure gluten flour
3-3/4 cups (850 ml) whole-
   wheat flour
1-1/2 cups (350 ml) hot water
   (120°F or 48°C)

1/4 cup (60 ml) safflower or corn oil
1/4 cup (60 ml) molasses or honey
1 tablespoon (15 ml) salt
2 tablespoons (30 ml) sesame seeds (optional)

In bowl of heavy-duty mixer, combine yeast, dry milk, cereal, gluten flour, 1-1/2 cups (350 ml) of the whole-wheat flour and water. Mix with dough hook until blended, then beat 3 minutes. Add oil, molasses, salt and sesame seeds and mix well. Gradually add remaining whole-wheat flour until dough cleans sides of bowl. Beat 10 minutes. With lightly oiled hands, remove to lightly oiled board and knead briefly. Divide into 3 equal portions and form into 3 loaves. Place in 3 oiled #3 loaf pans, cover with tea towel and let rise in warm place 1 hour or until double in size. Place in oven, set heat to 350°F (180°C) and bake 40 minutes or until bread tests done. Turn out onto wire rack, turn right side up and cool.

YAM BREAD

Potato bread does a hocus pocus and becomes a delightful new original: Yam Bread. Everyone who sampled the test bakings raved, and when we divulged how easy it is to accomplish, clamored for directions.

Texture and crust are excellent, and once again, toasting passed the critical test with yammers for more. (Remember, dark toast robs nutrition because of too much heat.)

Makes Two Large Loaves
2 tablespoons (30 ml) active dry yeast
1/2 cup (125 ml) lukewarm water
3 tablespoons (45 ml) butter, cut in bits
1-1/2 cups (350 ml) hot water 120°F or 48°C)
2 teaspoons (10 ml) salt
1 egg, at room temperature
1-1/4 cups (300 ml) mashed cooked yams
3 tablespoons (45 ml) firmly packed brown sugar
2 cups (500 ml) whole-wheat flour
4 cups (1 L) unbleached white flour, or as needed

Sprinkle yeast over lukewarm water, stir to dissolve and let stand until foamy. Stir butter and salt into hot water until melted, cool. In large bowl, beat egg lightly. Stir in yams, brown sugar, water and butter mixture and proofed yeast. Gradually beat in whole-wheat flour and 1 cup (250 ml) of the unbleached white flour. Beat vigorously 3 minutes until air bubbles form. Gradually add remaining unbleached flour to make a smooth, rather soft and pliable dough. Turn out onto floured board and knead, adding additional flour as needed to prevent sticking, 5 minutes. Dough will be slightly sticky on board but should not stick to hands. It should remain smooth and pliable. Form into smooth ball, place in oiled bowl, turn to coat all surfaces, cover with tea towel and let rise in warm place 1 hour or until double in bulk. Punch down, knead briefly, divide into 2 equal portions, cover with tea towel and let rest 10 minutes. Form into 2 loaves, place in 2 oiled #1 loaf pans, cover with tea towel and let rise in warm place 1 hour or until almost double in size. Place in oven, turn heat to 350°F (180°C) and bake 40 minutes or until bread tests done. Turn out onto wire rack, turn right side up and cool.

the yam is an edible root-tuber which produces a tall tropical vine with cinnamon-scented white flowers; it is not a true sweet potato

BANANA BREAD

Instead of a slightly sweet, quick banana bread that is more like a coffee cake, this whole-wheat yeast is a *bread* bread, with the flavor of banana enhanced by cinnamon and cardamom and the added texture of peanuts. It's hard to resist warm—the wafting scent will unnerve your nose—but make this a sharing loaf. Ask a neighbor in, give a half a loaf to your butcher (or baker?). Wrap a loaf in a new diaper and hand it to your pediatrician the next time you take baby in for a checkup, or wrap it in the *Wall Street Journal* and give it to your stockbroker, and watch your shares go up.

Makes One Large Loaf

1 tablespoon (15 ml) active
   dry yeast
1/2 cup (125 ml) lukewarm
   water
3 to 4 tablespoons (45 to 60 ml)
   honey
3 tablespoons (45 ml) safflower
   oil
1/2 cup (125 ml) milk, scalded
1 egg, at room temperature
1 tablespoon (15 ml) freshly
   grated orange peel
2 teaspoons (10 ml) ground
   cinnamon
1/2 teaspoon (2.5 ml) ground
   cardamom
1 cup (250 ml) mashed very
   ripe banana
1/2 tablespoon (7.5 ml) salt
2 cups (500 ml) whole-wheat
   flour
2-3/4 cups (650 ml) unbleached
   white flour, or as needed
1/2 cup (125 ml) chopped
   unsalted peanuts

Sprinkle yeast over water, stir to dissolve and let stand until foamy. Stir honey and oil into milk and let cool to lukewarm. In large bowl, beat egg lightly and stir in proofed yeast, milk mixture, orange peel, spices, banana and salt. Gradually beat in whole-wheat flour and 1 cup (250 ml) of the white flour. Beat vigorously until air bubbles form. Stir in peanuts and gradually beat in remaining white flour to form a stiff dough. Turn out onto floured board and knead, using additional flour as needed to prevent sticking, 5 minutes. Dough will be slightly sticky. Form into smooth ball, place in oiled bowl, turn to coat all surfaces, cover with tea towel and let rise in warm place 1-1/2 to 2 hours or until double in bulk. Punch down, turn out onto floured board and knead 2 minutes, adding flour if needed. Form into a loaf and place in an oiled #1 loaf pan, cover with tea towel and let rise 1-1/2 hours or until almost double in size. Bake in oven preheated to 375°F (190°C) 40 minutes or until bread tests done. Turn out onto wire rack, turn right side up and cool.

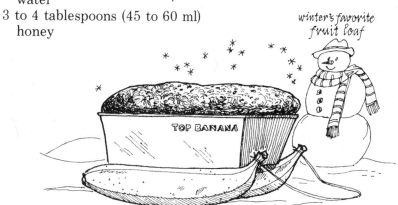

winter's favorite fruit loaf

TOP BANANA

GRANOLA BREAD

Granola is a mix of grains, seeds, dried fruits, honey and nuts that emerged as a part of the '60s culture—energy by the handful for body and spirit, and a boon for hikers, breakfast eaters and Zen meditators. It's available in packages or bulk at natural-foods stores and manufactured by cereal makers for supermarket distribution. What it does for bread is something no guru could have anticipated: gentle crunchiness, modest sweetness, nutrition and a nutty aftertaste. Spread a warm slice with unsalted butter for the first bite, then try pear or apple butter on it for transcendental alchemy. We were only moderately pleased with a toasted slice.

Makes Two Medium Loaves
1 cup (250 ml) boiling water
1 cup (250 ml) raisins
1-3/4 cups (400 ml) Granola Mix (see below)
1/4 cup (50 ml) sunflower seeds
1 teaspoon (5 ml) ground cinnamon
1/4 teaspoon (1.2 ml) ground nutmeg
3/4 cup (175 ml) milk, scalded
3 to 4 tablespoons (45 to 60 ml) honey
3 tablespoons (45 ml) active dry yeast
2 eggs, at room temperature
3 tablespoons (45 ml) peanut oil
2 teaspoons (10 ml) freshly grated lemon peel
2 teaspoons (10 ml) salt
2 cups (500 ml) whole-wheat flour
1-3/4 cups (400 ml) unbleached white flour, or as needed

Pour boiling water over raisins and let stand 10 minutes. Combine granola, sunflower seeds and spices; set aside. Drain raisins, set raisins aside and measure raisin water, adding more water if needed to make 3/4 cup (175 ml). Add to milk, stir in honey and let cool to lukewarm. Sprinkle yeast over, stir to dissolve and let stand until foamy. In large bowl, beat eggs lightly and blend in oil, lemon peel, yeast mixture and whole-wheat flour. Beat vigorously until air bubbles form, stir in granola, salt and raisins; blend in white flour to make a stiff dough. Turn out onto floured board and knead, adding additional flour to prevent sticking, 5 minutes. Lightly oil hands and board and continue kneading 3 minutes. Form into smooth ball, place in oiled bowl, turn to coat all surfaces, cover with tea towel and let rise in warm place 1-1/2 to 2 hours or until double in bulk. Punch down, knead briefly and divide into 2 equal portions. Cover with tea towel and let rest 10 minutes. Form into loaves and place in 2 oiled #2 loaf pans. Cover with tea towel and let rise in warm place 1-1/2 hours or until almost double in size. Place in oven, turn heat to 350°F (180°C) and bake 45 minutes or until bread tests done. Turn out onto wire rack, turn right side up and cool.

GRANOLA MIX Combine 1/2 cup (125 ml) *each* wheat flakes, soy flakes, triticale flakes, rye flakes and unhulled sesame seeds, and 1 cup (250 ml) *each* unprocessed rolled oats and untoasted wheat germ. Spread on a baking sheet and place in a preheated 300°F (140°C) oven 20 minutes, stirring often.

When dried foods are stored in open jars, losses of vitamins A, C and E occur from reactions with oxygen.

TRITICALE SANDWICH BREAD

As indicated in the beginning of this section, triticale is a grain, a pairing of wheat and rye, developed in the past 15 years. The result was first a superior feed for livestock (it is very high in proteins) and later introduced as a flour that would contribute more nutrition to bread. It is not, however, easily found, but don't give up. Natural-foods stores usually stock it. Triticale inherited its low-gluten level from the rye side of the family, so it is best when combined with whole-wheat or unbleached white flour. This sandwich loaf is good for peanut butter and jellying, will accommodate avocado and alfalfa sprouts for the veggie set, or stretch a hospitable point for the likes of creamed cheese and smoked salmon.

Makes Two Large Loaves
2 tablespoons (30 ml) active dry yeast
2-1/2 cups (600 ml) lukewarm water
6 tablespoons (90 ml) safflower oil
1/3 cup (75 ml) malt syrup
2 teaspoons (10 ml) liquid lecithin (optional)
1 tablespoon (15 ml) salt
1/4 cup (60 ml) non-instant nonfat dry milk
3 cups (700 ml) triticale flour
3-3/4 cups (775 ml) unbleached white flour, or as needed

In large bowl, sprinkle yeast over lukewarm water, stir to dissolve and let stand until foamy. Stir in oil, malt syrup, lecithin and salt, mixing well. Sift dry milk with 1 cup (250 ml) of the triticale flour and stir into yeast mixture. Gradually add remaining triticale flour and 1-1/2 cups (350 ml) of the unbleached white flour. Beat vigorously about 3 minutes until air bubbles form. Gradually add remaining unbleached flour to form stiff dough. Turn out onto floured board and knead, adding additional flour to prevent excessive sticking, 10 minutes until smooth and pliable. Form into smooth ball, place in oiled bowl, turn to coat all surfaces, cover with tea towel and let rise in warm place 1 hour or until double in bulk. Punch down and turn out onto floured board. If dough is sticky, knead in a little more flour to make a soft, relaxed dough. Form into 2 loaves and place in 2 oiled #1 loaf pans. Cover and let rise in warm place 1 hour or until almost double in size. Bake in oven preheated to 350°F (180°C) 35 minutes or until bread tests done. Turn out onto wire rack, turn right side up and cool.

CHEESE TRITICALE BREAD Stir into dough after beating vigorously 3/4 cup (175 ml) coarsely shredded Monterey Jack cheese; increase baking time 5 to 10 minutes.

The batter method differs from those of other yeast breads because there is no kneading. The gluten has to get in its licks, so beating, or battering, takes the place of kneading. If you have a heavy-duty mixer or food processor, you can make batter bread at the flip of a switch. The main advantage is that it is made more quickly than the familiar yeast method. An electric hand mixer with dough hook will barely get you started, but watch carefully for overheating of motor.

Since the dough isn't kneaded, you'll discover it takes less flour in proportion to the amount of liquid, and the dough will be slack. The finished breads will not be fine textured like kneaded breads. They are more like some baking-powder breads when cut, and the crust will be rough and chewy. Because they do not have the additional flour to support themselves, they bake better in deep casseroles or pans. Do not allow the rising in the container to go above the lip, as too much rising will cause a loaf to sink in the middle.

Batter Breads

95

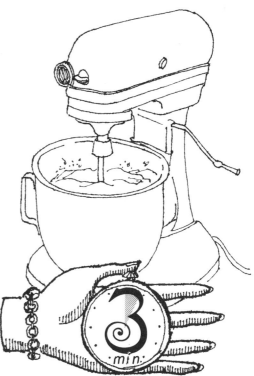

BATTER BREAD METHOD

The first step is to combine the proofed yeast with liquids and flavorings, and then beat in the portion of flour indicated in each recipe. Beat vigorously for three minutes, or 250 to 300 strokes. Then add the rest of the flour, one-half cup (125 ml) at a time, continuing beating and turning the bowl each time you scrape down the sides so that you get all the little gluten cells excited. A heavy-duty mixer is a blessing during these additions; you may find you have to take over by hand again during final additions if dough persists in "creeping" up the hook. Batter should be stiff, but not as firm as a kneaded batch. When pulled up with the wooden spoon it should come up in one mass, leaving only a little on edge of bowl. When the dough is hard to stir, try "stabbing" with a spoon and pulling up dough to get last flour integrated.

When you turn it into the heavily greased (don't stint!) pan or casserole, you may have to fight to get it into the corners. Use your fingers or a moistened spoon for this step and fill the vessel only two thirds full. The top will look like a plowed field but that adds to its baked charm. One good way to insure crusty bottom and sides is to remove bread from container when it tests done and place the loaf back in the oven for another five to seven minutes.

Batter breads do not have to cool completely before cutting, but control the urge for at least 15 minutes. Then, before anyone else can get near the loaf, "test" it for yourself by preempting the heel. Lucky you!

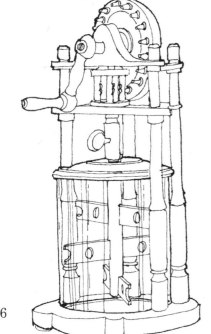

1790 wood and glass butter churn

96

OATMEAL BATTER BREAD

Samuel Johnson defined oats as "a grain which in England is generally given to horses, but in Scotland supports the people." Crafty Scots, they knew the oat was a horse of a different flavor—high in nutrition and a grain that was highly suited to their climate. The oat grain, called a "groat," rates high in protein, almost as high as soybeans. Unprocessed rolled oats have not been heat treated and are available in most natural-foods stores. If you can't find them use slow-cooking, old-fashioned rolled oats. Oats and molasses make congenial bread-fellows, giving a moist, mouth-watering flavor. The crumb is coarser than kneaded oatmeal bread, but again, the batter method is for in-a-hurry schedules, and this one is a pleaser.

Makes Two Medium Loaves

2-1/3 cups (550 ml) boiling water
1-1/3 cups (300 ml) unprocessed rolled oats
2 tablespoons (30 ml) butter, cut in bits
2/3 cup (150 ml) molasses
1/2 tablespoon (7.5 ml) salt
1 tablespoon (15 ml) active dry yeast
1/2 cup (125 ml) lukewarm water
1/2 cup (125 ml) pure gluten flour
2 cups (500 ml) whole-wheat flour
2-1/2 cups (600 ml) unbleached white flour, or as needed

Pour boiling water over oats, stir in butter to melt, and add molasses and salt. Let stand 20 to 30 minutes until lukewarm. While mixture is cooling, sprinkle yeast over lukewarm water, stir to dissolve and let stand until foamy. Stir into cooled oat mixture and beat in gluten flour and whole-wheat flour. Beat vigorously about 3 minutes until air bubbles form. According to general directions for batter breads, gradually add white flour. Let rise, uncovered, at room temperature or slightly warmer 2 hours or until double in bulk. Stir down and spoon into 2 well-greased #2 loaf pans. Let rise, uncovered, at room temperature 2 hours or until almost double in size. Place in oven, turn heat to 350°F (180°C) and bake 35 minutes or until bread tests done. Turn out onto wire rack, turn right side up and cool.

beating is a vigorous combination of mixing and stirring

ONION-HERB BATTER BREAD

This is a one-loaf project, just right for an evening's diversion. It can be frozen for later unveiling, or served up warm to the poker table (toasted, it makes a surprise "pizza" sandwich with filling of cheese, tomatoes and sausage). If you're limited for time, get out the heavy-duty mixer—and don't feel guilt if you have to yell "Uncle!" to the beat of the dough.

Makes One Medium Loaf
1 tablespoon (15 ml) active
   dry yeast
1/2 cup (125 ml) lukewarm
   water
1 tablespoon (15 ml) honey
1 cup (250 ml) whole-wheat
   flour
1 tablespoon (15 ml) butter,
   cut in bits

1/2 cup (125 ml) milk, scalded
1/4 cup (50 ml) untoasted
   wheat germ
1 teaspoon (5 ml) salt
1/4 cup (50 ml) minced onion
1 teaspoon (5 ml) minced
   garlic
1 teaspoon (5 ml) minced
   fresh chives
1/2 teaspoon (2.5 ml) minced
   fresh oregano
1/2 teaspoon (2.5 ml) minced
   fresh thyme
1 cup (250 ml) unbleached
   white flour, or as needed

In large bowl, sprinkle yeast over water, stir in honey and let stand until foamy. Stir in whole-wheat flour and beat vigorously about 3 minutes until air bubbles form. Stir butter into milk to dissolve; let cool to lukewarm and add to yeast mixture with wheat germ, salt, onion, garlic and herbs. Blend well. According to general directions for batter breads, gradually add white flour. Cover with tea towel and let rise in warm place 1-1/2 hours or until treble in bulk. Stir down and spoon into a well-buttered #2 loaf pan or casserole of comparable size. Cover with tea towel and let rise in warm place 1 hour or until almost double in size. Place in oven, turn heat to 350°F (180°C) and bake 35 minutes or until bread tests done. Turn out onto wire rack, turn right side up and cool.

CHIVE BATTER BREAD

A batter bread can be made in less than three hours, so it's a happy morning chore. You don't have to get up at six to "set" the bread to make a luncheon treat. This particular batter, with its blend of chives and garlic, will fill the house with bouquets of inviting odors. Guests who normally refuse to eat a single slice of bread will sigh for seconds, so don't be surprised if there are only crumbs after the invasion has left.

Makes One Round Loaf
1 tablespoon (15 ml) active
   dry yeast
1/4 cup (50 ml) lukewarm
   water
1 cup (250 ml) sour cream, at
   room temperature
1/4 teaspoon (1.2 ml) baking
   soda
1 egg, at room temperature
1-1/2 tablespoons (22.5 ml)
   honey
1 teaspoon (5 ml) salt
3 to 4 tablespoons (45 to 60 ml)
   chopped fresh chives
1/2 teaspoon (2.5 ml) minced
   garlic
2/3 cup (175 ml) whole-wheat
   flour
1-2/3 cups (400 ml) unbleached
   white flour, or as needed
Melted butter

Sprinkle yeast over lukewarm water, stir to dissolve and let stand until foamy. Combine sour cream and baking soda. In large bowl, beat egg lightly, stir in honey, salt, chives, garlic, proofed yeast, sour-cream mixture and whole-wheat flour. According to general directions for batter breads, gradually beat in unbleached flour. Spoon evenly into a well-buttered 9-inch (23 cm) round baking dish, brush lightly with melted butter and let rise, uncovered, in warm place 50 minutes or until almost double in size. Place in oven, turn heat to 350°F (180°C) and bake 40 minutes or until top is golden and bread tests done. Turn out onto wire rack, turn right side up and cool.

GRUYERE CHEESE BATTER BREAD

One good thing deserves another: that milk pale-yellow Swiss cheese from the Gruyere district turns up in a whole-wheat batter, and you'll be hard put to find a more satisfying live-in situation. If you have any prospector instincts, you'll immediately tackle this before anyone else gets the urge to try. Even if you've only made hardtack on a hunting trip, you'll find this recipe easier to follow than the tracks of your accountant through form 1044.

Makes Two Small Loaves

1 tablespoon (15 ml) active dry yeast
1/4 cup (60 ml) lukewarm water
3 tablespoons (45 ml) butter, cut in bits
1/2 cup (125 ml) hot water (120°F or 48°C)
1/2 cup (125 ml) evaporated milk
2 eggs, at room temperature
3 tablespoons (45 ml) honey
1/2 tablespoon (7.5 ml) salt
3/4 teaspoon (3.6 ml) paprika
1 cup (250 ml) grated Gruyere cheese
1-1/2 cups (350 ml) whole-wheat flour
1/2 cup (125 ml) pure gluten flour
1 cup (250 ml) unbleached white flour, or as needed

Sprinkle yeast over lukewarm water, stir to dissolve and let stand until foamy. Stir butter into hot water until melted, add evaporated milk and cool to lukewarm. In large bowl, beat eggs lightly; add proofed yeast, butter mixture, honey, salt, paprika, cheese and whole-wheat flour and mix well. Add gluten flour. According to general directions for batter breads, gradually beat in unbleached flour. Cover with tea towel and let rise in warm place 1 hour or until double in bulk. Stir down and spoon into 2 well-greased #3 loaf pans. Cover with tea towel and let rise in warm place 45 minutes or until almost double in size. Place in oven, turn oven heat to 350°F (180°C) and bake 35 minutes or until bread tests done. Turn out onto wire rack, turn right side up and cool.

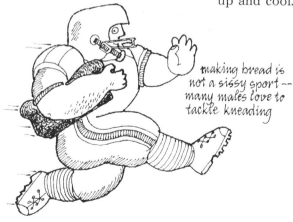

making bread is not a sissy sport -- many males love to tackle kneading

PARMESAN CHEESE BATTER BREAD

Mark this recipe for Sunday night supper . . . of a warm summer's evening on the patio, or around the kitchen table in January. Since there is no kneading and one rising, it takes less than three hours from start to bread board. And the extra-moist inside under crusty top spreads an earthy fragrance you can't resist.

Makes One Large Loaf
2 tablespoons (30 ml) active
   dry yeast
2 cups (500 ml) lukewarm
   chicken broth
2 tablespoons (30 ml) granulated sugar
1 teaspoon (5 ml) salt
2 tablespoons (30 ml) butter,
   softened
1/2 cup (125 ml) freshly grated
   Parmesan cheese
1 tablespoon (15 ml) crumbled
   dried oregano
3-1/2 cups (825 ml) unbleached
   white flour, or as needed
1 tablespoon (15 ml) freshly
   grated Parmesan cheese for
   topping

In large bowl, sprinkle yeast over broth, stir in sugar and let stand until foamy. Stir in salt, butter, 1/2 cup (125 ml) Parmesan cheese, oregano and 2 cups (500 ml) of the flour. Blend well and then beat vigorously about 3 minutes until air bubbles form. According to general directions for batter breads, gradually add remaining flour. Cover with tea towel and let rise in warm place 45 minutes to 1 hour or until more than double in bulk. Stir down batter for 30 strokes and turn into a well-buttered 2-quart (2 L) casserole. Sprinkle with 1 tablespoon (15 ml) Parmesan cheese and bake in oven preheated to 375°F (190°C) 1 hour or until bread tests done. Turn out onto wire rack, turn right side up and cool.

Grate cheese onto a wet plate—it slips right off.

Swedish wire beater

RYE BATTER BREAD

When is a rye bread awry? When it neither looks nor feels like the familiar long, fine-textured, dark rye loaf, as in this peasanty batter rye. The wheel shape that comes out of the casserole is a natural for buffet or patio-table centerpiece, crowned with a small braid wreath of gaudy yellow and orange nasturtiums to feed the eye. The rough crusty outside covers an extra-moist inside—the makings of a self-rising success.

Makes One Loaf
2 tablespoons (30 ml) active
   dry yeast
1 cup (250 ml) lukewarm water
3 tablespoons (45 ml) molasses
1 teaspoon (5 ml) liquid
   lecithin (optional)
2 tablespoons (30 ml) butter,
   cut in bits
1 cup (250 ml) milk, scalded
2 to 3 teaspoons (10 to 15 ml)
   caraway seeds
2 teaspoons (10 ml) salt
1-1/2 cups (350 ml) rye flour
2-1/4 cups (525 ml) unbleached
   white flour, or as needed

Sprinkle yeast over water, stir to dissolve and let stand until foamy. Stir in molasses and lecithin. Stir butter into milk and let cool to lukewarm. Add caraway seeds and salt to milk mixture, then combine with yeast mixture. Beat in rye flour and 1 cup (250 ml) of the unbleached flour. According to general directions for batter breads, gradually add remaining unbleached flour. Cover with tea towel and let rise in warm place until triple in bulk. Beat down and let rise until double in bulk. Stir down and spoon into a *well*-greased 1-1/2-quart (1.5 L) straight-sided casserole or souffle dish. Place in oven, turn heat to 375°F (190°C) and bake 40 to 45 minutes or until bread tests done. Bake as above, turn out onto wire rack, turn right side up and cool.

SALLY LUNN

Rooting out origins of breads, particularly with a name like Sally Lunn, can lead down many lanes. One gossip has it that Beau Brummel munched Sally's cakes in her tiny bakery in Bath. Elizabeth David, in her comprehensive *English Bread & Yeast Cookery,* writes that it was called a "rich French breakfast cake"; she also indicates that it was made in a bun shape with scalded clotted cream

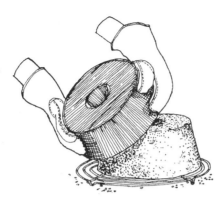

(a cholesterol nightmare!). This recipe uses only a modest one-third cup of butter, the traditional lemon peel and currants and is a soft-dough batter bread. A tube pan bakes a beautiful ring, though the originals were hoop-shaped. The hoops were sliced horizontally into two or three layers, spread with thick cream or butter, then assembled again. We think you'll enjoy knowing Sally as in this recipe, however, without the butter and cream calories.

Makes One Bundt or Tube Loaf
1 tablespoon (15 ml) active dry yeast
1/2 cup (125 ml) lukewarm water
2 tablespoons (30 ml) honey
1/3 cup (75 ml) butter, cut in bits

1/2 cup (125 ml) milk, scalded
3 eggs, at room temperature
1 teaspoon (5 ml) salt
1 tablespoon (15 ml) freshly grated lemon peel
4 cups (1 L *sifted*) unbleached white flour
2/3 cup (150 ml) dried currants

Sprinkle yeast over water, stir in honey and let stand until foamy. Stir butter into milk to dissolve; cool to lukewarm. In large bowl, beat eggs lightly and stir in proofed yeast, milk mixture, salt and lemon peel. Beat in 2 cups (500 ml) of the flour until well blended. Stir in currants. According to general directions for batter breads, gradually beat in remaining flour. Cover with tea towel and let rise in warm place 45 minutes or until double in bulk. Beat down and spread evenly in a well-buttered Bundt or large tube pan, cover with tea towel and let rise in warm place 45 minutes or until a little over double in size. Bake in oven preheated to 375°F (190°C) 35 minutes or until bread tests done. If top seems to be browning too fast, cover loosely with foil. Run knife down sides and center of pan to loosen bread, turn out onto wire rack, turn right side up and cool.

Rolls & Small Breads

the snail

the "U"

the knot

the "8"

the butterfly

the Parker House

the braid

the lifesaver

the hand

fun with small yeast rolls

Small is not only beautiful, it's also bountiful: Here are hard rolls and soft, supper rolls and whole-wheat refrigerator ones, English muffins and bagels, pocket bread and a whole bunch of bread stick recipes.

We saw it in New York: at ten in the morning, a Brooks Brothers suit striding up Madison Avenue, munching a Zum-Zum sausage on hard roll. We saw it in Seattle: two pretty young women on Fifth Avenue, window-looking during the lunch hour with hands full of stuffed pita bread. If the past decade has brought any eating habit out of the social closet into popular acceptance, surely "finger" food is it. Lunch bags, school buckets and picnics have always lined up for finger food—primarily something wrapped in bread—and no one would dream of questioning them. But it's the relaxation of custom all over the country that has brought this new interest in finger food, and little breads are the quick answer for any time of day or night, for any occasion. They can be eaten simply warm with butter, filled with truffled pate or corned beef and sauerkraut, or slathered with preserved wild blackberries from Washington's burnt-over meadows.

Bake a batch of herb or bacon buns, freeze them and you're ready for a dozen lunch boxes. Cheese rolls are easy and raisin bagels are a mad morning's pursuit.

FRENCH BREAD ROLLS

There is something very basic about tearing apart a fresh hard roll and fighting that first bite without waiting for butter. Attack one of these rolls and its fragrance and crust will be your award for kneading and patience. They're superior envelopes for a juicy hamburger patty, or for salami, onions and three kinds of cheese. And don't forget that they slice like tiny bread, can be dipped in egg and will come up delicious French toast for one.

Makes Sixteen to Twenty
3-3/4 cups (850 ml) unbleached
   white flour, or as needed
2 cups (500 ml) lukewarm
   water
1 tablespoon (15 ml) active dry
   yeast
1/2 tablespoon (7.5 ml) salt
Yellow cornmeal
Egg White Wash, page 222

In large mixing bowl, measure 2-1/2 cups (600 ml) of the flour. Make a well in center and pour in 1/3 cup (75 ml) of the water. Sprinkle yeast over, stir to dissolve, cover with tea towel and let stand until foamy. Gradually beat in remaining water until well blended. Beat vigorously about 3 minutes until air bubbles form. Cover with tea towel and let rest 30 minutes or up to 8 hours. Sprinkle salt over, stir in and gradually beat in remaining flour to make stiff dough. Turn out onto lightly floured board and knead at least 10 minutes, adding additional flour only as needed, until smooth and pliable but still soft. Form into smooth ball, place in lightly floured bowl and sprinkle top lightly with flour. Cover with plastic wrap and lightly dampened terry towel. Let stand at room temperature 1-1/2 to 2 hours or until double in bulk. Punch down, knead briefly, cover with tea towel and let rest 10 minutes. Divide into 16 to 20 equal portions approximately 2 ounces (56 g) each, form into smooth balls, cover with tea towel and let rise 1 hour. With palm of hand, flatten each ball slightly, fold in long edges as if forming a loaf and shape into ovals. Rolls may also be reformed into balls. Arrange on greased baking sheet sprinkled with cornmeal, cover with tea towel and let rise 45 minutes or until almost double in size. For baking instructions, see French Bread, page 66.

Just before baking, with scissors snip a pattern (see sketch) on top of each roll and brush lightly with Egg White Wash. After 10 minutes of baking, remove pan of water and turn baking sheet around for even browning. Mist several times during remaining baking. Rolls

flatten each ball slightly

-- then fold into ovals and pinch as if forming a loaf

snip with scissors just before baking

103

will brown in approximately 20 minutes in all. Remove to wire rack and serve hot. Or cool, place in brown paper bag (not plastic) and reheat directly on oven shelf 10 minutes in 350°F (180°C) oven.

NOTE Dough may rise in the refrigerator up to 24 hours. Two hours before shaping into balls, remove to room temperature and proceed as above. Dough will be slightly more sticky, resulting in extra-light texture.

DUTCH CRUNCH ROLLS

You've probably looked at bakers' rolls and breads with a thick crack-strewn, floury topping. *That* is Dutch crunch, and a new taste sensation if you haven't bitten into a Dutch crunch roll. We turned up a generous friend who could lead us to the proper ingredients, and here they are. The rice flour is the surprise—but *don't* make the mistake of buying *sweet* rice flour because that's not the bread baker's kind. In metropolitan areas, the right kind is available in stores selling Oriental foods; otherwise, try a natural-foods store.

Makes Sixteen
1 recipe French Bread Rolls, page 103

Dutch Crunch Topping
2 tablespoons (30 ml) active
    dry yeast
1 cup (250 ml) lukewarm water
4 teaspoons (20 ml) granulated
    sugar
2 tablespoons (30 ml) safflower
    or corn oil
1-2/3 cups (410 ml) rice flour
1/2 tablespoon (7.5 ml) salt

Prepare French Bread Rolls. After second rising, form into 16 smooth balls and set aside to rise. Twenty minutes before ready to bake, make topping. Sprinkle yeast over water, stir in 1 teaspoon (5 ml) of the sugar and let stand until foamy. Stir in remaining sugar, the oil, flour and salt. Beat well and set aside. Place a shallow pan on bottom shelf of oven and preheat oven to 375°F (190°C). Just before baking, beat topping and dip a ball of dough in mixture to coat top one third. Place dipped side up on baking sheet. Repeat with remaining balls, beating topping several times during process to make sure it remains well mixed. Pour 1/2 cup (125 ml) water into heated pan in oven. Place baking sheet of rolls on rack above pan and bake 20 minutes or until golden, removing water pan after 10 minutes. Transfer to wire rack and serve warm.

LUNCHEON ROLLS

These rich, yielding rolls can be hustled into your luncheon menu if you start about 9 A.M. Jog a couple miles while they're rising, come back and shape them, and you'll still have time to get yourself and the lunch organized by the time they come to the table basketed and cuddled in a crisp, white linen napkin. Handmade rolls are a gracious compliment to guests.

*Makes Approximately
Four Dozen*
1 tablespoon (15 ml) active dry
    yeast
1/4 cup (60 ml) lukewarm
    water
2 tablespoons (30 ml) honey
1/2 cup (125 ml) heavy cream,
    scalded
1-1/4 cups (300 ml) unbleached
    white flour, or as needed
Double recipe Milk Wash,
    page 222

Sprinkle yeast over water, stir to dissolve and let stand until foamy. Stir honey into cream, cool to lukewarm and combine with proofed yeast. Gradually beat in flour to make stiff dough. Turn out onto floured board and knead, adding additional flour only to prevent sticking, 5 minutes. Dough will be quite soft. Form into smooth ball, place in oiled bowl, turn to coat all surfaces, cover with tea towel and let rise in warm place 1 hour, or until double in bulk. Punch down, knead briefly and roll out and/or pat into rectangle or oval 1/3 inch (1 cm) thick. With 1-1/2-inch (4 cm) cookie cutter, cut into rounds. Place rounds 1 inch (3 cm) apart on buttered baking sheets, cover with tea towel and let rise in warm place 45 minutes or until almost double in size. Bake in oven preheated to 375°F (190°C) 12 to 15 minutes, or until golden. Brush with Milk Wash and return to oven for 2 minutes. Remove to wire rack and serve hot.

POTATO ROLLS

These natural children of that delicious Potato Egg Bread are enriched by milk. They play dress-up as Garlic-Potato Rolls, and sugary Pecan Rolls, and even masquerade as down-home croissants. Let them play on your imagination and in your kitchen. (Can't afford to give your girl a Rolls? Scoop out a potato roll, wrap it around diamond earrings and tie with a ribbon.)

Makes Sixteen
1/2 recipe Potato Egg Bread, page 64
1/2 cup (125 ml) milk, scalded and cooled to lukewarm

Prepare Potato Egg Bread dough, substituting milk for 1/2 cup (125 ml) of the potato cooking water or water. After dough rests, divide into 16 equal portions, approximately 2 ounces (56 g) each. Roll each portion into a smooth ball and place in 16 buttered muffin wells. Cover with tea towel and let rise in warm place 45 minutes, or until almost double in size. Bake in oven preheated to 350°F (180°C) 35 minutes or until rolls test done. Serve hot.

CRESCENT ROLLS Roll each half portion into a circle 9 inches (23 cm) in diameter. Cut each circle into 8 wedges and roll in the same manner as a croissant, page 116. Let rise and bake as above.

GARLIC-POTATO ROLLS Add to dough with milk 2 teaspoons (10 ml) finely minced garlic. Before baking, brush lightly with Egg White Wash, page 222, and sprinkle with coarse salt.

PECAN ROLLS Roll dough into a rectangle approximately 3/8 inch (1 cm) thick. Brush lightly with melted butter. Starting at a long side, roll tightly like a jelly roll. Cut into 1-1/2-inch (4 cm) slices (page 138). Butter 4-inch (10 cm) foil tart pans. Sprinkle brown sugar, ground cinnamon and freshly grated orange peel in each pan. Arrange pecan halves in pans, round side down. Place 1 slice, cut side up, on top of mixture in each pan. Let rise and bake as above. Turn out so that nut mixture is on top. Eat hot.

105

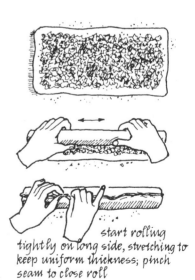

start rolling tightly on long side, stretching to keep uniform thickness; pinch seam to close roll

CHEESE ROLLS

Two cheeses, low-fat cottage cheese and that pale-gold Swiss Emmentaler with its slightly nutty flavor, impart a special magnetism to these generous country-style small breads. Minced onions and chives, a generous portion of nutritious whole-wheat flour, and that sprinkling of coarse salt make them downright irresistible when served hot with a crock of unsalted butter.

Makes One Dozen

2 teaspoons (10 ml) active dry yeast
2/3 cup (150 ml) lukewarm water
1 teaspoon (5 ml) honey
1-1/2 cups (350 ml) unbleached white flour, or as needed
1/4 cup (60 ml) finely minced onion
1 tablespoon (15 ml) olive oil
3/4 cup (175 ml) whole-wheat flour
1/4 teaspoon (1.2 ml) baking soda
1-1/2 cups (350 ml) lightly packed finely shredded Emmentaler cheese
1 tablespoon (15 ml) chopped fresh chives
2/3 cup (150 ml) low-fat cottage cheese
Egg White Wash, 222
Coarse salt

In large bowl, sprinkle yeast over water, stir in honey and let stand until foamy. Stir in 1 cup (250 ml) of the unbleached white flour and beat vigorously about 3 minutes until air bubbles form. Cover with tea towel and let rise in warm place 30 to 40 minutes. Combine whole-wheat flour and baking soda and toss with Emmentaler cheese and chives. Stir into yeast sponge with onions and cottage cheese. Gradually add remaining unbleached white flour to make a slightly sticky dough. Turn out onto floured board and knead, adding additional unbleached flour as needed to prevent excessive sticking, 5 minutes. Dough will remain slightly sticky; oil hands and board lightly last 2 minutes of kneading. Form into ball, place in oiled bowl, turn to coat all surfaces, cover with tea towel and let rise in warm place 1-1/2 hours or until double in bulk. Punch down and divide into 3 equal portions. Divide each portion into 4 equal portions. Roll each portion into a smooth ball, place them in 9-inch (23 cm) round baking pan and prick with tines of fork. Brush with wash and sprinkle with coarse salt. Cover with tea towel and let rise in warm place 1 hour and 15 minutes or until almost double in size. Bake in oven preheated to 350°F (180°C) 30 minutes or until rolls test done. Transfer to wire rack, cool slightly and serve warm.

QUICK YEAST BISCUIT ROLLS

Say "biscuit" and a picture of a fluffy, baking-powder round pops into mind. But you have a pleasant surprise if you switch images and make these jolly little buttermilk rolls. It'll be hard to stop popping them in your mouth. The yeast subtly transforms the slightly bitter baking-powder aftertaste (self-rising flour has both baking powder and baking soda in its makeup) to a nice new taste sensation. Chalk up another breakaway from the humdrum.

*Makes Approximately
Twenty-eight*

1/2 tablespoon (7.5 ml) active
   dry yeast
1/4 cup (60 ml) lukewarm
   water
1 tablespoon (15 ml) granulated
   sugar
1/4 cup (60 ml) safflower oil
1 cup (250 ml) buttermilk,
   at room temperature
2-3/4 cups (650 ml) self-rising
   white flour

In large bowl, sprinkle yeast
over water, stir in sugar and let
stand until foamy. Stir in remaining ingredients, mix well,
cover tightly with plastic wrap
and refrigerate several hours or
up to 1 week.

When ready to bake, with
floured hands (if using metric
measures, you might need a
little more flour) divide into 28
small balls approximately 1
ounce (28 g) each. Place balls
in buttered miniature muffin-
tin wells and bake in oven
preheated to 350°F (180°C) 15
minutes or until golden and
test done. Serve immediately.

ONION SUPPER CLOVERLEAFS

Another winning idea for supper-
tamers, given about three hours
notice. These get their charms
from onions, bacon, minced
fresh herbs, cheese and whole-
wheat flour with the white.
They're so complete you can
lean the menu on them and one
main dish, or a plate of cold
meats and cheeses and the
meal will become a legend.

Makes One Dozen

1 tablespoon (15 ml) active
   dry yeast
1/2 cup (125 ml) lukewarm
   water
1 tablespoon (15 ml) honey
1 cup (250 ml) whole-wheat
   flour
1 tablespoon (15 ml) butter,
   melted and cooled slightly
1 egg, at room temperature and
   lightly beaten
1/2 cup (125 ml) sieved ricotta
   cheese, at room temperature
3 tablespoons (45 ml) finely
   minced onion
3 tablespoons (45 ml)
   crumbled crisply cooked
   bacon
1/2 teaspoon (2.5 ml) salt
2 teaspoons (10 ml) minced
   fresh chives
1 teaspoon (5 ml) minced fresh
   oregano or marjoram
1 cup (250 ml) unbleached
   white flour, or as needed

In large warmed bowl, sprinkle
yeast over water, stir to dissolve
and let stand until foamy. Stir
in honey and whole-wheat flour.
Beat vigorously about 3 minutes
until air bubbles form. Beat in
butter, egg, cheese, onion, bacon,
salt and herbs. Gradually beat
in unbleached white flour to
form stiff dough. Turn out onto
floured board and knead, adding
additional flour as needed to
prevent sticking, 5 minutes. If
dough is still quite sticky, lightly
oil board and hands; continue
kneading 3 more minutes until
smooth and pliable. Form into
smooth ball. Place in oiled
bowl, turn to coat all surfaces,
cover with tea towel and let
rise in warm place 1 hour and
15 minutes or until double in
bulk. Punch down, form into
ball, cover with tea towel and
let rest 5 minutes. Divide into
12 equal portions approximately
2 ounces (56 g) each. Then
divide each portion into 3 equal
parts and roll each into a
smooth ball. Place 3 balls in
each of 12 buttered muffin-tin
wells. Cover with tea towel and
let rise 40 minutes or until
almost double in size. Bake in
oven preheated to 350°F (180°C)
25 to 30 minutes until browned
and test done. Serve hot.

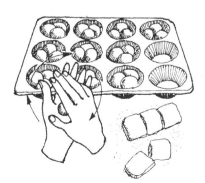

WHOLE-WHEAT BARBECUE BUNS

Here is a serious problem you'll have to face: Try *our* burger buns and you may never be able to eat a run-of-the-franchise triple-decker again. Goodbye to faceless, cottony white buns and hotdog rolls. Even kids with vinyl palates will probably agree, and certainly the family budget will smack its lips. Now's the time to lead young burger snatchers into the fun of making and baking—a great Saturday project. Let them do it alone— the only valid way to learn.

Makes Six to Eight

1 tablespoon (15 ml) active
    dry yeast
1 cup (250 ml) lukewarm
    water
2 tablespoons (30 ml) brown
    sugar
1-2/3 cups (400 ml) unbleached
    white flour, or as needed
3 tablespoons (45 ml) non-
    instant nonfat dry milk
3 tablespoons (60 ml) butter,
    cut in bits and softened
1/2 teaspoon (2.5 ml) salt
1 cup (250 ml) whole-wheat
    flour
Egg White Wash, page 222
Sesame seeds, poppy seeds,
    caraway seeds or dried onion
    flakes

In large bowl, sprinkle yeast over water, stir in sugar and let stand until foamy. Sift 1 cup (250 ml) of the unbleached white flour with dry milk and stir into proofed yeast. Beat vigorously about 3 minutes until air bubbles form, cover with tea towel and let rest at room temperature 30 to 45 minutes. Beat in butter and salt until blended and gradually add whole-wheat flour and remaining unbleached flour, blending well. Turn out onto lightly floured board and knead, adding addi- tional flour as needed to pre- vent sticking, 5 minutes or until smooth and pliable. Form into smooth ball, place in oiled bowl, turn to coat all surfaces, cover with tea towel and let rise in warm place 1 hour or until double in bulk. Punch down, knead briefly, cover with tea towel and let rest 5 to 10 minutes. Divide into 6 to 8

for large buns, foil tart pans or a Yorkshire pudding pan

equal portions, approximately 3 ounces (84 g) to 4 ounces (112 g) each. For hamburger buns, form each portion into a ball and place in 6 or 8 buttered 4-inch (10 cm) foil tart pans arranged on baking sheet. Flatten balls slightly, cover with tea towel and let rise in warm place until half again double in size. For hotdog buns, form into 6 to 8 logs approximately 5 to 7 inches (13 to 18 cm) long. Place on buttered baking sheet and let rise as above. Brush buns lightly with Egg White Wash and sprinkle with seeds or onion flakes. Place in oven, turn heat to 350°F (180°C) and bake 20 minutes or until buns are lightly golden and test done. Turn out onto rack, turn right side up and cool.

ONION BUNS Saute 1 medium onion, very thinly sliced, in 1 to 2 tablespoons (15 to 30 ml) butter until soft. Just before baking, spread on top of buns.

HERB BUNS Add with salt 1/4 cup (60 ml) minced fresh chives, 2 tablespoons (30 ml) dill seed or 2 to 3 teaspoons (10 to 15 ml) celery seeds.

BACON BUNS Substitute for 2 tablespoons (30 ml) of the but- ter 2 tablespoons (30 ml) bacon drippings. Add with salt 1/3 cup (75 ml) crumbled crisply cooked bacon.

WHOLE-WHEAT REFRIGERATOR ROLLS

Holiday dinners and luncheons are hard to plan for, and these wholesome rolls have saved and enhanced the reputations of many a harried kitchen maid—or man—by waiting in the wings in the refrigerator. This is "convenience" baking in the fullest sense of the word: Set them up before a big party, wrap and stash in the cool box (not freezer) for up to 24 hours. Allow about 60 minutes from the moment you remove from the refrigerator to the table.

Makes Eighteen

1-1/2 tablespoons (22.5 ml) active dry yeast
1/4 cup (60 ml) lukewarm water
2 tablespoons (30 ml) brown sugar
4 tablespoons butter, cut in bits, or lard, at room temperature
1/2 cup (125 ml) milk, scalded
1/4 cup (60 ml) water
1 egg, at room temperature
1-1/2 cups (350 ml) whole-wheat flour
1 to 1-1/2 teaspoons (5 to 7.5 ml) salt
1/3 cup (75 ml) poppy seeds
1-1/2 cups (360 ml) unbleached white flour, or as needed
Melted butter

Sprinkle yeast over lukewarm water, stir in 1 teaspoon (5 ml) of the sugar and let stand until foamy. Add butter to milk, stir to melt and add sugar to dissolve. Add water and let cool to lukewarm. In large bowl, beat egg lightly and stir in proofed yeast, milk mixture and whole-wheat flour. Beat vigorously about 3 minutes until air bubbles form. Sprinkle salt and poppy seeds over, blend well and gradually beat in 1-1/4 cups (300 ml) of the unbleached white flour. Sprinkle board with remaining 1/4 cup (60 ml) unbleached flour and knead, adding additional flour as needed to prevent sticking, 5 minutes until smooth and pliable. Divide dough into 3 equal portions and divide each portion into 6 equal parts. Roll each part into a smooth ball and flatten with palm to make a circle. Brush circles with melted butter. Score the center of each circle with a knife, fold in half and place in buttered muffin-tin wells. Repeat with remaining dough. Cover with plastic wrap and refrigerate 2 hours or up to 24 hours. Remove from refrigerator, let rise in warm place 40 minutes or until almost double in bulk and bake in oven preheated to 375°F (190°C) 20 minutes or until rolls test done. If rolls seem to be browning too quickly, cover with foil last 5 minutes. Serve hot.

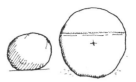

flatten ball into circle; press the back of a knife into dough, above the center and fold on crease, then place in buttered muffin tin

A small amount of soy flour added to yeast breads will keep bread fresh longer by slowing rancidity of fats.

ENGLISH MUFFINS

A 1754 cookbook warns "... don't touch them with a knife either to spread or cut them open, if you do they will be heavy as Lead." That advice still holds. Always split a muffin with fork or fingers to get that raggedy surface that toasts so invitingly. If you read a dozen books, you'll get a dozen directions for making these airy, chewy rounds. But then it's contradiction that makes baking such a challenge. Start with our viewpoint and we promise you'll be pleased.

110

An added hint (from an English source): Heat the flour in a 250°F (120°C) oven for ten minutes before mixing it into the yeast sponge. This is said to insure the lightly crusted outside and the honeycombed inside that waits for the butter. Also, an iron griddle may overheat in the center if you're using gas; a square aluminum one distributes heat more evenly (oil lightly before using).

Makes Approximately
Six to Eight
1 tablespoon (15 ml) active dry yeast
1 cup (250 ml) lukewarm water
1 teaspoon (5 ml) honey
1-1/2 cups (350 ml) unbleached white flour, or as needed
1 cup (250 ml) pure gluten flour
2 tablespoons (30 ml) butter, cut in bits and softened
2 teaspoons (10 ml) salt
1 cup (250 ml) whole-wheat flour
Yellow cornmeal

use a clean tuna can, without top or bottom, for cutting muffins

In large bowl, sprinkle yeast over water, stir to dissolve, stir in honey and let stand until foamy. Add 1 cup (250 ml) of the unbleached white flour and the gluten flour. Beat vigorously approximately 3 minutes until air bubbles form. Beat in butter, salt, whole-wheat flour and remaining unbleached flour to form stiff dough. Turn out onto lightly floured board and knead, adding additional white flour only to prevent sticking, 8 minutes or until smooth and pliable. Form into smooth ball, place in oiled bowl, turn to coat all surfaces, cover with tea towel and let rise in warm place 1-1/2 hours or until slightly more than double in bulk. Punch down, knead briefly and with rolling pin roll out 3/4 inch (2 cm) thick. Cut into 3-1/2-inch (9 cm) rounds, sprinkle both sides with cornmeal and place on baking sheet 1-1/2 inches (4 cm) apart. Knead scraps briefly and reroll and cut. Cover loosely with tea towel and let rise in warm place 50 minutes or until almost double in size. Preheat skillet to 375°F (190°C) and cook muffins, without crowding, 7 to 8 minutes per side. Cool on wire rack.

POCKET BREAD

Like bagels, pita has an ancient heritage from the Middle East. It's a pocket bread for marvelous fillings, but it can also be the fork, spoon and plate for the Arabs. It has several names, but the recipe is basically the same. The secret is to form the dough into balls and then pat flat into circles, as one would shape tortillas. The final size can vary, but the thickness is stable. And a very hot oven is important to make the breads puff up, so you can "separate" top from bottom. Your baking sheet should be heavy, as heat will warp a lightweight one and cause uneven baking. They'll keep in the freezer, wrapped in foil, for up to six months.

Makes Eight Rounds
1 tablespoon (15 ml) active dry yeast
1-1/2 cups (350 ml) lukewarm water
1 tablespoon (15 ml) honey
1-1/2 cups (350 ml) unbleached white flour, or as needed
1-1/2 cups (350 ml) whole-wheat flour
1 teaspoon (5 ml) salt
Yellow cornmeal

In large bowl, sprinkle yeast over water, stir in honey and let stand until foamy. Beat in unbleached white flour and 1/4 cup (60 ml) of the whole-wheat flour. Beat vigorously until air bubbles form. Beat in salt and remaining whole-wheat flour to form stiff dough. Turn out onto board lightly floured with white flour and knead, adding additional flour only as needed to prevent sticking, 5 minutes or until dough is smooth and pliable. Form into smooth ball, place in oiled bowl, turn to coat all surfaces, cover with tea towel and let rise in warm place 1 hour or until double in bulk. Punch down, cover and let rise until again double in bulk. Punch down, knead briefly and divide into 8 equal portions. Knead each portion briefly and

form into a ball. Cover with tea towel and let rest 20 to 30 minutes. Turn oven heat to 500°F (260°C) and place baking sheet on lower rack to preheat. Keeping balls covered and working with 1 at a time, roll into a 7-inch (18 cm) circle approximately 1/8 inch (3 mm) thick and place on surface lightly dusted with cornmeal; cover with tea towel and repeat with remaining balls. When first 2 circles have rested 10 minutes, quickly transfer to heated baking sheet and bake on lowest rack of preheated oven 5 to 8 minutes, depending upon crispness desired, until golden and puffed. Remove to wire rack and repeat with remaining circles, continuing to bake 2 at a time.

111

There is no need to sift flour for yeast bread except when you want to blend in spices or dry ingredients that will form lumps.

WHOLE-WHEAT BAGELS

Many years ago in New York there was a famous Jewish baker who advertised on subway posters with a large photograph of someone holding a bagel. The someone was always a Chinese lady or an Indian chief. The line underneath read: "You don't have to be Jewish to like them!" Today nearly everybody (with strong molars) likes them. The roll-with-a-hole has a special place in breadmaking because it is simmered lightly in water before it is baked. This clinches the tough, unforgiving texture, which, when toasted and spread with cream cheese and smoked salmon, is the promised land for countless weary travelers. It's hard to top the taste of a plain whole-wheat bagel, but try adding raisins, almonds, onions or poppy seeds. Slice one in half and put it under the broiler or in the toaster. A sure hit.

Makes Twenty to Twenty-four
1 tablespoon (15 ml) active dry yeast
2 cups (500 ml) lukewarm potato cooking water
3 tablespoons (45 ml) malt syrup or honey
5 cups (1.2 L) unbleached white flour, or as needed
2 eggs, separated
1 teaspoon (5 ml) cold water
3 tablespoons (45 ml) corn or safflower oil
1 teaspoon (5 ml) salt
2 cups (500 ml) whole-wheat flour
Yellow cornmeal
2 to 3 teaspoons (10 to 15 ml) granulated sugar (optional)
Sesame or poppy seeds, or chopped onion sauteed in butter until soft (optional)

In large warmed bowl, sprinkle yeast over 1/4 cup (50 ml) of the potato water, stir to dissolve and let stand until foamy. Add remaining potato water, malt syrup and 3 cups (700 ml) of the unbleached white flour. Beat vigorously about 3 minutes until air bubbles form. Cover with tea towel and let stand at room temperature 30 to 45 minutes.

Beat egg yolks, remove 1 tablespoon (15 ml) and beat with cold water; set aside. Beat remaining yolks lightly with whites and add to yeast mixture with oil, salt and whole-wheat flour. Mix well and gradually add remaining white flour to make a stiff dough. Turn out onto floured board and, adding additional flour only as needed to prevent sticking, knead 10 minutes. Form into smooth ball, place in oiled bowl, turn to coat

shape each rope into a ring, moisten ends so they stick when overlapped

all surfaces, cover with tea towel and let rise in warm place 1-1/2 hours or until double in bulk.

Punch down and divide into 20 to 24 equal portions. Knead 1 portion briefly, roll into a rope approximately 3/4 inch (2 cm) in diameter and 9 inches (23 cm) long, and in palm of hand, form a circle. Pinch ends together, using water if needed to seal. Place on surface lightly sprinkled with cornmeal and repeat with remaining portions of dough. Cover with tea towel and let rise 20 to 30 minutes.

While bagels are rising, bring a large kettle of water to a gentle, rolling boil, adding sugar if desired. Set oven heat to 425°F (220°C), allowing plenty of time to reach heat. Starting with first bagels formed, drop 2 or 3 at a time into boiling water, depending upon size of pot. Boil 1-1/2 minutes, turn and boil 1-1/2 minutes on second side. Lift out with slotted spoon, draining well, and place at least 1-1/2 inches (4 cm) apart on greased baking sheet. When all bagels are boiled, brush evenly with reserved egg yolk-water mixture, being careful not to let it run down onto sheet. Sprinkle with seeds or sauteed onions, if desired. Place in preheated oven and bake 20 to 25 minutes or until golden. Remove to wire racks and let cool.

RAISIN BAGELS Add to dough with whole-wheat flour 1/2 cup (125 ml) chopped raisins.

ALMOND BAGELS Add to dough with whole-wheat flour 1/2 cup (125 ml) chopped almonds and 1 teaspoon (5 ml) freshly grated lemon peel.

ONION BAGELS Add to dough with whole-wheat flour 2/3 cup (150 ml) minced onion sauteed in butter until soft. Top bagels with additional sauteed onions before baking.

POPPY-SEED BAGELS Add to dough with whole-wheat flour 1/2 cup (125 ml) poppy seeds and 2 teaspoons (10 ml) freshly grated orange peel. Top bagels with additional poppy seeds before baking.

FRENCH BREAD STICKS

Crisp bread sticks are best eaten while waiting patiently for minestrone or a salad. They are also naturals to drive home a point in an argument and are comforters when you want something to eat but don't know what you want. We have clustered together a clan of different flavors—French bread, whole-wheat spirited with Parmesan, herbs or pine nuts, and a fragrant dark rye. Store them in a glass container with tightly fitting lid so you can enjoy

looking at them. Five minutes in a warm oven will freshen stale ones. Remember, it's not your fault if people can't keep hands off of bread sticks . . . they're addictive.

Makes Thirty-two
1 recipe French Bread Rolls, page 103
Egg White Wash, page 222
Coarse salt, poppy seeds or sesame seeds

Prepare dough for French Bread Rolls. After letting balls rise, divide each ball in half and roll each half into a rope approximately 10 inches (25 cm) long. Arrange on buttered baking sheet 1 inch (3 cm) apart, cover with tea towel and let rise until half again as large. Brush with Egg White Wash and sprinkle with coarse salt, poppy seeds or sesame seeds. Bake as directed for rolls 15 to 18 minutes or until golden and test done. Cool on wire rack.

113

To pour water into pan used to make steam for baking French bread (preheat empty pan), use long-spout watering can—keep hands away from pan area to protect from steam burn.

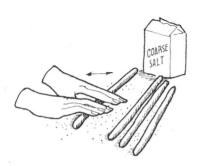

WHOLE-WHEAT BREAD STICKS

Makes Approximately Twenty-eight
1 tablespoon (15 ml) active
   dry yeast
3/4 cup (175 ml) lukewarm
   water
1 tablespoon (15 ml) honey
1/4 cup (60 ml) olive oil
1/2 cup (125 ml) milk, scalded
1 cup (250 ml) whole-wheat
   flour
1-3/4 cups (400 ml) unbleached
   white flour, or as needed
1/2 teaspoon (2.5 ml) salt
1 egg white, beaten until stiff
   but not dry
Egg Wash, page 222
Coarse salt

In large bowl, sprinkle yeast over water, stir to dissolve and let stand until foamy. Stir honey and oil into milk; cool to lukewarm. Combine with proofed yeast and stir in whole-wheat flour and 1/2 cup (125 ml) of the unbleached flour. Beat vig-orously about 3 minutes until air bubbles form. Sprinkle salt over, stir in and then stir in egg white. Gradually beat in remaining unbleached flour to make stiff dough. Turn out onto floured board and knead, adding additional flour as needed to prevent sticking, 8 minutes until dough is smooth and pliable. Form into smooth ball, place in oiled bowl, turn to coat all surfaces, cover with tea towel and let rise in warm place 1 hour or until double in bulk. Punch down and knead briefly. Pinch off 28 small balls approximately 1 ounce (28 g) each. Form each ball into oval and then roll into a rope 11 to 12 inches (28 to 30 cm) long, making sure diameter stays even. Arrange ropes 1 inch (3 cm) apart on oiled or greased baking sheets, cover with tea towel and let rise in warm place 30 minutes or until half again as large. Brush with Egg Wash and sprinkle with coarse salt. Bake in oven preheated to 375°F (190°C) 12 to 15 minutes until golden and test done. Cool on wire rack.

PARMESAN BREAD STICKS Omit Egg Wash and salt. Three minutes before they have finished baking, dip sticks in melted butter, roll in freshly grated Parmesan cheese and return to oven until done.

HERB BREAD STICKS Add with salt 1 teaspoon (5 ml) freshly grated lemon peel and 1/4 teaspoon (1.2 ml) each crumbled dried oregano, crumbled dried basil and minced garlic.

PINE-NUT BREAD STICKS Add with salt 2 teaspoons (10 ml) freshly grated orange peel and 1/2 cup (125 ml) finely chopped pine nuts.

RYE BREAD STICKS

Makes Approximately Two Dozen
1/2 recipe Dark Rye Bread,
   page 88
Egg White Wash, page 222
Caraway seeds

Prepare Dark Rye Bread dough. After first rising, pinch off small pieces of dough approximately 1 ounce (28 g) each. Form each ball into an oval and then roll into a rope approximately 10 inches (25 cm) long, making sure diameter is even. Place ropes on buttered baking sheet 1 inch (3 cm) apart, cover with tea towel and let rise until half again as large. Brush with Egg White Wash and sprinkle with caraway seeds. Bake as directed 20 minutes or until test done. Cool on wire rack.

CHINESE STEAMED BUNS

Halfway around the world from Boston and brown bread another steamed bread is the staple of millions of Chinese: steamed buns, or *bao*. They go with a number of dishes, such as Peking duck, or alone as a filling finger food, in which case they can be served plain, or filled before steaming with heavenly mixtures. We suggest a filling of plum sauce, barbecued pork (or ham or chicken), minced green onions and sesame oil. The unfilled buns are smooth and soft, and the filled ones look like pale pokes, little pleated bags with twisted top. Both are as delicate as an opening apple blossom.

Makes One Dozen

1 tablespoon (15 ml) active dry
    yeast
1-1/2 cups (350 ml) lukewarm
    water
3 tablespoons (45 ml) granu-
    lated sugar
4 cups (1 L) unbleached white
    flour, or as needed
2 tablespoons (10 ml) peanut
    or corn oil (optional)
1 teaspoon (5 ml) salt

In large bowl, sprinkle yeast over water, stir in 1 tablespoon (15 ml) of the sugar and let stand until foamy. Add remaining sugar and 2 cups (500 ml) of the flour. Beat vigorously

about 3 minutes until air bubbles form. Stir in oil and salt; gradually add remaining flour to make stiff dough. Turn out onto floured board and knead, adding additional flour as needed to prevent sticking, 5 minutes. Form into smooth ball, place in oiled bowl, turn to coat all surfaces, cover with tea towel and let rise in warm place 1 hour or until double in bulk. Punch down, form into 2 equal balls, cover with tea towel and let rest 10 to 20 minutes. Knead each portion briefly and divide into 6 equal portions. Form each portion into a smooth ball, sealing seam. Place each, seam side down, on a 4-inch (10 cm) square of waxed paper. Transfer to 4 9-inch (23 cm) bamboo steamer racks, cover with tea towel and let rise in warm place 45 minutes or until almost double in size. Stack bamboo racks, cover and place over wok filled with water to within 1/2 inch (1.5 cm) of bottom of steamer rack. Bring water to gentle boil, lower heat to keep water simmering but not boiling hard and steam 20 minutes or until buns are shiny and springy to the touch. Remove from wok and let cool, covered, 2 or 3 minutes. Serve warm.

FILLED STEAMED BUNS Pat each ball into a 4-inch (10 cm) circle. In center of each circle place 1 teaspoon (5 ml) hoisin or plum sauce, 1 tablespoon (15 ml) shredded cooked ham, barbecued pork or cooked fowl, 1/2 teaspoon (2.5 ml) minced green onion and a dash of Oriental sesame oil. Pull dough up to enclose filling, pleating and twisting top to seal. Place twisted side up on waxed paper squares and proceed as with unfilled buns.

bamboo
steamer

Croissants & Brioche

CROISSANTS
(From Bobbie's Kitchen)

This tender crescent-shaped, flaky-crisp roll is almost a ceremonial bread. Served with sweet butter and eye-opening strong coffee, it is Paris in spring, ambrosia in the first waking hour. Croissants are the ultimate achievement of breadbaking; unfortunately, their reputation for being impossible to make in a family kitchen is unwarranted. There are simple rules and a few dos and don'ts. Keep these in mind as you make your first batch and you'll have the world at your door. But don't be disappointed if the first few times your shapes are not uniform, or the layers not quite flaky enough—it takes practice.

- Keep dampened cloths handy for covering waiting dough; don't let the skin of the unbaked dough get dry or a crust will form and gum up the works.
- Butter is the only acceptable shortening; don't cheat. Unsalted butter is essential because it gives you control over the salt content of the croissants.
- Use parchment paper under and over the butter when flattening it; waxed paper will sometimes tear in the pounding/rolling.
- Work quickly; if you're timid, the dough may get the upper hand and leave you with disappointment.
- If you do not have a large enough work space, divide dough, rolling out half at a time.
- When rolling out dough, scrape away excess flour on work surface, then toss a fresh sprinkling of flour onto surface. Do this frequently.
- If the butter begins to ooze through the dough while rolling out, pat flour on trouble spot and then rush dough back to the refrigerator for 15 minutes. Cold will save the day and also slow the leavening action of the yeast.
- When cutting the dough and the triangular shapes (see pattern), use a pizza cutter; it runs a straight line so you can dispense with rulers, which take more time to maneuver.
- When baking, use a plaque (heavy-duty baking sheet with 1-inch or 3-cm sides) or other heavy baking sheet.
- If you have a gas stove or an electric stove with elements covered, just before baking throw three to four ice cubes onto bottom of oven to create steam.
- Finally, although the fragrance will excite your senses when the rolls come out of the oven, *don't* eat one immediately. They are still "baking," so wait 15 to 20 minutes. *Then* it's lift-off time (although you can wait longer and reheat).
- Parisians like their croissants dark. If you plan to freeze them, however, you may want them to be a bit paler. Achieve the right dark look when they're reheated in a 350°F (180°C) oven. Do not wrap for freezing until completely cooled.

Makes Two Dozen

4 cups (1 L) unbleached white
   flour, or as needed
2 teaspoons (10 ml) salt
2 tablespoons (30 ml) granulated sugar
1/4 cup (50 ml) instant nonfat
   dry milk
1 tablespoon (15 ml) active
   dry yeast
1-3/4 cups (450 ml) warm water
   (105° to 115°F or 42° to 46°C)

1/2 pound (250 g) unsalted
   butter, at room temperature
Egg Wash, page 222

In bowl of heavy-duty mixer, combine 2 cups (500 ml) of the flour, the salt, sugar, dry milk and yeast. Stir in water and mix 2 minutes, stirring in remaining flour 1/2 cup (125 ml) at a time to make a soft, slightly sticky dough. If dough appears excessively sticky, beat in a little more flour. Dough should clean sides of bowl. When thoroughly blended, cover bowl with plastic wrap and refrigerate 1 to 1-1/2 hours or up to 2 days.

Place butter between 2 layers of parchment paper, and with heavy rolling pin, beat the butter into a rectangle uniformly 1/4 inch (6 mm) thick. Remove top paper, and with steel baker's scraper, trim the butter into a 6- by 12-inch (15 by 30 cm) rectangle, fitting excess pieces where there is not enough to form the shape. Replace the top paper and refrigerate until butter has hardened and dough is ready.

Turn chilled dough out onto well-floured work surface that is at least 20 by 33 inches (50 by 82 cm). Pound the dough with a heavy rolling pin to flatten slightly, then roll and stretch into a 8- by 20-inch (20 by 50 cm) rectangle. Use fingers to shape square corners. Place the butter on the dough as shown in diagram. Fold unbuttered third of dough over onto the middle third, covering one half of the butter. Then fold the last third over on top of the pile of dough. Your dough will be folded exactly like a business letter with 2 separate layers of butter inside. Thus you will have a layer of dough, butter, dough, butter and dough. Flatten with rolling pin and roll into a 8- by 16-inch (20 by 40 cm) rectangle. Again fold into thirds and turn the dough so that the open edge of the fold is on the righthand side, like a book. Flatten and roll a third time, repeating same steps. Wrap dough tightly in a cloth that has been soaked in water and wrung out, place package in plastic bag, fold top of bag over and refrigerate 2 hours.

After chilling, pound and roll dough flat and fold in thirds as before. Give a half turn, roll and fold again. Dampen cloth, rewrap and refrigerate overnight.

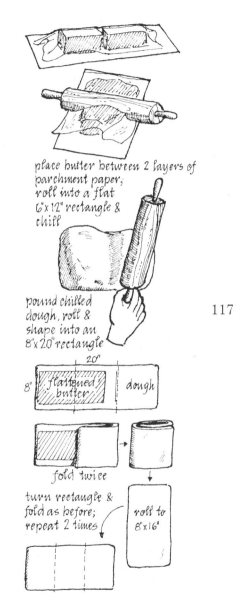

place butter between 2 layers of parchment paper; roll into a flat 6"x 12" rectangle & chill

pound chilled dough, roll & shape into an 8"x 20" rectangle

8" — 20" — flattened butter — dough

fold twice

turn rectangle & fold as before; repeat 2 times

roll to 8"x16"

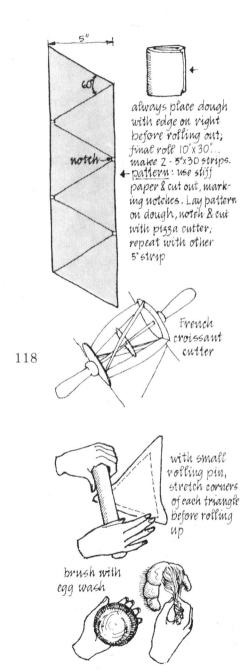

5"

60°

notch →

always place dough
with edge on right
before rolling out;
final roll 10"x30"...
make 2 - 5"x30 strips.
← pattern: use stiff
paper & cut out, mark-
ing notches. Lay pattern
on dough, notch & cut
with pizza cutter;
repeat with other
5" strip

French
croissant
cutter

118

with small
rolling pin,
stretch corners
of each triangle
before rolling
up

brush with
egg wash

The next morning, place dough on well-floured surface and roll out to a long rectangle 10 by 30 inches (25 by 75 cm). Cut in half lengthwise and put 1 strip, rewrapped, back in plastic bag; refrigerate. You are now working with a piece of dough 5 by 30 inches (13 by 75 cm). Lay pattern (as shown in sketch) on dough strip and cut notches to mark triangles. Remove pattern, cut dough and place triangles on upper edge of work surface so you have room to work quickly. As you work, frequently scrape excess flour from work surface and toss fresh flour onto surface and dough; excess flour on dough can be dusted off with a pastry brush after triangles are cut and as they are being formed. With wide end of tri-angle nearest you, use a short rolling pin to stretch point away and to widen base. Tri-angles will be approximately 7 inches (18 cm) from tip to bot-tom and bottom edge will be 1 to 1-1/2 inches (3 to 4 cm) wider than original triangle.

With thumbs and forefingers, start crescent roll at base, dusting off excess flour with pastry brush and rolling tightly—and rapidly. Form crescent so point is underneath top of curve facing away from curve. With mister, spray plaque or baking sheet with water. Form

each roll into a U-shape on pan, with hidden point facing toward the bottom of the U, as shown in drawing. Arrange the rolls at least 1 inch (3 cm) apart. (When baked, the shape modifies to a C.) Being careful not to drip onto pan, brush croissants evenly with Egg Wash.

Repeat with other half of dough after rerolling to 5- by 30-inch (13 by 75 cm) rectangle. Let croissants rise, uncovered, approximately 2 hours or until almost double in size. Allowing plenty of time to preheat oven, turn heat to 450°F (230°C). Brush rolls again with Egg Wash. Bake 10 minutes, check to see if they are browning too fast (in which case cover loosely with foil), turn plaque around in oven for even baking and bake 5 minutes longer or until croissants are desired color. Transfer to wire rack and cool.

Unsalted butter is the key to controlling the salt content of breads like croissants and brioche.

BRIOCHE

This is the golden bread of breads. When you have mastered it, you have earned the baker's crown. Brioche is an elegant butter-and-egg dough, halfway between a bread and a cake. It is fine textured and fragrant, usually baked in a fluted pan and identified by a fat brown topknot. This is called a *brioche a tete.* The large one is *grosse,* the small *petit.* Shaped into a ring, it becomes a crown brioche, elaborate with dough decorations; it converts into wrappings for sausages, for pates, for cheese. A tall one, baked in a coffee can, is *brioche mousseline.* In its most tantalizing form, it is the *petit pain au chocolat* so loved by French school children. (The long roll hides a thick stick of grainy milk chocolate. It is kept in the pocket to warm—and to be devoured at recess. Leave out the currants.)

Brioche dough is no more complicated than any yeast dough, but it takes time and it takes attention to method, and should never be rushed in rising.
● Strenuous mixing by heavy-duty mixer or by hand gives the springy, feather-light texture. Enlist the help of a strong tennis arm if you don't have the former.
● If you've forgotten to take the eggs out of the refrigerator

grosse brioche à tête

ahead of time, warm them in hot water to help them mix into the dough more readily.
● Prolonged chilling is very important to make the dough firm enough to handle.
● Muffin or small pie tins can be used to bake *brioche a tete,* but if you're going to present something so special, the fluted pans will add fillip and are worth the investment. Liberally brush the pan with melted butter before shaping dough.
● Cutting fresh brioche with a knife is not done in France. Breaking off pieces is considered *de rigueur.*
● The bread is very durable. Well-wrapped loaves will keep fresh at room temperature four to five days, or can be frozen. Reheat in a 350°F (180°C) oven ten minutes after thawing.

Makes One to Two Dozen Petit and One Grosse Brioche
4 cups (950 ml) unbleached white flour, or as needed
2 tablespoons (30 ml) instant nonfat dry milk
2 teaspoons (10 ml) salt
3 tablespoons (45 ml) granulated sugar
1/2 teaspoon (2.5 ml) ground ginger
1 tablespoon (15 ml) active dry yeast
1/4 cup (60 ml) warm water (115°F or 46°C)
6 eggs, at room temperature
1/2 pound (250 g) unsalted butter, at room temperature
1 cup (250 ml) dried currants, plumped in 2 tablespoons (30 ml) dark rum or white wine
Egg Wash, page 222

In bowl of heavy-duty mixer, combine 2 cups (500 ml) of the flour, the milk, salt, sugar, ginger and yeast. Add water and mix 1 to 2 minutes. One at a time and beating after each addition, add eggs. Mix for at least 2 minutes. Gradually add 1 cup (250 ml) more flour. When well blended, cut butter into 1/2-inch (1.5 cm) pieces and gradually beat into dough. Squeeze liquid out of currants and add them to dough. Gradually add remaining flour and continue beating 2 minutes longer.

Dough will be very floppy when you turn it out onto a

heavily floured board. Use a steel baker's scraper to lift and fold dough, turning it as you do, in a kind of rolling rather than kneading pattern. An additional 1/2 cup (125 ml) flour may be needed during the 5-minute kneading time. Dough should still be quite soft and pliable, but not sticky. Form into smooth ball, place in oiled bowl, turn to coat all surfaces, cover with plastic wrap and let rise in warm place 1 hour or until double in bulk. Punch down, turn over in bowl, cover with moist cloth and refrigerate 2 hours. Punch down, turn over in bowl, cover with tea towel and let stand at room temperature 2 hours. Again punch down, cover with moist cloth and refrigerate overnight.

PETIT BRIOCHE Bake these tiny brioche in 2 dozen 2-1/4-inch (6 cm) or 1 dozen 3-inch (8 cm) fluted pans that have been liberally brushed with melted butter. Divide dough into 2 equal portions, returning 1 covered portion to refrigerator. Divide remaining portion into 3 equal portions; chill 2 while working with the first. With both hands, roll first portion into a log 1 inch (3 cm) in diameter. With ruler laid next to the log, carefully cut off 1- or 2-inch (3 or 5 cm) pieces, weighing approximately 1 ounce (28 g) or 2 ounces (56 g) re-

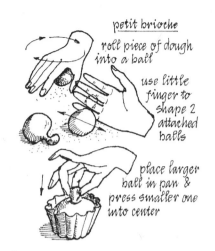

petit brioche
roll piece of dough into a ball
use little finger to shape 2 attached balls
place larger ball in pan & press smaller one into center

spectively. Under palm of hand, roll each piece, in a gentle circular motion, into a round, smooth ball. Then, with side of little finger slightly off center of ball, "cut" back and forth until you have a large ball on the lefthand side still connected to a tiny one on the right. Gently turn the large ball onto its bottom, and using quite a bit of pressure, stuff into fluted pan; with other hand press the tiny ball into the center. Repeat with remaining pieces and rest of first half of dough. Brush evenly with Egg Wash and let rise, uncovered, in warm place 1-1/2 hours or until almost double in size.

Allowing plenty of time to preheat oven, set oven heat at 450°F (230°C) and place a plaque, or other heavy baking sheet, in oven to heat. Just before baking, brush dough

again with Egg Wash, transfer the flutes to the heated pan, place in oven and bake 10 to 15 minutes or until cake tester inserted in center comes out clean. If browning too fast, cover loosely with foil. Turn out onto wire rack, turn right side up and cool.

GROSSE BRIOCHE A TETE Brush a 6-cup (1.4 L) fluted mold liberally with melted butter. Form three fourths of second half of dough into a smooth round ball and place in bottom of mold. With fingers, make a funnel-shaped hole in center of dough 2-1/2 inches (6 cm) wide at the top and at least 2 inches (5 cm) deep. Form a ball from remaining dough and with fingers form into a teardrop shape. Insert pointed end of teardrop into hole in dough, making a topknot. Brush with Egg Wash and let rise, uncovered, in warm place 1-1/2 to 2 hours or until almost double in size. Preheat oven to 475°F (245°C) 20 minutes, placing plaque or heavy baking sheet in oven to heat. Place filled brioche pan on plaque and bake 20 minutes. If browning too fast, cover loosely with foil. Reduce oven heat to 350°F (180°C) and bake an additional 20 to 25 minutes, or until cake tester inserted in center comes out clean. Turn out onto wire rack, turn right side up and cool.

Filled Breads

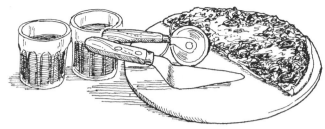

PIZZA

Mark Twain and Henry James were hooked on the spicy Italian "pie." Caruso and D'Annunzio loved them. Even the Pompeiians had a pizzeria warmed up the day Vesuvius blew its top in 79 A.D. Millions of Americans clamor for them every day.

In Naples, where pizza was born, so they say, the dough is lovingly made with a light crust, no thick rim, no doughy center. It is bathed in olive oil, doused with a number of earthy things— fresh chopped tomato, cheeses, minced garlic, black mushrooms, sausages, anchovies— though not all at the same time. Italians like their pizzas small, with wine, as appetizers, or as a midnight snack in front of the television. Just like in America, only here size has no limits, nor does choice of toppings.

Try these toppings or make up your own:
● olive oil, hot sausage, chopped green onions, thinly sliced green peppers
● olive oil, chopped fresh tomatoes, onions, mushrooms, anchovies
● olive oil, mozzarella (grated or sliced), prosciutto and black olives
● pesto made of olive oil, fresh basil, pine nuts, minced garlic and Parmesan
● over the above: basil, rosemary, marjoram, capers, parsley, black pepper, in any combination that pleases you

Makes One Large Pizza
1 tablespoon (15 ml) active dry yeast
1/4 cup (60 ml) lukewarm water
1 teaspoon (5 ml) honey
1/2 cup (125 ml) milk, scalded and cooled to lukewarm
2 tablespoons (30 ml) olive oil
3/4 cup (175 ml) whole-wheat flour
1/2 teaspoon (2.5 ml) salt
3/4 cup (175 ml) unbleached white flour, or as needed
Olive oil

In large bowl, sprinkle yeast over water, stir in honey and let stand until foamy. Combine milk and oil and stir into proofed yeast with whole-wheat flour. Beat vigorously about 3 minutes until air bubbles form. Stir in salt and gradually add unbleached white flour to make stiff dough. Turn out onto floured board and knead, adding additional flour only to prevent sticking, 8 minutes, or until smooth and pliable. Form into smooth ball, place in oiled bowl, turn to coat all surfaces, cover with tea towel and let rise in warm place 1 hour and 10 minutes or until double in bulk. Punch down, knead briefly, cover with tea towel and let rest 10 to 15 minutes. Roll and pat into a circle a little larger than a 14-inch (35 cm) pizza pan. Dough will be approximately 1/8 inch (3 mm) thick. Transfer to pizza pan oiled with olive oil and build up sides slightly to form a rim. Brush lightly with olive oil and bake in oven preheated to 425°F (220°C) 8 minutes. If dough puffs, prick gently with tines of fork to release steam. Top as desired and return to oven for 20 minutes or until nicely browned.

PIZZA TURNOVERS

Here is an earthy peasant-bread package that can be served with sterling service, or eaten out of hand. The Italians call them *calzoni* and serve them warm, with a fresh garden salad and a robust red wine. You may want to pack a picnic hamper with freshly baked turnovers (loosely wrapped in foil so the steam won't soften the crust) and reheat them on the edge of a charcoal brazier. Add a thermos of hot tomato-clam juice and a basket of summer fruits, and head for Via Italiano.

Makes Two Large Turnovers
1 recipe Pizza dough, page 121
Thinly sliced mozzarella, Cheddar or Monterey Jack cheese
Crumbled crisply cooked bacon
Crumbled dried or minced fresh oregano
Minced fresh parsley
Freshly ground black pepper

Prepare Pizza dough. After rising, knead dough briefly, cover with tea towel and let rest 10 to 15 minutes. Knead 2 to 3 minutes, divide into 2 equal portions and roll each portion into an oval approximately 1/4 inch (6 mm) thick. Down the center of each oval layer the cheese slices, overlapping them about half. Sprinkle with bacon, oregano, parsley and pepper. Pulling long sides out to 1/8-inch (3 mm) thickness, fold one side over filling, then repeat with other long side to encase completely. Seal, using a little water if necessary. Place on well-buttered baking sheets and bake in oven preheated to 400°F (210°C) 15 minutes or until browned. Serve immediately, cut into slices.

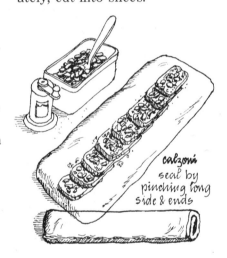

calzoni
seal by
pinching long
side & ends

focaccia

press
dimples in
with fingertips

FOCACCIA

This is northern Italy's version of pizza, usually baked on a large plaque and served cut into rectangles. It has a thicker, softer texture and is baked at 400°F (210°C) so that it can rise more in the oven. In San Francisco's Genovese bakeries, there are three popular toppings beside sugar. All start with a heavy brushing of olive oil. First, a simple sprinkling of coarse salt; second, chopped green onion; and third, a good tomato sauce and Parmesan cheese. To cut, use a pair of kitchen shears rather than a bread knife.

Makes One Large Rectangle
1 recipe Pizza dough, page 121

Prepare Pizza dough, omitting honey and substituting unbleached white flour for the whole-wheat flour. After rising, roll and pat into a rectangle approximately 1/3 inch (1 cm) thick. Cover with tea towel and let rise in warm place 40 minutes or until double in size. Top as described in introduction. Bake in oven preheated to 400°F (210°C) 20 to 30 minutes. Serve hot.

ONION PIE

In Germany during World War II, every male was called up to serve and women were left behind to run the street cars, shovel the snow and do all the hard jobs. They were drafted into heavy labor, often out of big cities to farms to help grow food for the army. Because food for workers was scarce, it took ingenuity to make the one main meal of the day. This simple pie is one example. Our version is a motherly bread meal to share on a Sunday night with old friends, accompanied with a carafe of wine and bowls of fresh cold peaches slathered with thick cream.

Makes Two Nine-inch Pies

Dough
1 tablespoon (15 ml) active dry yeast
1/4 cup (60 ml) lukewarm water
1 cup (250 ml) buttermilk
1 tablespoon (15 ml) butter, cut in bits
3/4 teaspoon (3.6 ml) salt
1/2 teaspoon (2.5 ml) malt powder (optional)
1/4 teaspoon (1.2 ml) ground ginger
2-3/4 cups (650 ml) unbleached white flour, or as needed

Sprinkle yeast over water, stir to dissolve and let stand until foamy. Heat together buttermilk and butter, stirring to melt butter. Sift together salt, malt powder, ginger and 1-1/2 cups (375 ml) of the flour. Beat into buttermilk with proofed yeast. Beat vigorously about 3 minutes until air bubbles form. Gradually add remaining flour to make stiff dough. Turn out onto floured board and knead, adding additional flour to prevent sticking, 5 to 7 minutes or until dough is smooth and pliable. Form into smooth ball, place in oiled bowl, turn to coat all surfaces, cover with *lightly* dampened towel and let rise in warm place 1 hour, or until double in bulk. Punch down, form into ball, cover with tea towel and let rest 10 minutes. Divide into 2 equal portions. On a lightly floured board, pat and then roll out each portion into a circle 10 inches (25 cm) in diameter. Transfer each circle to a buttered 9-inch (23 cm) pie tin. Gently pat into tins and form rims around edges, building up slightly. Cover with tea towel and let rise in warm place 20 minutes or until half again as large.

Topping
1-1/2 pounds (675 g) yellow onions, thinly sliced
3 tablespoons (45 ml) butter
2 tablespoons (30 ml) unbleached white flour
1 teaspoon (5 ml) cumin seed
1/4 teaspoon (1.2 ml) salt
2 eggs
1-1/2 cups (375 ml) sour cream
1/2 teaspoon (2.5 ml) sweet paprika

Saute onions in butter until translucent; cool and stir in flour, cumin seed and salt. When the pie shells have finished rising, cover bottom of each with an equal amount of onion mixture. Combine eggs and sour cream, beat lightly and pour over the onions. Sprinkle with paprika and bake in oven preheated to 375°F (190°C) 45 to 50 minutes or until custard is set and edges of dough are golden. Cut into wedges and serve immediately.

123

Use plain yoghurt in place of sour cream if you are on a diet; substitute skimmed milk for whole.

Sweet Breads

SWEET SUCCESS: FRUIT BREADS, BUNS,
BREADS FOR HOLIDAYS AND FESTIVALS

Toothsome sculptures that look difficult float from the hands of a
nine-year old; wreathes and braids rise up in splendor. A sturdy
panettone is proudly lifted from the oven by his smug grand-
father. Both are artists playing joyfully with dough. Whether one
is innocent or old, the art of baking pretty breads never ceases to
catch enthusiasm. Results may not be perfect, perhaps, but are
still satisfying: Given a glaze and sprinklings of nuts or poppy
seeds, even an *un*even coffee cake has charm to soothe the
savage yearning to express independence.

Many of the special breads in this section start with one
Basic Sweet Dough, which means you can play a whole scale of
tantalizing breads without practicing. We've provided directions
to make the pretty shapes. And if you're hesitant to try, start by
finding decorative pans which will give handsome, sculpted
forms—Turk's caps, the *Kugelhopf*-fluted tube, gelatin molds. And
remember, a snow-drifting of powdered sugar over the top has
boosted the rating of many a modest sweet bread.

BASIC SWEET DOUGH

Unfortunately, many people feel that baking a yeast coffee cake is too much work, takes too much time in complicated schedules. The key to release time is to pick a day when there's a sick child at home to be comforted, or you need to put together papers for the tax man. Making yeast doughs allows spaces between risings and bakings so you don't feel panic; in fact, the kneading time will erase your frustrations as you push and shove and turn (just imagine it's the IRS you're pummeling). These coffee cakes freeze well and are reputation-savers when you go into unexpected-company shock. Just remember that icings do not freeze well and should be applied after the cake is thawed. The recipe is generous so you can double your interest.

1 tablespoon (15 ml) active
  dry yeast
1/4 cup (60 ml) lukewarm
  water
3 tablespoons (45 ml) honey
6 tablespoons (90 ml) butter,
  cut in bits
1/2 cup (125 ml) milk, scalded

2 eggs, at room temperature
Grated peel of 1 or 2 lemons
1/2 teaspoon (2.5 ml) salt
  (optional)
1 teaspoon (5 ml) pure
  vanilla extract (optional)
3 cups (700 ml) unbleached
  white flour, or as needed

Sprinkle yeast over water, stir to dissolve and let stand until foamy. Add butter and honey to milk, stir well and cool to lukewarm. In large bowl, beat eggs lightly. Stir in proofed yeast, milk mixture, lemon peel, salt and vanilla extract. Gradually beat in 1-3/4 cups (400 ml) of the flour. Beat vigorously about 3 minutes until air bubbles form. Beat in 3/4 cup (175 ml) more of the flour. Cover with tea towel and let rise in warm place 1 hour or until double in bulk. Stir down and turn out onto board floured with the remaining 1/2 cup (125 ml) of flour. Knead, adding additional flour only to prevent sticking, 5 minutes until smooth and pliable. Dough should snap when kneaded and when squeezed should feel buttery but not sticky. Use as directed in specific recipes.

Sweet rolls and coffee cakes need less salt because of the sugar.

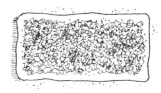

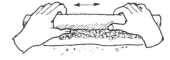

start rolling tightly on long side, stretching to keep uniform thickness; pinch seam to close roll

almand
coffee cake

candied
fruit
wreath

POWDERED
SUGAR

bake with custard cup in the center
to prevent hole from closing

ALMOND COFFEE CAKE

Makes Two Large Pretzels
1 recipe Basic Sweet Dough,
   page 125
1/2 teaspoon (2.5 ml) ground
   cinnamon
1/2 teaspoon (2.5 ml) almond
   extract
Melted butter
1 recipe Almond Filling,
   page 223
Coffee Glaze, page 222
Lightly toasted slivered
   blanched almonds

Prepare Basic Sweet Dough,
adding cinnamon and almond
extract to eggs and omitting
vanilla extract. After kneading,
divide in half. Working with 1
portion at a time and keeping
other one covered with a towel,
roll and pat into an 8- by 15-
inch (20 by 38 cm) rectangle.
Brush with melted butter and
spread with half the filling. Roll
up jelly-roll fashion, then form
into pretzel shape. Repeat with
second portion. Transfer to buttered baking sheet and cover
lightly with tea towel. Let rise
in warm place 30 minutes or
until half again double in size.
Bake in oven preheated to
350°F (180°C) 25 to 30 minutes. Transfer to wire rack,
cool slightly and drizzle glaze
over. Sprinkle with almonds.

CANDIED FRUIT COFFEE CAKE

Makes One Large Wreath
1 recipe Basic Sweet Dough,
   page 125
3/4 teaspoon (3.6 ml) ground
   allspice
1/4 teaspoon (1.2 ml) ground
   nutmeg
Melted butter
1 recipe Candied Fruit Filling,
   page 223
Powdered sugar

Prepare Basic Sweet Dough,
adding allspice and nutmeg to
eggs. After kneading, roll and
pat into an 8- by 24-inch (20
by 61 cm) rectangle. Brush with
melted butter and crumble
Candied Fruit Filling evenly
over, leaving a 1-inch (3 cm)
border on each long side. Roll
up jelly-roll fashion. Transfer
to buttered baking sheet and
form a ring, joining ends by
pinching together. With scissors,
cut slashes 2 inches (5 cm) long
and 1 inch (3 cm) apart. Cover
with tea towel and let rise in
warm place 30 minutes or until
half again double in size. Bake
in oven preheated to 350°F
(180°C) 25 to 30 minutes. Transfer to wire rack, brush liberally
with melted butter and sprinkle
well with powdered sugar.

DATE COFFEE CAKE

Makes One Ring
1 recipe Basic Sweet Dough,
  page 125
1 recipe Date Filling,
  page 224
Powdered sugar

Prepare Basic Sweet Dough. After kneading, divide in half and form each half into a ball. Working with 1 ball at a time and keeping other one covered with a towel, flatten slightly and form into a ring. Place ring in well-oiled Bundt pan, flatten slightly and carefully cover with filling. Form a ring from second ball of dough and place on filling, pressing down gently. Cover with tea towel and let rise in warm place 30 minutes or until half again double in size. Bake in oven preheated to 350°F (180°C) 35 to 40 minutes or until golden. Invert onto wire rack, sprinkle with powdered sugar and cool.

Too much liquid and the coffee cake will be soggy and sink in the middle; too little and it will be dense and dry, and bulge in the center.

DRIED CURRANT COFFEE CAKE

Makes One Coffee Cake
1 recipe Basic Sweet Dough,
  page 125
Melted butter
Brown sugar
Ground cinnamon
Freshly grated orange or
  lemon peel
Dried currants
Coffee, Orange or Lemon
  Glaze, page 222

Prepare Basic Sweet Dough. After kneading, roll and pat dough into an 8- by 30-inch (20 by 76 cm) rectangle. Brush with melted butter, sprinkle with light coating of brown sugar, dust with cinnamon and strew citrus peel and currants over all. Roll up jelly-roll fashion. Starting in the center of a 10-inch (25 cm) cast-iron skillet, form a coil with the roll. Cover with tea towel and let rise in warm place until half again double in size. Bake in oven preheated to 350°F (180°C) 30 to 35 minutes. Transfer to wire rack, cool slightly and drizzle glaze over.

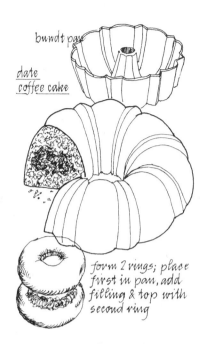

bundt pan

date coffee cake

form 2 rings; place first in pan, add filling & top with second ring

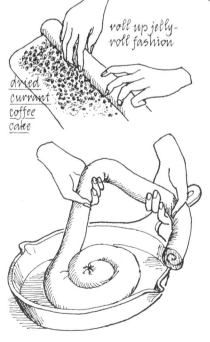

roll up jelly-roll fashion

dried currant coffee cake

127

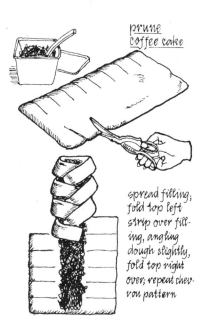

fresh fruit coffee cake

prune coffee cake

spread filling; fold top left strip over filling, angling dough slightly, fold top right over; repeat chevron pattern

FRESH FRUIT COFFEE CAKE

Served warm from the oven, with the heady fragrance of cinnamony peaches overflowing the kitchen, this cakelike bread could easily win you an all-expenses-paid, round-the-table trip, packed with compliments. It is simple to put together in a hurry for Sunday brunch, for an impromptu buffet or for a picnic basket. Fresh apricots, plums from your own tree or tart apples will slice in place of the peaches. This recipe makes 12 generous pieces and can be doubled to serve a crowd; bake on a 13- by 18-inch (33 by 46 cm) plaque or baking pan.

Makes One Cake
1/2 recipe Basic Sweet Dough, page 125
1 egg yolk
2 teaspoons (10 ml) water
2 to 2-1/2 pounds (1 kg to 1.25 kg) peaches or apples, peeled and sliced, or unpeeled apricots or plums, sliced
1 recipe Streusel, page 224

Prepare Basic Sweet Dough. After kneading, roll and pat dough into a well-buttered 8- by 12-inch (20 by 30 cm) *shallow* baking pan. Cover with tea towel and let rise in a warm place 30 minutes until slightly puffy. Beat together egg yolk and water and evenly brush over surface of dough. In overlapping rows, arrange prepared fruit on top of dough. Crumble Streusel evenly over fruit and bake in oven preheated to 350°F (180°C) 30 to 35 minutes. Cool slightly before serving.

PRUNE COFFEE CAKE

Makes Two Medium Coffee Cakes
1 recipe Basic Sweet Dough, page 125
1 recipe Prune Filling, page 225
Melted butter
Powdered sugar

Prepare Basic Sweet Dough. After kneading, divide in half. Working with 1 portion at a time and keeping other one covered with a towel, roll and pat into a 9- by 14-inch (23 by 35 cm) rectangle. Spread half of filling down center of rectangle. With scissors, make 3-inch (8 cm) cuts 1 inch (3 cm) apart along long sides of rectangle. Fold "fingers" in to form a chevron pattern as shown. Place on buttered baking sheet and repeat with second half of dough. Cover with tea towel and let rise in warm place 30 minutes or until half again double in size. Bake in oven preheated to 350°F (180°C) 25 to 30 minutes. Transfer to wire rack, brush liberally with butter and sprinkle with powdered sugar.

POPPY-SEED TWIST

Makes One Large Twist
1 recipe Basic Sweet Dough,
    page 125
1 recipe Poppy-Seed Filling,
    page 224
Melted butter
Poppy seeds

Prepare Basic Sweet Dough. After kneading, divide in half, reserving a piece of dough the size of a golf ball. Working with 1 portion at a time and keeping other one covered with a towel, roll and pat into a 9- by 14-inch (23 by 35 cm) rectangle. Spread with half the filling. Roll up jelly-roll fashion, seal seam well and position it on the side of the roll. Repeat with second portion of dough. Place the 2 rolls on a buttered baking sheet. With a sharp knife dipped in flour, cut each roll in half lengthwise as shown, keeping cut sides up. Form a twist with each cut pair, keeping cut sides up. Shape each twist into a semicircle to form a ring. Pinch ends together. Using small ball of reserved dough, form 2 flat ribbons and place over joints to conceal them. Cover with tea towel and let rise in warm place until half again double in size. Bake in oven preheated to 350°F (180°C) 25 to 30 minutes. Transfer to wire rack, brush liberally with melted butter and sprinkle with poppy seeds.

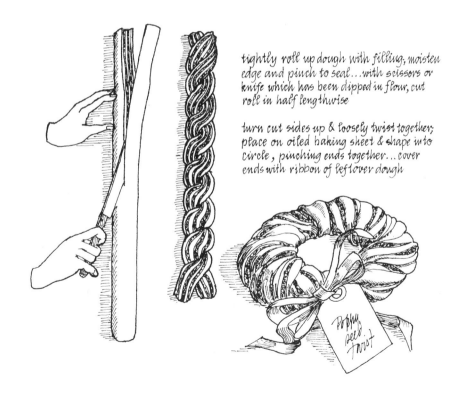

tightly roll up dough with filling, moisten edge and pinch to seal...with scissors or knife which has been dipped in flour, cut roll in half lengthwise

turn cut sides up & loosely twist together; place on oiled baking sheet & shape into circle, pinching ends together...cover ends with ribbon of leftover dough

Poppy seed Twist

tahini
coffee cake

form filled dough into jelly roll
shape, pinch to seal & place on baking
sheet; at 1"intervals, cut ⅔ way into
roll with scissors & shape into cres-
cent...starting at right, spread
first cut flat, continue turning
rest of cuts, each overlapping the
one before
     (tahini is the paste made
     from ground sesame seeds)

walnut-honey
coffee cake

form filled dough into jelly roll
shape, pinch to seal; place on bak-
ing sheet & form an S; repeat with
other roll to make a cross

130

TAHINI COFFEE CAKE

Makes Two Crescents
1 recipe Basic Sweet Dough,
     page 125
1 recipe Tahini Filling,
     page 225
Egg Wash, page 222
Lemon or Orange Glaze,
     page 222

Prepare Basic Sweet Dough.
After kneading, divide in half.
Working with 1 portion at a
time and keeping other portion
covered with a towel, roll and
pat into a 9- by 12-inch (23 by
30 cm) rectangle. Spread with
half the filling, leaving a 1-inch
(3 cm) border on each long
edge. Roll up jelly-roll fashion.
Transfer to buttered sheet. With
scissors, cut slashes two thirds
of the way through 1 inch
(3 cm) apart. Starting at right
end of roll, turn first cut flat.
Continue turning remaining cuts,
each overlapping the one before.
Repeat with second half of
dough. Cover with tea towel
and let rise in warm place 30
minutes or until half again
double in size. Brush with wash
and bake in oven preheated to
350°F (180°C) 25 to 30 minutes. Transfer to wire rack,
cool slightly and drizzle glaze
over.

WALNUT-HONEY COFFEE CAKE

Makes One Coffee Cake
1 recipe Basic Sweet Dough,
     page 125
Melted butter
1 recipe Walnut-Honey Filling,
     page 225
Powdered sugar
Coarsely ground walnuts

Prepare Basic Sweet Dough.
After kneading, divide in half.
Working with 1 portion at a
time and keeping other portion
covered with a towel, roll and
pat into an 8- by 15-inch (20
by 38 cm) rectangle. Brush with
butter and spread with filling,
leaving a 1-inch (3 cm) border
on each long edge. Roll up
jelly-roll fashion and place on a
buttered baking sheet in an
"S" shape. Repeat with second
half of dough and place on
sheet to form a cross as shown.
Cover with tea towel and let
rise in warm place 30 minutes
or until half again double in
size. Bake in oven preheated to
350°F (180°C) 30 to 35 minutes. Transfer to wire rack,
brush generously with butter
and sprinkle with powdered
sugar and walnuts.

Store brown sugar with a
slice of orange rind in a
cool, dry place.

KUGELHOPF

A famous coffee-house bread originating in Poland centuries ago and claimed by both Germans and Austrians. The secret of its continuing appeal is the butter-yeast-sugar-raisin proportions. The other secret is earnest beating (no kneading).

Makes One Coffee Cake
1/2 cup (125 ml) milk, scalded
1/4 pound (125 g) butter, cut in bits
1/2 cup (125 ml) granulated sugar
1/2 teaspoon (2.5 ml) salt
1 tablespoon (15 ml) active dry yeast
1/4 cup (50 ml) lukewarm water
3 eggs, lightly beaten
Grated peel of 1 lemon
3 cups (700 ml) sifted unbleached white flour
3/4 cup (175 ml) golden raisins or dried currants
Dry bread crumbs
1/4 cup (60 ml) sliced blanched almonds
Powdered sugar

Combine milk, butter, sugar and salt. Stir to melt butter and let cool to lukewarm. In large bowl, sprinkle yeast over water, stir to dissolve and let stand until foamy. Stir in milk mixture, eggs and lemon peel. Beat in 2 cups (500 ml) of the flour until well blended. Toss raisins with 2 tablespoons (30 ml) of the flour and set aside. Scraping sides of bowl often, gradually beat in remaining flour; continue beating 10 minutes. Mix in floured raisins, cover with tea towel and let rest 1-1/2 hours or until double in bulk. Do not hurry the rising. Grease a heavy Bundt or other decorative tube mold with butter or solid shortening. Dust with bread crumbs and press almonds against bottom and sides of pan. Beat down dough and turn into pan. Cover with tea towel and let rise in warm place 1 hour until almost double in size, or until top is almost level with top of pan. Bake in oven preheated to 350°F (180°C) 55 to 60 minutes, or until cake tester comes out clean. Top should be a rich dark brown. Turn out onto wire rack, sprinkle with powdered sugar and cool.

Store raisins or currants in sherry or brandy the night before using; refrigerate. Scrumptious.

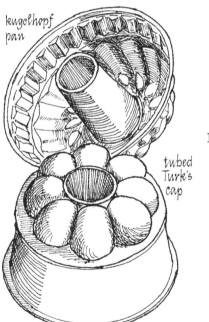

kugelhopf pan

tubed Turk's cap

PANETTONE

An Italian cake bread, sometimes simply made with raisins and anise, but we've chosen to make it a fruity celebration. Legend tells of a baker named Tony who became rich and famous in the 15th century because he created a bread using newly imported golden raisins and candied lemon peel. The bread was called *pan de Tonio.* It is formed into a round loaf, glazed with egg or butter and makes a fragrant toast. In fact, leftover and stale, it makes a good rusk by careful drying in a warm oven. It is also a surprise breakfast treat dipped in egg and cooked in a waffle iron, then dusted with powdered sugar.

Makes One Round Coffee Cake

Fruit Mixture (Day One)
1/2 cup (125 ml) mixed
  chopped candied fruits
1/4 cup (60 ml) chopped
  candied cherries
1/4 cup (60 ml) dried currants
1/3 cup (75 ml) pine nuts or
  chopped blanched almonds
2 teaspoons (10 ml) freshly
  grated lemon peel
1/2 teaspoon (2.5 ml) anise
  extract
1/2 teaspoon (2.5 ml) crushed
  anise seed
1/4 cup (60 ml) bourbon

Dough (Day Two)
1 tablespoon (15 ml) active
  dry yeast
1/4 cup (60 ml) lukewarm
  water
1/3 cup (75 ml) granulated
  sugar
1/4 pound (125 g) butter,
  cut in bits
3/4 cup (175 ml) milk, scalded
2 eggs, at room temperature
1 egg yolk
1/2 teaspoon (2.5 ml) salt
  (optional)
3-1/2 cups (850 ml) unbleached
  white flour, or as needed

Egg Wash, page 222
Melted butter
Powdered sugar (optional)

To make the fruit mixture, combine all ingredients and let stand, stirring often, 24 hours.

The following day, make the dough. Sprinkle yeast over water, stir in 1 teaspoon (5 ml) of the sugar and let stand until foamy. Stir butter into milk to melt, add remaining sugar to dissolve and cool to lukewarm. In large bowl, beat eggs and egg yolk with salt. Add proofed yeast, milk mixture and 2 cups (500 ml) of the flour. Beat vigorously about 3 minutes until air bubbles form. Stir in fruit mixture and 1 cup (250 ml) of the remaining flour. Dough will be stiff and a bit sticky. Cover with tea towel and let rise in warm place 1 hour and 15 minutes or until double in bulk. Punch down and turn out onto board floured with 1/2 cup (125 ml) flour. Knead well and, adding additional flour (up to 1/4 cup or 60 ml) as needed to prevent sticking, continue to knead 5 minutes to make a smooth and pliable dough. Form into a large ball and place in well-buttered 2-quart (2 L) souffle dish or casserole. Cover with tea towel and let rise in warm place 30 minutes or until half again double in size. Brush with Egg Wash. Bake in oven preheated to 350°F (180°C) 35 minutes or until cake tester comes out clean. Turn out onto wire rack, turn right side up, brush liberally with melted butter and sprinkle with powdered sugar.

KULICH

Among Easter breads, the Russian *kulich* stands tall, some say to represent the domes of old churches. It's always baked in a round tin, and wears a white, powdered-sugar icing that drips down the sides. Traditionally, a rose crowns the loaf, made of icing if you don't have a handy bush. In the old days, walking with heavy boots through the kitchen was forbidden until the delicate bread was safely in the oven (a good excuse today for keeping skates outside). Strips of dough were placed on top of the loaf to form the letters "XV," meaning Christ is Risen. *Kulich* has a rich, cakelike texture and is filled with a wanton lot of fruits and nuts that have marinated in brandy overnight. Sometimes a pinch of saffron is added to the marinade. The bread is served in round slices, preferably with sweet butter, and the top is saved to put back on the cut loaf.

Makes One Large Coffee Cake

Fruit Mixture (Day One)
1/4 cup (60 ml) golden raisins
1/4 cup (60 ml) chopped
  candied citron
2 tablespoons (30 ml)
  chopped candied cherries
1/4 cup (60 ml) chopped
  blanched almonds
2 teaspoons (10 ml) freshly
  grated orange peel
1 teaspoon (5 ml) freshly
  grated lemon peel
1/4 teaspoon (1.2 ml) ground
  cardamom
2 to 3 tablespoons (30 to
  45 ml) brandy

Dough (Day Two)
1 tablespoon (15 ml) active
  dry yeast
1/4 cup (60 ml) lukewarm
  water
3 tablespoons (45 ml) firmly
  packed brown sugar
6 tablespoons (90 ml) butter,
  cut in bits
1/2 cup (125 ml) milk, scalded
1 egg, at room temperature
2 egg yolks
Grated peel of 1 lemon
1 teaspoon (5 ml) pure vanilla
  extract
3 cups (700 ml) unbleached
  white flour, or as needed

Powdered Sugar Glaze,
  page 223

To make the fruit mixture, combine all ingredients and let stand, stirring often, 24 hours.

The following day, make the dough. Sprinkle yeast over water, stir in 1 teaspoon (5 ml) of the sugar and let stand until foamy. Stir butter into milk to melt, add remaining sugar to dissolve and let cool to lukewarm. In large bowl, beat egg and egg yolks with lemon peel and vanilla extract. Add proofed yeast, milk mixture and 2 cups (500 ml) of the flour. Beat vigorously about 3 minutes until air bubbles form. Beat in fruit mixture and 3/4 cup (175 ml) of the remaining flour. Cover with tea towel and let rise in warm place 1 hour and 15 minutes or until double in bulk. Punch down and turn out onto board floured with 1/4 cup (60 ml) flour. Knead well and, adding additional flour as needed to prevent sticking, continue to knead for 5 minutes to make a smooth and pliable dough. Form into an oval. Make a heavy foil collar around a 2-pound (1 kg) coffee can, butter collar and can well and place dough inside can. Cover with tea towel and let rise in warm place 1 hour or until half again double in size (approximately 1 inch or 3 cm from top of can). Bake in oven preheated to 350°F (180°C) 40 minutes or until cake tester comes out clean. If top browns too fast, cover loosely with foil. Carefully remove from can and set upright on wire rack. Cool slightly and drizzle glaze over, allowing glaze to drip down sides of cake.

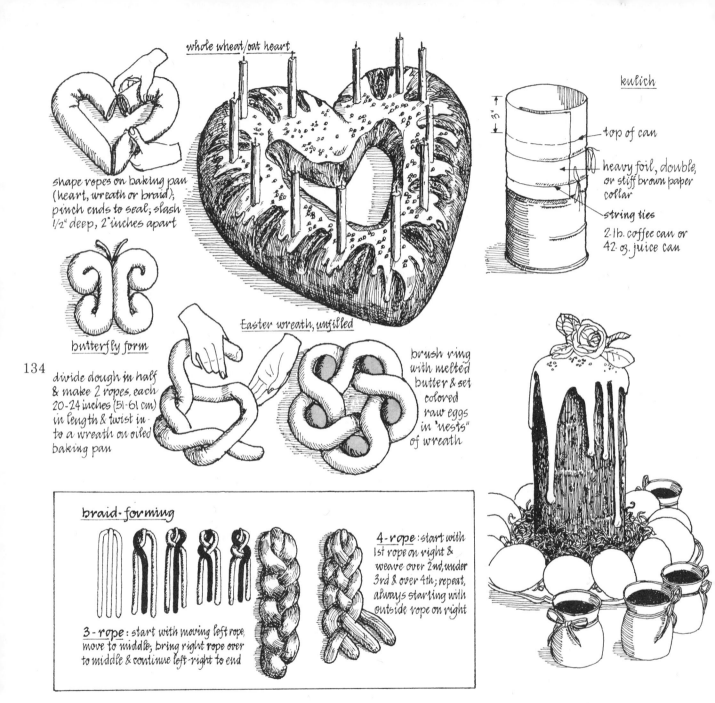

whole wheat/oat heart

shape ropes on baking pan (heart, wreath or braid); pinch ends to seal; slash 1/2" deep, 2"inches apart

butterfly form

134

divide dough in half & make 2 ropes, each 20-24 inches (51-61 cm) in length & twist into a wreath on oiled baking pan

Easter wreath, unfilled

brush ring with melted butter & set colored raw eggs in "nests" of wreath

kulich

3"

top of can

heavy foil, double, or stiff brown paper collar

string ties

2-lb. coffee can or 42-oz. juice can

braid-forming

4-rope: start with 1st rope on right & weave over 2nd, under 3rd & over 4th; repeat, always starting with outside rope on right

3-rope: start with moving left rope, move to middle; bring right rope over to middle & continue left-right to end

WHOLE WHEAT-OAT HEART

Feel like flaunting tradition? Hurray for another kind of birthday cake for someone who can't stand icings. This salubrious whole-wheat and rolled-oats cake, dressed up with a ring of candles, will make any celebrant feel sound of wind and limb. And it's within the reach of a fourth-grader to hatch because it is direct, uncomplicated. Making sweet yeast bread can intimidate even a seasoned baker, but success here is almost guaranteed. Young bakers need only one milk-and-honey success to get the urge to try again. This dough can be recast into a wreath or become a butterfly to "take off" a new year.

Makes One Large Heart
1 tablespoon (15 ml) active dry yeast
1-1/2 cups (350 ml) lukewarm water
1/4 cup (60 ml) honey
2-1/4 cups (525 ml) unbleached white flour, or as needed
1-1/2 cups (350 ml) whole-wheat flour
1/3 cup (75 ml) non-instant nonfat dry milk
3/4 teaspoon (3.6 ml) salt
1/4 teaspoon (1.2 ml) ground mace
1 egg, at room temperature
2/3 cup (150 ml) unprocessed rolled oats
4 tablespoons (60 ml) butter, melted and cooled slightly
1 tablespoon (15 ml) freshly grated orange peel
Walnut Honey Filling, page 225
1/2 teaspoon (2.5 ml) ground cinnamon
1/2 to 2/3 cup (125 to 150 ml) raisins

In large warmed bowl, sprinkle yeast over water, stir to dissolve and let stand until foamy. Beat in honey, 1-1/2 cups (350 ml) of the unbleached white flour and 1 cup (250 ml) of the whole-wheat flour. Beat vigorously about 3 minutes until air bubbles form. Sift in dry milk, salt and mace and beat well. Beat in egg, oats, butter and 1 tablespoon (15 ml) orange peel. Gradually beat in remaining flours to make stiff dough. Turn out onto board floured with 2 tablespoons (30 ml) additional white flour and knead well to incorporate. Adding up to 2 tablespoons (30 ml) additional flour, knead 5 minutes until smooth. If dough is still sticky, lightly oil hands and board to continue the kneading process. Dough should be soft and pliable. Form into a ball, place in oiled bowl, turn to coat all surfaces, cover with tea towel and let rise in warm place 1 hour and 15 minutes or until double in bulk. Punch down, knead briefly and divide in half. Working with 1 portion at a time and keeping other portion covered with a towel, roll and pat into a 10- by 18-inch (25 by 46 cm) rectangle. Combine Walnut Honey Filling and ground cinnamon and brush rectangle liberally with mixture, reserving some for topping. Strew raisins over. Roll up jelly-roll fashion. Repeat with second half of dough. Transfer rolls to a buttered baking sheet and form them together into a heart shape as shown. With a razor blade, cut slashes 1/2 inch (1.5 cm) deep and 2 inches (5 cm) apart. Cover with tea towel and let rise in warm place 1 hour or until half again double in size. Bake in oven preheated to 350°F (180°C) 40 to 45 minutes. Transfer to wire rack and brush with remaining Honey Glaze mixture.

Baking bread with an experienced baker will give you more confidence than any written word. (Thank you, Meg!)

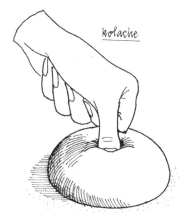

kolache

make a deep indentation with thumb and fill with a teaspoon of filling

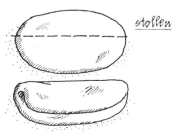

stollen

pat dough into oval & fold top down to within 1" of bottom

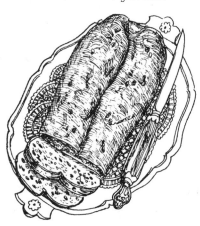

STOLLEN

This is an elegant folded bread from Germany, also enfolding many chopped dried fruits and peels—and a double ration of rum or brandy. The story handed down by word of mothers to posterity is that it represents the Christ child in swaddling clothes. But whatever its ancestry, *Stollen* is one of the prettiest of Christmas breads and becomes a great handmade gift. This recipe makes three generous loaves for three special friends.

Makes Three Coffee Cakes

Fruit Mixture (Day One)
1/2 cup (125 ml) dried currants
1/2 cup (125 ml) golden raisins
1/2 cup (125 ml) chopped candied orange
1/2 cup (125 ml) chopped candied citron
2 tablespoons (30 ml) chopped angelica (optional)
1/2 cup (125 ml) slivered or chopped blanched almonds
2 teaspoons (10 ml) freshly grated lemon peel
1 teaspoon (5 ml) pure vanilla extract
1 teaspoon (5 ml) anise extract
2 tablespoons (30 ml) almond paste
1/2 cup (125 ml) brandy or dark rum

Dough (Day Two)
4 cups (1 L) unbleached white flour, or as needed
1-1/4 cups (300 ml) milk, scalded
4 tablespoons (60 ml) active dry yeast
1/2 cup (125 ml) granulated sugar
1/2 pound (250 g) butter, melted and cooled slightly
Grated peel of 1 or 2 lemons

Melted butter
Powdered sugar

To make the fruit mixture, combine all ingredients and let stand, stirring often, 24 hours.

The following day, make the dough. Into large bowl, measure 3-1/2 cups (850 ml) of the flour. Make a well in center, pushing flour aside, and pour in milk. Let milk cool to lukewarm, sprinkle yeast over, add 1 teaspoon (5 ml) of the sugar and stir gently without incorporating much of the flour. Cover with tea towel and let stand until yeast is foamy. Add remaining sugar, the butter and lemon peel. Mix well, stirring in all of the flour in bowl and beating vigorously about 3 minutes until air bubbles form. Beat in fruit mixture, cover with tea towel and let rise in warm place 1 hour and 15 minutes or until double in bulk.

Punch down, turn out onto floured board and knead, adding additional flour only to prevent sticking, 5 minutes. Dough should be soft and pliable. Divide into 3 equal portions. Working with 1 portion at a time and keeping the others covered with a towel, roll and pat into a flat oval approximately 1/2 inch (1.5 cm) thick. Flip one long side over to within 1 inch (3 cm) of other long edge as shown. Place on buttered baking sheet and repeat with remaining 2 portions of dough. Cover and let rise in warm place 40 minutes or until half again double in size. Bake in oven preheated to 350°F (180°C) 40 to 45 minutes or until cake tester comes out clean. Remove to wire rack, brush liberally several times with melted butter and sprinkle well with powdered sugar.

Almonds: To remove skin, soak two to five minutes in hot water, pour off water and slip off skins. This works for pistachios also.

KOLACHE
(Czech Christmas-Eve Bread)

Makes Twenty to Twenty-four
1 recipe Basic Sweet Dough, page 125
1/2 teaspoon (2.5 ml) ground nutmeg
Prune, Apricot, Cottage Cheese or Walnut-Honey Filling, pages 223 through 225
Melted butter
Powdered sugar

Make Basic Sweet Dough, adding nutmeg to egg mixture. After kneading, divide into 20 to 24 equal portions, kneading each briefly. Form each portion into a ball and place 2 inches (5 cm) apart on buttered baking sheets. Make an indentation in each ball and fill with approximately 1 teaspoon (5 ml) of filling. Cover with tea towel and let rise in warm place 30 minutes or until almost double in size. Bake in oven preheated to 350°F (180°C) 15 minutes or until golden. Transfer to wire rack, brush liberally with butter and sprinkle with powdered sugar.

hot cross buns

HOT CROSS BUNS

Makes Sixteen
1 recipe Basic Sweet Dough, page 125
1 teaspoon (5 ml) ground cinnamon
1 to 1-1/2 cups (250 to 350 ml) raisins
Powdered Sugar Glaze, page 223

Prepare Basic Sweet Dough, adding cinnamon to eggs. Last 2 minutes of kneading process, knead in raisins. Divide dough into 16 equal portions. Roll portions into smooth balls and place 1 inch (3 cm) apart on buttered baking sheet. Cover with tea towel and let rise in warm place 30 minutes or until half again double in size. Bake in oven preheated to 350°F (180°C) 20 minutes or until golden. Transfer to rack, cool completely and make a cross on each bun with glaze.

cinnamon rolls

for crisp rolls, place on pan, flatten with spatula

cut a thick slice part way through and spread apart

to slice rolled breads, slip a thread under roll, cross ends and pull

CINNAMON ROLLS

Makes Two Dozen

1 recipe Basic Sweet Dough, page 125
2 tablespoons (30 ml) freshly grated orange peel
Melted butter
Brown sugar
Ground cinnamon
Ground nutmeg
Raisins or dried currants
Chopped pecans, walnuts, almonds or filberts (optional)
Heavy cream (optional)
Coffee, Orange or Lemon Glaze, page 222

Prepare Basic Sweet Dough, adding orange peel to egg. After kneading, divide in half. Working with 1 portion at a time and keeping other one covered with towel, roll and pat into an 8- by 14-inch (20 by 38 cm) rectangle. Brush generously with butter. Lightly and evenly cover with brown sugar, leaving a 1-inch (3 cm) border on each long edge. Sprinkle with cinnamon and nutmeg and strew raisins and nuts over. Roll up jelly-roll fashion. Using thread method as shown, carefully cut into 12 equal slices.

Place slices with a cut side up in lightly buttered 4-inch (10 cm) foil tart pans or arrange at least 1 inch (3 cm) apart on buttered baking sheet. Repeat with second half of dough. Cover with tea towel and let rise in warm place until half again double in size. Drizzle about 1 teaspoon (5 ml) cream over each roll, if desired. Bake in oven preheated to 350°F (180°C) 15 minutes or until golden. Transfer to wire rack, let cool slightly and drizzle glaze over.

SAFFRON BUNS

Saint Lucia Day, December 13, begins before daybreak in Sweden. It is the custom for the young daughters of the house to bring steaming coffee and saffron buns to their parents. A very pretty custom, but the golden yellow buns are too good to withhold from the rest of the year. The aroma of saffron, even a quarter teaspoon, is intense and exotic (this is the world's most costly herb, taking 70,000 blossoms to produce one pound). In Sweden, the buns are made in the shapes of cats, wheels, or simple "S" figures and decorated with raisins. It's also possible to simply divide the dough into small loaves.

Makes Approximately Sixteen
1 tablespoon (15 ml) active dry yeast
1/2 cup (125 ml) lukewarm water
4 tablespoons (60 ml) butter, cut in bits
2/3 cup (150 ml) milk, scalded
1/2 cup (125 ml) granulated sugar, mixed with 1/4 teaspoon (1.2 ml) powdered saffron
3-1/2 cups (850 ml) unbleached white flour, or as needed
1 egg, lightly beaten
1/4 teaspoon (1.2 ml) salt
Egg Wash, page 222
Raisins
Blanched almonds, halved

In large warmed bowl, sprinkle yeast over water, stir to dissolve and let stand until foamy. Stir butter into milk to melt and then stir in sugar and saffron; cool to lukewarm. Add to proofed yeast with 2 cups (500 ml) of the flour. Blend and beat vigorously about 3 minutes until air bubbles form. Beat in egg and salt. Gradually beat in remaining flour to form stiff dough. Turn out onto floured board and knead, adding additional flour as needed to prevent sticking, 8 minutes. Dough should stick slightly to your hands but not to the board. Form into smooth ball, place in oiled bowl, turn to coat all surfaces, cover with tea towel and let rise in warm place 1-1/2 hours or until double in bulk. Punch down, knead briefly, form into ball, cover with tea towel and let rest 15 minutes. Divide into 16 equal portions. Roll each portion into an 8-inch-long (20 cm) log. Form logs into "S" shapes placed 1 inch (3 cm) apart on buttered baking sheets. Cover with tea towel and let rise in warm place 45 minutes or until half again double in size. Brush with wash and decorate with raisins and almonds as shown. Bake in oven preheated to 375°F (190°C) 15 minutes or until golden. Transfer to wire rack and cool 3 to 4 minutes. Serve warm.

form 8" logs into "S" shapes, add raisins or almonds at each curved end & brush with egg wash

cut 2 strips as shown to make cross on plain bun

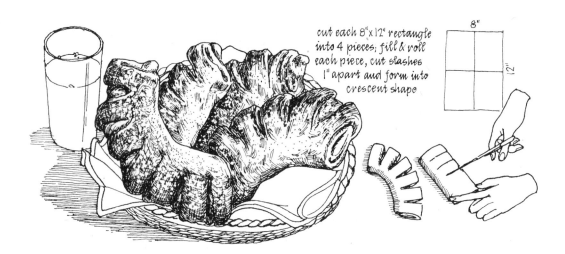

cut each 8"x12" rectangle into 4 pieces; fill & roll each piece, cut slashes 1" apart and form into crescent shape

8"

12"

CARDAMOM BEAR CLAWS

Makes Eight Bear Claws
1 recipe Basic Sweet Dough,
   page 125
1 teaspoon (5 ml) ground
   cardamom
2 teaspoons (10 ml) freshly
   grated orange peel
1 recipe Apricot Filling,
   page 223
Melted butter
Powdered sugar

Prepare Basic Sweet Dough, adding cardamom and orange peel to egg and omitting vanilla extract. After kneading, divide in half. Working with 1 portion at a time and keeping other portion covered with a towel, roll and pat into an 8- by 12-inch (20 by 30 cm) rectangle. Cut the rectangle into 4 equal portions as shown. Repeat with second half of dough. Divide filling equally among the 8 portions, spreading it to cover centers. Fold each portion like a business letter and place on buttered baking sheets. With scissors, make cuts on open edge halfway through and 1 inch (3 cm) apart as shown. Cover with tea towel and let rise in warm place 30 minutes or until half again double in size. Bake in oven preheated to 350°F (180°C) 15 to 20 minutes. Transfer to wire rack, brush liberally with melted butter and sprinkle with powdered sugar.

PHILADELPHIA STICKY BUNS

A famous upside-down cinnamon bun of unique flavor, with a shameless slathering of sweetness—a legend as famous to the Quaker city as sourdough is to San Francisco.

Makes Eighteen

Dough
1-1/2 cups (350 ml) milk, scalded
1 tablespoon (15 ml) active dry yeast
1/4 cup (60 ml) lukewarm water
5 cups (1.2 L) unbleached white flour, or as needed
1/2 tablespoon (7.5 ml) salt
2 tablespoons (30 ml) honey
1/2 cup (125 ml) granulated sugar
1/4 pound (125 g) butter, at room temperature
2 eggs

Filling
4 tablespoons (60 ml) butter, melted
1/2 cup (125 ml) firmly packed brown sugar
2 teaspoons (10 ml) ground cinnamon
1/2 cup (125 ml) raisins
1/2 cup (125 ml) chopped walnuts
1 cup (250 ml) light corn syrup, or mixture of half maple and half light corn syrup

To make the dough, cool milk to lukewarm and set aside. In large mixing bowl, sprinkle yeast over water, stir to dissolve, add milk and let stand until foamy. Add 2 cups (500 ml) of the flour, salt and honey, beating until smooth. Cover and set aside in warm place. In another mixing bowl, cream together granulated sugar and butter. Add eggs, one at a time, beating after each addition. Stir into proofed yeast. Gradually beat in remaining flour. Cover with tea towel and let rise in warm place 1 hour or until double in bulk. Turn dough out onto floured board and, adding additional flour as needed to prevent sticking, knead 8 or 10 times until smooth. Divide in half. Working with 1 portion at a time and keeping the other one covered with a towel, roll and pat into an 8- by 12-inch (20 by 30 cm) rectangle. To fill, brush with melted butter, sprinkle with brown sugar and cinnamon, strew raisins and walnuts over and drizzle lightly with 1/4 cup (60 ml) corn syrup. Roll up jelly-roll fashion and cut into 9 equal slices (page 138). Butter a deep 9-inch (23 cm) square baking pan and spread with 1/4 cup (60 ml) of the corn syrup. Stand rolls, cut side up, in prepared pan. Repeat with remaining half of dough and a second pan. Cover with tea towel and let rise in warm place 1 hour or until almost double in size. Bake in oven preheated to 350°F (180°C) 40 minutes or until golden. Immediately turn out onto foil sheet or large platter and serve warm.

Sourdough

SOURDOUGH STARTERS
SOURDOUGH BREADS

SOURDOUGH STARTER

Sourdough "starter" is a living, leavening agent, just like yeast, but delivering powerfully good flavor and aroma that yeast can't match. Sourdough is a slowpoke when it's rising, so don't try to hurry it along. Adding some dry yeast will speed up the action, but a real s/d purist would rather wait than adulterate.

A "starter" is the beginning of all sourdough breads; it looks like thick pancake batter, is basically flour and water (some call for dry milk, another for potato water, etc.) that is set in a warm place where it will, you hope, capture wild yeast spores out of the air and maintain them. Starter can be begged from a friend or purchased in dehydrated form in a package in a natural-foods store. Best of all, you can make it, and we've included several starter recipes in different flavors for you to experiment with. The older the starter, the more tangy its behavior.

Suggestions for launching a starter: (1) Make sure all utensils are spanking clean; use stoneware, glass or plastic containers, because long exposure to metal will change the taste. A crock with a loose lid is a fine way to store the starter in the back of the refrigerator; always be sure there's a way for any expanding gases to escape the container. (2) Temperature is vital to success in making starters; a thermometer is essential to keep warmth about 85°F (29°C). Place the crock or bowl, covered with a clean towel, in a warm spot, such as over a pilot light or on top of the refrigerator or water heater. The mixture should be stirred several times each day; it will take from three to five days to become light and bubbly.

To use, add to it one cup (250 ml) flour and a little more than three-fourths cup (200 ml) of lukewarm water (the kind of flour depends on which starter you've chosen to make); the mixture will be lumpy, but fermentation will dissolve those lumps in a few hours. Empty the starter into a good-sized, warmed bowl, mix in the flour and liquid and cover with plastic wrap and an old bath towel. Warning: Use a good-sized bowl or the starter may bubble over the top. Let the bowl sit in a warm place for 12 hours—it should be bubbly and raring to go in that amount of

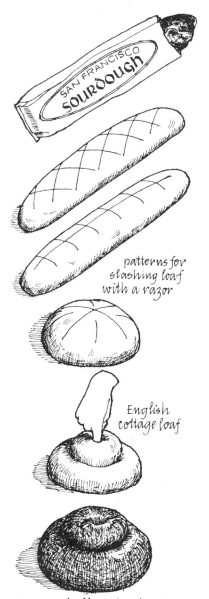

patterns for slashing loaf with a razor

English cottage loaf

form two balls of dough, place smaller on top of larger & poke finger through both

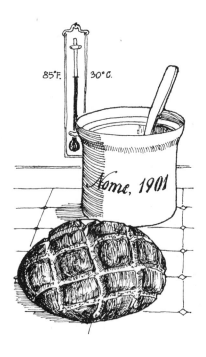

85°F. 30°C.

Nome, 1901

144

time. On cool nights it may take longer, on hot nights, less. And it won't be ruined if it sits another six hours before you get around to using it.

The next morning, measure out the amount to be used in the recipe and refrigerate the rest; it must be kept cold or it will work itself to death. A starter may rest four to six months in the back of the box and not spoil, but others recommend refreshing it every two or three weeks with more flour and water.

We don't add more than one cup (250 ml) of flour in any 12-hour period; if the recipe calls for more starter, wait the 12 hours, then add another cup (250 ml) and liquid and wait 12 hours longer. There should always be *at least* one cup (250 ml) of starter to store, though we recommend two because it's easier to stir in the flour. Don't add anything else. If you want an even more sour taste, let the starter you've measured stand for another day before using.

Consolation department: If by the fifth day of a new starter's life there is no bubbling action, start over. Also, when s/d stands for a long time in the refrigerator, a yellowish liquid separates to the top. Don't worry, stir it down and the starter will be all right. If, however, you see a rainbow of colors and mold, kiss it goodbye and start over. It is possible to freeze a starter, but we suggest you keep it viable—and quickly usable—in the refrigerator section. Once you've become hooked on sourdough, you'll find you want to bake up a storm every week.

BASIC STARTER

1 large baking potato, peeled
  and cubed
1 cup (250 ml) unbleached
  white flour
1/2 tablespoon (7.5 ml) active
  dry yeast
1 teaspoon (5 ml) granulated
  sugar

Cook potato in water to cover until tender. Pour off liquid to measure 1 cup (250 ml), saving potato for other use. Let potato water cool to lukewarm. In a glass or ceramic bowl that has been scalded, place flour, yeast and sugar; add lukewarm potato water and stir in well. Cover with plastic wrap and pierce plastic with fork to release gases. Place in a warm, draft-free location at an even 85°F (29°C) for 2 days; stir several times daily. (Do not let sourdough starter rise above 95°F [35°C] because higher temperatures are favorable to less desireable microorganisms.) Refrigerate until ready to use.

Replenish as directed in introduction at end of first week and let stand overnight or 12 hours in a warm location before refrigerating again. When replenishing, add lukewarm water with flour. Starter should be at room temperature when using in recipes, always after having stood 12 hours from addition of replenishing flour and water. At least 1 cup (250 ml) should remain to refrigerate.

RYE STARTER

2 cups (500 ml) rye flour
1 tablespoon (15 ml) active
  dry yeast
1-1/2 cups (375 ml) lukewarm
  water (110°F or 44°C)
1 onion slice (optional)

In a glass or ceramic bowl or jar that has been scalded, combine flour and yeast, add water and blend well. Add onion slice, cover with plastic wrap and pierce plastic with fork to release gases. Place in a warm, draft-free location, at an even 85°F (29°C) for 3 days; stir several times daily. Remove onion slice and refrigerate until ready to use.

Onion imparts a strong flavor and this starter can only be used with compatible rye recipes; rye starter without onion can be used in any rye sourdough recipe. To replenish, always use rye flour. If starter does not seem bubbly after replenishing and standing 12 hours, sprinkle 1 teaspoon (5 ml) active dry yeast over and stir in well. Like whole-wheat starter, you may have to plan longer rising times for dough made with this one.

WHOLE-WHEAT STARTER

1-1/2 cups (375 ml) whole-
  wheat flour
1 teaspoon (5 ml) active dry
  yeast
1-1/2 cups (375 ml) lukewarm
  water (110°F or 44°C)

In a glass or ceramic bowl or jar that has been scalded, combine flour and yeast, add water and blend well. Cover with plastic wrap and pierce plastic with fork to release gases. Place in a warm, draft-free location at an even 85°F (29°C) for 18 to 24 hours; stir several times daily. Refrigerate until ready to use.

If you have several starters, keep whole-wheat separate from others to preserve its own distinctive flavor. Whole-wheat starter does not have as much rising action as that made with white flour; you may have to plan longer rising times. To replenish, always use whole-wheat flour.

145

The Klondike sourdough depended on his starter for survival—took it to bed on cold nights so it wouldn't freeze.

YOGHURT STARTER

1 cup (250 ml) low-fat milk
2 tablespoons (30 ml) *natural* plain yoghurt
1 cup (250 ml) unbleached white flour

Heat milk to 100°F (38°C) on thermometer. Remove from heat and stir in yoghurt. Pour into scalded glass jar or bowl, cover with plastic wrap and place in a warm location for 18 hours. Consistency will be like thin yoghurt. Stir in flour until well blended, cover again with plastic and pierce plastic with fork to release gases. Place in a warm, draft-free location at an even 85°F (29°C) for 2 days; stir several times each day. It should have a strong sourdough smell and show bubbles. Refrigerate until ready to use. When replenishing starter, add lukewarm milk instead of water.

In the early days of America, well-established sourdough starters were valuable and often a part of a bride's dowry.

SOURDOUGH SAN FRANCISCO BREAD

The barely burnt tough crust—you play tug-of-war with every bite—the snowy soft insides, slathered with unsalted butter or soft brie. *This* is the bread that ruins diets and for which tourists leave home.

Each bakery in the city guards its recipe jealously; each has its secret starter, its unique oven. So, making a sourdough loaf in a kitchen to compete with a "bought" loaf is pure second guessing. Needless to say there are many guessers, each boasting the true secret. This is a better than fair try. See if you can resist its wicked aroma right out of the oven.

Makes Two Loaves
1 tablespoon (15 ml) active dry yeast
1-1/2 cups (350 ml) warm water (110° to 115°F or 44° to 46°C)
1 cup (250 ml) sourdough starter
1 tablespoon (15 ml) granulated sugar
1/2 tablespoon (7.5 ml) salt
2 tablespoons (30 ml) cider vinegar
5-1/2 cups (1.3 L) unbleached white flour, or as needed
1/2 teaspoon (2.5 ml) baking soda
Yellow cornmeal

In large warmed bowl, sprinkle yeast over water, stir to dissolve and let stand until bubbly. Blend in starter, sugar, salt and vinegar. Gradually beat in 3 cups (700 ml) of the flour. Beat vigorously at least 3 minutes. Turn batter into a large oiled glass or ceramic bowl, cover with tea towel and let rise in warm place 1 hour or until double in bulk. Combine 1 cup (250 ml) of the remaining flour with baking soda. Stir batter down and add flour-baking soda mixture. Gradually add remaining flour to make a stiff dough. Turn out onto floured board and knead, adding additional flour only as needed to prevent sticking, approximately 300 strokes of folding and turning or until dough is smooth and elastic. Sprinkle a greased baking sheet or double baguette pan with cornmeal. Form dough into 2 oblong loaves and place on sheet or in pans. Cover with tea towel and let rise in warm place 1 to 1-1/2 hours or until not quite double in size. With sharp razor, slash the tops of loaves diagonally to a depth of at least 1/2 inch (1.5 cm). Mist with water and bake in oven preheated to 450°F (230°C) 10 minutes. Reduce heat to 400°F (210°C) and bake 35 minutes longer or until bread tests done. For a harder crust, place a pan of hot water on bottom of oven and mist with water several times during baking. Remove pan of water after 15 minutes of baking. Turn out onto wire rack and cool.

NOTE If you like your sourdough very dark, remove the baked bread from the pan or sheet and place under the broiler about 2 minutes, or until rich brown in color.

SOURDOUGH BACKWOODS WHOLE-WHEAT BREAD

Crusty, earthy—a natural adjunct to back-of-the-stove soups and corned beef that has been glazed with fruit. Slice it thinly and pass it with goat cheese and a mug of dark beer. Stays moist for days if covered with plastic wrap and stored in the refrigerator.

Makes Two Loaves

Day One
1 cup (250 ml) unbleached white flour
1 cup (250 ml) whole-wheat flour
1 cup (250 ml) sourdough starter, at room temperature
1 cup (250 ml) lukewarm beef broth
1 tablespoon (15 ml) honey

Combine flours. In large bowl, mix starter, broth and honey. Stir in flour mixture and beat until well mixed. Cover with plastic wrap and tea towel and let rise in warm place 24 hours.

Day Two
1 tablespoon (15 ml) active dry yeast
1 cup (250 ml) lukewarm beef broth
1 tablespoon (15 ml) honey
1-1/2 cups (350 ml) unbleached white flour, or as needed
1/2 tablespoon (7.5 ml) salt
1/4 teaspoon (1.2 ml) ground sage
1/2 cup (125 ml) untoasted wheat germ
2 cups (500 ml) whole-wheat flour
Melted butter

In large warmed bowl, sprinkle yeast over broth, stir in honey and let stand until foamy. Add sourdough mixture from Day One and beat vigorously 3 minutes. Gradually add 1 cup (250 ml) of the unbleached white flour, the salt, sage and wheat germ, mixing well. Gradually add whole-wheat flour and beat until dough comes away clean from sides of bowl. Turn out onto board floured with remaining unbleached white flour and knead, adding additional flour only as needed to prevent sticking, 5 minutes. Form into smooth ball, place in oiled bowl, turn to coat all surfaces, cover with tea towel and let rise in warm place 1-1/2 hours or until double in bulk. Punch down and let rise 1-1/2 hours or until double in bulk. Punch down once more, knead briefly and cover with tea towel. Let rest 10 minutes. Divide dough into 2 equal portions. Form each into a long, thin loaf and place, seam side down, in 2 oiled baguette pans. With sharp razor, slash the tops of loaves diagonally to a depth of 1/2 inch (1.5 cm). Cover with dampened tea towel and let rise in warm place 1 hour or until almost double in size. Brush with melted butter and bake in oven preheated to 425°F (220°C) 50 to 55 minutes or until bread tests done. A shallow pan of water set on lowest oven rack and misting with water as you put loaves in oven will give a crisper crust. Remove pan of water after 15 minutes of baking. When done, turn out onto wire rack, turn right side up and cool.

SOURDOUGH POTATO-RYE BREAD

This is a coarse rye, with sour pumpernickel gusto. The dough spreads during baking and slices are usually wide and approximately one and a half inches (4 cm) tall, a compatible dimension for sausage.

Makes Two Long Loaves

Day One
1 cup (250 ml) sourdough starter, at room temperature
1/4 cup (60 ml) molasses
1 cup (250 ml) potato cooking
   water, at room temperature
2 cups (500 ml) whole-wheat
   flour

In large warmed bowl, combine starter, molasses, potato water and whole-wheat flour. Stir well, cover with plastic wrap and a heavy towel and let rise in warm place overnight or at least 12 hours.

Day Two
1 cup (250 ml) beef broth
1/4 cup (60 ml) nondegerminated yellow cornmeal
1 cup (250 ml) riced potatoes
1 tablespoon (15 ml) active
   dry yeast
1/4 cup (60 ml) lukewarm
   water or potato water
1 tablespoon (15 ml) salt
4 tablespoons (60 ml) butter,
   melted
1/2 teaspoon (2.5 ml) ground
   mace
1/2 teaspoon (2.5 ml) ground
   nutmeg
1/2 cup (125 ml) rye meal (see
   Note)
2 cups (500 ml) rye flour
2 cups (500 ml) unbleached
   white flour, or as needed
Egg White Wash, page 222
Poppy seeds

Bring broth to boil, add cornmeal and, stirring constantly, cook 2 minutes. Remove from heat, stir in potatoes and cool to lukewarm; add to starter mixture.

Sprinkle yeast over lukewarm water, stir to dissolve and let stand until foamy. Add to starter mixture with salt, butter and spices. Beating constantly, add rye meal, rye flour and unbleached white flour. Dough will be sticky and heavy. Turn out onto floured board and, adding additional flour as needed to prevent sticking, knead 8 minutes. If dough is still sticky after 5 minutes, lightly oil board and hands and finish kneading. Dough will be slightly sticky to hands but should not stick to board. Form into smooth ball, place in oiled bowl, turn to coat all surfaces, cover with tea towel and let rise in warm place 1 hour or until double in bulk. Punch down and turn out onto floured board; knead for 20 turns. Cover with tea towel and let rest 5 to 10 minutes. Divide into 2 equal portions and form each into a long loaf. Place side by side on large greased baking sheet. With sharp razor, cut 3 slashes from end to end 1/2 inch (1.5 cm) deep. Brush evenly with Egg White Wash, being careful not to spill onto baking sheet, and sprinkle generously with poppy seeds. Let rise, uncovered, in warm place 45 minutes or until almost double in size. Bake in oven preheated to 400°F (210°C) 20 minutes; reduce heat to 375°F (190°C) and bake 30 minutes longer or until bread tests done. To give top a shiny dark look, place under broiler and, being careful of scorching, broil until dark. Transfer to wire rack and cool.

NOTE If rye meal is unavailable, substitute rye flakes ground in a blender.

148

SOURDOUGH
DARK RYE RING

This is a great loaf for a big buffet party. Its ethnic source is near-east European, where the sourdough starter, probably a rye one, was made three days early for festive breads. We have substituted the classic white flour starter, which happily changes the bitter chocolate, the black coffee and molasses into a rare rye treat with no loss of authenticity.

Makes One Large Loaf

2 cups (500 ml) strong brewed
   coffee
1 square (1 ounce or 28 g)
   unsweetened chocolate, cut up
1/4 cup (60 ml) molasses
1 tablespoon (15 ml) active
   dry yeast
1/2 cup (125 ml) lukewarm
   water
2 tablespoons (30 ml) honey
2 cups (500 ml) sourdough
   starter, at room temperature
1 tablespoon (15 ml) salt
2-1/2 cups (600 ml) unbleached
   white flour, or as needed
2 cups (500 ml) unprocessed
   bran
1/2 teaspoon (2.5 ml) ground
   ginger
2 tablespoons (30 ml) caraway
   seeds
3 cups (700 ml) rye flour
Egg White Wash, page 222

Bring coffee to boil, add chocolate, remove from heat and stir until chocolate is melted. Stir in molasses and cool to lukewarm. In large bowl, sprinkle yeast over water, stir in honey and let stand until foamy. Add starter, coffee mixture, salt and 1 cup (250 ml) of the unbleached flour. Blend well and beat in bran, ginger and caraway seeds. Continuing to beat, gradually add rye flour. Dough will be heavy and sticky. Mound remaining unbleached white flour on board and turn dough out onto it. Using steel baker's scraper, work in flour until dough can be kneaded. Adding additional flour as needed to prevent sticking, knead 6 to 8 minutes. Form into smooth ball, place in oiled bowl, turn to coat all surfaces, cover with tea towel and let rise in warm place 1 to 1-1/2 hours or until double in bulk. Punch down, turn out onto floured board and shape into a ring 12 to 14 inches (30 to 40 cm) in diameter. Carefully transfer to greased baking sheet and, with fingers, continue to enlarge the hole in center to a 4-inch (10 cm) diameter. Brush with Egg White Wash and let rise, uncovered, in warm place 45 minutes. Again brush with Egg White Wash and bake in oven preheated to 400°F (210°C) 25

minutes. Reduce heat to 350°F (180°C) and continue baking 20 minutes more or until bread tests done. Transfer to wire rack and cool.

place a small custard cup or ramekin in hole in center before baking; fill with butter or cheese when bread cools

leaf decoration: slash edges, moisten leaf on underside when applying to loaf.

If yeast is added to a sourdough starter, it competes with natural yeasts in starter and may keep crust from browning, but it does shorten proofing time.

to make a "mushroom" shape, cut a ring of cardboard & attach to can top with tape

fold down tabs

SOURDOUGH WHOLE-WHEAT BATTER BREAD

Carry to a picnic in the coffee can in which it is baked (cover the can with bright wrapping paper and a sassy note: "No Additives, You Subtract"). A nourishing loaf, light and rich with respectable texture and that elusive, slightly sour, over-tone. Makes wonderful toast, served with homemade berry preserves or wild honey.

Makes One Large or
Two Small Loaves
1 tablespoon (15 ml) active
   dry yeast
1/4 cup (60 ml) lukewarm tea
1/4 cup (60 ml) honey
1/4 teaspoon (1.2 ml) ground
   ginger
1 can (13 ounce or 384 g)
   evaporated milk
1 cup (250 ml) sourdough
   starter, at room temperature
2 tablespoons (30 ml) safflower
   oil
1 teaspoon (5 ml) salt
2 cups (500 ml) stone-ground
   whole-wheat flour
2 cups (500 ml) unbleached
   white flour, or as needed
1/2 cup (125 ml) untoasted
   wheat germ
1/2 cup (125 ml) walnuts,
   finely ground

In large ceramic, glass or plastic bowl, sprinkle yeast over tea, stir in 1 tablespoon (15 ml) of the honey and let stand until foamy. Stir in remaining honey and the ginger. Add milk, starter oil and salt, beating until smooth. Combine flours, wheat germ and ground walnuts. Beating constantly, add flour mixture to starter mixture 1/2 cup (125 ml) at a time according to general directions for batter breads (page 96), adding additional unbleached flour only if needed.

Thoroughly grease a clean 2-pound (1 kg) coffee can or 2 1-pound (500 g each) coffee cans. Pat dough in can(s). Cover with oiled plastic wrap and tea towel and let rise in warm place 1 hour or until dough pushes up wrap. Bake on lowest rack in oven preheated to 350°F (180°C) 1 hour or until bread tests done. Loosen around sides of can with long slim knife and turn out onto wire rack. Turn right side up and cool.

Moisture during baking is absolutely necessary to attain the hard, crackly crust of sourdough bread.

SOURDOUGH RAISIN-OAT BREAD

A chewy bread, excellent for toast, with a subtle sourdough aftertaste. Allow at least five and a half hours on your time schedule, from start to finish, as the dough is a slow riser because it has no yeast to give it a boost. The starter should have at least eight hours "working time."

Makes Two Medium Loaves
1 cup (250 ml) lukewarm
   evaporated milk
1-1/2 cups (350 ml) sourdough
   starter
1/2 cup (125 ml) molasses
1/4 cup (60 ml) honey
4 tablespoons (60 ml) butter or
   margarine, melted
1/2 tablespoon (7.5 ml) salt
1 teaspoon (5 ml) ground
   allspice
2 cups (500 ml) unprocessed
   rolled oats
3/4 cup (175 ml) raisins, tossed
   lightly with a little flour
2-1/2 cups (600 ml) unbleached
   white flour, or as needed

In large warmed bowl, combine milk, starter, molasses, honey, butter, salt and allspice. Gradually add oats, a small amount at a time, mixing in well, then stir in raisins. Beat in flour, 1/2 cup (125 ml) at a time, to form a stiff dough. Turn out onto floured board and knead 5 to 7 minutes, adding additional flour only as needed to prevent sticking. Form into smooth ball, place in oiled bowl, turn to coat all surfaces, cover with dampened tea towel and let rise in warm place at least 2 hours or until double in bulk. Punch down, turn out onto board and knead briefly. Cover with tea towel and let rest 10 minutes. Divide dough into 2 equal portions, form into loaves and place in 2 #2 loaf pans. Cover with tea towel and let rise in warm place 1-1/2 hours or until almost double in size. Bake in oven preheated to 375°F (190°C) 35 to 40 minutes or until bread tests done. Turn out onto wire rack, turn right side up and cool.

TANGY SOURDOUGH CASSEROLE LOAF

A quick, moist bread to make after supper for a special next-morning treat: fragrant toast full of currants, almonds and a delightful sourdough-orange taste worth rushing to the breakfast table for.

Makes One Loaf
2 tablespoons (30 ml) active
   dry yeast
1/2 cup (125 ml) lukewarm
   fresh orange juice
2 tablespoons (30 ml) honey
1 cup (250 ml) sourdough
   starter, at room temperature
1 can (13 ounce or 384 g)
   evaporated milk
Grated peel of 1 orange
1 teaspoon (5 ml) salt
1 teaspoon (5 ml) ground allspice
3-1/2 cups (825 ml) unbleached
   white flour, or as needed
1 cup (250 ml) dried currants
1/2 cup (125 ml) blanched
   almonds, finely chopped
2 tablespoons (30 ml) candied
   lemon peel, finely chopped

In large bowl, sprinkle yeast over orange juice, stir in honey and let stand until foamy. Stir in starter, milk, orange peel, salt and allspice. According to general directions for batter breads, page 96, beat in 3 cups (700 ml) of the flour. Combine remaining flour with currants, almonds and lemon peel and stir in to make batter-bread consistency, adding additional flour if needed. Transfer to 2-1/2-quart (2.5 L) straight-sided casserole. Cover with plastic wrap and a tea towel and let rise in warm place 1 hour. Bake in oven preheated to 375°F (190°C) 1 hour or until bread tests done. Turn out onto wire rack, turn right side up and cool.

shape circle of dough over foil pan with fingers

SOURDOUGH HERB "TRENCHERS"

Long before the poor had plates in Merrie Old England, juicy chunks of meat were served on bowl-shaped rounds of bread called trenchers. The bread was probably more like hardtack, as the poor couldn't afford good flour or yeast. Anyway, once the meat was eaten and the juices or gravy had soaked into the trencher, it was eaten, too. We've pepped up a present-day bread plate with herbs to give you a new post-game supper idea, and a way to get kids safely around a vegetable stew.

Makes Six

1-1/2 cups (350 ml) sourdough starter
1 tablespoon (15 ml) honey
1/2 teaspoon (2.5 ml) salt
4 tablespoons (60 ml) butter, melted and cooled
1 egg, lightly beaten
1 cup (250 ml) whole-wheat flour
1-1/2 cups (350 ml) unbleached white flour, or as needed
1 tablespoon (15 ml) chopped fresh parsley
1/2 teaspoon (2.5 ml) celery seeds
1/4 teaspoon (1.2 ml) ground thyme
Additional melted butter

In large bowl, combine starter, honey, salt and 4 tablespoons (15 ml) melted butter; beat in egg. Combine whole-wheat flour, 1 cup (250 ml) of the unbleached white flour and herbs. Gradually add to starter mixture, beating until dough cleans side of bowl. Turn out onto board floured with remaining unbleached white flour and knead in flour. Adding additional flour only as needed to prevent sticking, knead until dough is smooth and pliable. Form into smooth ball, place in oiled bowl, turn to coat all surfaces, cover with dampened tea towel and let rise in warm place at least 2 hours or until double in bulk. (Don't hurry the rising. Without yeast it will be slower.) Punch down, turn out onto floured board and knead briefly. Roll out to 1/2-inch (1.5 cm) thickness. With a 6-inch (15 cm) diameter bowl as a pattern, set bowl rim on dough and cut around edge with a sharp knife. Generously grease outsides of 6 4-inch foil tart pans. Place pans upside down on baking sheet and drape dough circle over bottom of inverted pan; shape onto sides. Let trenchers stand 15 minutes, brush with melted butter and bake in oven preheated to 375°F (190°C) 20 minutes. If dough spreads out or begins to puff up, protect hand with hot pad or mitt and gently press back into shape. Transfer to wire rack and cool.

NOTE Trenchers may be made ahead, stored in an airtight container and reheated 10 minutes in a 350°F (180°C) oven before serving. If you make a double recipe, cover and refrigerate half of dough while you bake the first batch.

SOURDOUGH BANANA LITTLE LOAVES

The flavor of fruits, nuts and spices is even richer when used with sourdough. Try this nutty banana for starters. Also, you can substitute cooked prunes or apricots in place of bananas. Keep little loaves handy in the freezer for future giving, for quick dessert substitute, for zipping up the school lunch box. Always moist; toasts well.

Makes Four Miniature Loaves
1 cup (250 ml) whole-wheat
  flour
1-1/2 cups (350 ml) unbleached
  white flour
1/2 teaspoon (2.5 ml) salt
1 teaspoon (5 ml) double-
  acting baking powder
1/2 teaspoon (2.5 ml) baking
  soda
1 teaspoon (5 ml) ground
  nutmeg
2 eggs, lightly beaten
1/3 cup (75 ml) firmly packed
  brown sugar
1/3 cup (75 ml) honey
1/3 cup (75 ml) safflower oil
1 cup (250 ml) sourdough
  starter, at room temperature
2 large ripe bananas, mashed
Grated peel of 1 lemon
1 cup (250 ml) blanched
  almonds, finely chopped

Sift together flours, salt, baking powder, baking soda and nutmeg into a mixing bowl; add kernels left in sifter to flour mixture. Combine eggs, sugar, honey and oil and blend well. Stir in starter, bananas and lemon peel. Continue beating until well mixed. Add flour mixture all at once and stir just until dry ingredients are moistened. Fold in almonds and spoon into 4 prepared (page 165) #4 loaf pans. Bake in oven preheated to 375°F (190°C) 50 minutes or until bread tests done. Cool on wire rack 10 minutes, turn out, turn right side up, remove waxed paper and cool.

An ancient treatment for anemia: Stick a rusty nail into a green apple, let it stand overnight; remove the nail and eat the apple.

SOURDOUGH APPLE SORCERY

This is a bewitching combination of tart applesauce and sourdough. The flavor even improves if kept in the refrigerator a day or two, provided it doesn't disappear immediately while warm. Bake in small loaves for giving away or for freezing. Makes good toast.

Makes Four Miniature Loaves
3/4 cup (200 ml) unbleached
  white flour
3/4 cup (175 ml) whole-wheat
  flour
2/3 cup (150 ml) lightly toasted
  wheat germ
1/2 teaspoon (2.5 ml) salt
1/2 teaspoon (2.5 ml) baking
  soda
1 teaspoon (5 ml) double-
  acting baking powder
1/2 teaspoon (2.5 ml) ground
  cinnamon
1 egg
1/2 cup (125 ml) firmly packed
  brown sugar
1/2 cup (125 ml) safflower oil
1 cup (250 ml) sourdough
  starter, at room temperature
1 cup (250 ml) unsweetened
  thick applesauce

Combine flours, wheat germ, salt, baking soda, baking powder and cinnamon and blend well. In large bowl, beat egg lightly and blend in sugar and oil. Mix in starter and applesauce and mix well. Add mixture and stir just until dry ingredients are moistened. Spoon into 4 prepared (page 165) #4 loaf pans and bake in oven preheated to 350°F (180°C) 50 minutes or until bread tests done. Cool on wire rack 10 minutes, turn out, turn right side up, remove waxed paper and cool.

153

SOURDOUGH SQUARE ENGLISH MUFFINS

Ask a proper Britisher about the origin of these muffins and he'll tell you they're just Yankee crumpets. But then, he's probably never sampled sourdough—or he might claim *a priori* rights. Instead of cutting the muffins with a large biscuit cutter, we've cut them into squares. Fits the cheese, among other things, without overhangs.

Makes One Dozen

Day One
1 cup (250 ml) milk, at room temperature
1/2 cup (125 ml) sourdough starter, at room temperature
2-3/4 cups (650 ml) unbleached white flour, or as needed

In large pottery or glass bowl, combine milk, starter and 2 cups (500 ml) of the flour. Blend well, cover with plastic wrap and let stand at room temperature at least 8 hours.

Day Two
1 tablespoon (15 ml) granulated sugar
1/2 teaspoon (2.5 ml) salt
1/2 teaspoon (2.5 ml) baking soda
1/4 cup (50 ml) nondegerminated yellow cornmeal

Combine 1/2 cup (125 ml) of remaining flour, sugar, salt and baking soda. Sprinkle over starter mixture, mix thoroughly and turn out onto board floured with remaining flour. Knead in flour and, adding additional flour only as needed to prevent sticking, continue kneading 3 to 4 minutes until dough is smooth and no longer sticky. Roll out to 1/2-inch (1.5 cm) thickness and with floured sharp knife cut into 3-inch (8 cm) squares.

Pour half of the cornmeal into a medium-mesh sieve and sprinkle over a large baking sheet. Place muffins on cornmeal, at least 1 inch (3 cm) apart, and sprinkle tops with remaining cornmeal. Cover with tea towel and let rise in warm place 45 minutes or until almost double in size. Bake on greased griddle or in electric skillet over medium-low heat, 8 minutes per side. Check to be sure they're not getting too brown. Serve warm, or split and toast.

NOTE Timing problems? Muffins can be refrigerated after letting them rise 30 minutes instead of 45; leave cover on and refrigerate overnight. Bake when you are ready, allowing a few extra minutes per side. In a hurry? Use 2 griddles.

Prop a recipe book open with two clothespins, one on each side of the center fold.

SOURDOUGH BISCUITS

Makes Approximately Fourteen

Day One
1/2 cup (125 ml) sourdough
    starter
1 cup (250 ml) milk
1-1/2 cups (350 ml) unbleached
    white flour, or as needed

Combine starter, milk and 1 cup (250 ml) of the unbleached white flour. Blend well, cover with tea towel and let rise at room temperature overnight.

Day Two
1 tablespoon (15 ml) honey
1 teaspoon (5 ml) double-
    acting baking powder
1/2 teaspoon (2.5 ml) baking
    soda
3/4 teaspoon (3.6 ml) salt
1 cup (250 ml) whole-wheat
    flour
Bacon drippings, heated with
    equal amount of safflower or
    corn oil or butter

The next day, stir in honey. Combine remaining unbleached white flour, baking powder, baking soda and salt. Stir into starter mixture and beat well. Mound whole-wheat flour on board, turn dough out onto board and knead in flour. Adding additional unbleached white flour as needed to prevent sticking, knead lightly to form a soft dough. Roll dough out to 1/2-inch (1.5 cm) thickness and cut into 2-1/2-inch (6 cm) rounds. Dip each round into bacon dripping mixture and arrange close together in a 9-inch (23 cm) square baking pan. Cover with tea towel and let rise in warm place 30 minutes. Bake in oven preheated to 375°F (190°C) 30 to 35 minutes. Serve hot.

SOURDOUGH CINNAMON ROLLS

Makes Approximately Sixteen

Day One
1/2 cup (125 ml) sourdough starter, at room temperature
1 cup (250 ml) evaporated milk
2 cups (500 ml) unbleached white flour, or as needed

Combine starter, evaporated milk and 1-1/4 cups (300 ml) of the unbleached white flour. Cover with tea towel and let stand overnight.

Day Two
4 tablespoons (60 ml) butter, softened
1/4 cup (60 ml) honey
2 eggs, lightly beaten
1-1/2 cups (350 ml) whole-wheat flour
1 teaspoon (5 ml) double-acting baking powder
1/2 teaspoon (2.5 ml) baking soda
3/4 teaspoon (3.6 ml) salt

Filling
1/2 cup (125 ml) chopped dates
Grated peel of 1 orange
1/4 cup (60 ml) fresh orange juice
Melted butter
1/4 cup (60 ml) firmly packed brown sugar
1/2 tablespoon (7.5 ml) ground cinnamon

Melted butter for dipping
Powdered Sugar Glaze, page 223

The next morning, prepare filling: Simmer dates and orange peel in orange juice 10 minutes and set aside to cool while finishing dough.

Returning to dough, beat together softened butter, honey and eggs and stir into starter mixture. Combine whole-wheat flour, 1/2 cup (125 ml) of the white flour, baking powder, baking soda and salt; stir into dough and turn out onto board floured with white flour. Knead, adding additional unbleached flour only as needed to prevent sticking, 5 to 7 minutes. Roll out into 8- by 14-inch (20 by 35 cm) rectangle and brush generously with melted butter. Strew date mixture over and sprinkle with brown sugar and cinnamon. Starting at a long side, roll tightly like a jelly roll. Seal seam by pinching together dough and closing ends. Cut roll into approximately 16

slices (see page 138). Dip top and bottom of each slice into melted butter and place cut side up on jelly-roll pan. Cover loosely with tea towel and let rise in warm place approximately 1 hour or until almost double in size. Bake in oven preheated to 375°F (190°C) 30 to 35 minutes. While hot, frost with Powdered Sugar Glaze and serve warm.

SOURDOUGH SCONES

Served warm from the oven, they're wicked! At a block party, the whole lot disappeared in three minutes. They reheat well when split and put under the broiler. For singles, the recipe can be cut in half.

Makes Eighteen

Day One
1 cup (250 ml) sourdough starter, left at room temperature at least 12 hours
1-1/2 cups (350 ml) milk, at room temperature
4-1/2 cups (1 L) unbleached white flour, or as needed

In large warmed bowl, mix starter, milk and 3 cups (700 ml) of the flour. Cover with tea towel and let stand in warm place overnight or least 8 hours.

156

Day Two
6 tablespoons (90 ml) butter, melted
1/2 cup (125 ml) granulated sugar
1/2 teaspoon (2.5 ml) salt
1 teaspoon (5 ml) baking soda
1/2 cup (125 ml) dried currants
Melted butter for dipping

Pour melted butter over top of starter mixture and stir in; it will take considerable effort to blend. In another bowl, combine 1 cup (250 ml) of the remaining flour, sugar, salt and baking soda. Sprinkle over dough, add currants and beat in thoroughly. Turn out onto board floured with remaining flour and knead, adding additional flour only as needed to prevent sticking, 5 minutes or until dough is no longer sticky. Divide into 2 equal portions and roll each into a 9-inch (23 cm) square. With floured sharp knife, cut each square into 3-inch (8 cm) squares. Dip each scone into melted butter and arrange in 2 9-inch (23 cm) square baking pans. Cover with tea towel and let rise in warm place 45 minutes or until almost double in size. Bake in oven preheated to 375°F (190°C) approximately 35 minutes. Serve immediately with butter and jam. Or cool on wire rack and wrap for freezing.

SOURDOUGH GRIDDLE-CAKES AND WAFFLES

When you're eating these delicate treats, you'll swear they could be air-borne if you didn't anchor them down with your fork—probably the most delicate of flour-based foods, with none of the usual macho pancake temperament. And the waffles, so light and tender, freeze very well, returning to ambrosia via the toaster. But best of all, it's that sourdough fragrance and flavor to linger over on a lazy, rainy Saturday morning.

Serves Four Generously
2 eggs, separated
2 tablespoons (30 ml) safflower oil
2 cups (500 ml) sourdough starter, at room temperature
2 tablespoons (30 ml) granulated sugar
1 teaspoon (5 ml) salt
1 teaspoon (5 ml) baking soda

In large bowl, lightly beat egg yolks, add oil and stir in starter. In a small bowl, combine sugar, salt and soda. Sprinkle sugar mixture over starter mixture and fold in. Mixture will increase in size because of soda's action on sourdough. Beat egg whites until stiff but not dry and fold in. Cook according to directions for griddlecakes (page 207) or waffles (page 210).

old cast-iron fireplace waffle iron

Quickly Made Breads

QUICK BREADS & COFFEE CAKES
CORN BREADS
SODA BREADS
SELF-RISING FLOUR BREADS
BISCUITS & MUFFINS
UNLEAVENED BREADS
CRACKERS

The *bread* also rises, Mr. Hemingway, without yeast or starters. It wasn't until the 1850s that an efficient bread riser appeared that would change the pattern of baking: a mixture of sodium bicarbonate (baking soda) and cream of tartar. At first it was used to lighten homemade biscuits, and then housewives found they could make delicate "lady" cakes and lemon cookies, gingerbreads and Johnny cakes, without waiting for dough to rise, without long kneadings.

Breads had been made earlier with buttermilk or sour milk that depended on soda, an alkali, to form the gas that immediately started batter "working." Women found they had to work rapidly and get the batch into the oven before the gases lost their vigor. (Commercial bakers were always men; women were always in the home.)

The same need for speed holds true today for breads, coffee cakes and small breads made with baking powder or soda. Don't dawdle over quick breads. Let the phone ring off the wall. Ignore the doorbell.

GUIDELINES FOR MAKING QUICK BREADS

When the recipe indicates an amount of baking powder, be sure it is double-acting. That is, it starts working while you're mixing, and it continues acting in the oven. It must be fresh. If you are not sure of the age of some you have on the shelf, drop a teaspoonful into a half cup (125 ml) of hot water. If it bubbles and fizzes, it's still active. When baking soda is called for, sift it with the flour and other dry ingredients so that it is thoroughly mixed in. Don't add it to the liquids.

There may be slight variations in directions for assembling quick breads, but generally they will follow a basic pattern. First, sift the dry ingredients into a large bowl and be sure they are well blended. Then make a well in the center. Combine the liquids in another bowl and pour into the well all at once, stirring until dry ingredients are just moistened.

In recipes that start with creaming butter and sugar, as for cakes, add the eggs (always room temperature and fresh) and then add the flour alternately with the liquid. But, most important, don't overdo mixing—too much and you'll need a forklift to ease the bread to the table. Muffins are particularly allergic to overstirring and will develop tunnels like a gopher run. Add fruits and nuts last, and spoon batter into a buttered and

lightly floured pan (no flouring for muffins).

Quick breads can't take the molten-lava heat that French bread needs: 325° to 375°F (140° to 190°C) oven temperature will deliver a respectable brown. Don't push your luck by turning up the heat. Also, you can't use the *thump* test to decide whether a quick bread is done. Rely on a toothpick or cake tester inserted into the middle of a loaf; if sticky dough clings to it, the bread is not ready and needs more time. When the sides pull away from the pan, that's usually a sign it is finished. Baking time can vary five minutes on either side of the recommended amount in our recipes, depending on humidity, on the contents—fruits, nuts, kind of flour available in your area, etc.—so not to worry.

Quick breads keep up to six months in the freezer if well-wrapped in foil or plastic. They will thaw in two to three hours at room temperature. Quickly baked breads are breads of hospitality, open hand, warm heart. Always keep them on hand, or keep the makings handy. They outrank the analyst's couch.

THOUGHTS ON MAKING QUICK BREADS

- Don't double a recipe. Make two batches, if necessary.
- Always assemble all ingredients before you start.
- Preheat oven in plenty of time, so you can pop the bread in without waiting; if baking in glass, lower temperature 25°F (12.5°C).
- Dust raisins, nuts, chopped fruits with a little of the measured flour so they won't sink to the bottom of the loaf.
- Bake in the middle of the oven. If your stove bakes unevenly, rotate pan halfway through the baking time.
- If you don't have correct-sized pan: too large and loaf will be flat; too small and batter will run over the sides, making a mess. Bake in smaller pans, filled two-thirds full, or muffin tins. The smaller pans (#4) are ideal giveaway size. Bake breads in the lightweight folded aluminum ones found in packages in supermarkets.
- Leave a quick bread huddling in its pan for 10 minutes before turning out on a wire rack to cool. The bread continues "baking" for a few minutes right out of the oven and the brief waiting time helps it set up. You don't have to wait until it's cool to satisfy a healthy curiosity: Hot breads may be crumbly but will firm as they cool. And the only way to eat a muffin is piping hot.

160

Glass jars are best for storing dried foods. Just remember light affects nutrient levels—store in a dark place.

QUICK BREAD MIX

*Makes Approximately
Nine Cups (2 L)*

It's like having *moussaka* ready in the freezer when your rich Greek uncle stops by unexpectedly—a quick-bread mix that you prepare ahead of time and store in a jar in the refrigerator. This is a basic whole-wheat/dry milk/soy flour mix with baking powder, the *good* things ready to stir up coffee cakes, pancakes and your imagination. Don't be without it.

*Makes Approximately
Nine Cups (2 L)*
3-1/2 cups (825 ml) un-
    bleached white flour
3 cups (700 ml) whole-wheat
    pastry flour
1-1/2 cups (350 ml) soy flour
1 cup (250 ml) non-instant
    nonfat dry milk
1/3 cup (75 ml) double-acting
    baking powder
2 tablespoons (30 ml) salt

In two portions (two are recommended for manageability), sift together all ingredients. Store in covered container in refrigerator.

QUICK-BREAD MIX
TEA LOAVES

That label, tea loaves, belongs to another generation, when everyone ran out and looked up if they heard airplane engines. But it surprisingly translates to today's living: People are taking time to share mid-afternoon tea or coffee with other people . . . and with warm breads. The small loaves cut into polite little slices no one wants to resist. This is a non-sweet, deeply indebted to Swiss cheese, mustard, dill weed and the Quick-Bread Mix waiting in the fridge.

Makes Four Miniature Loaves
3 cups (700 ml) Quick-Bread
    Mix, preceding
3/4 teaspoon (3.6 ml) dry
    mustard
1 teaspoon (5 ml) dill weed
1/4 teaspoon (1.2 ml) salt
Dash cayenne pepper
1-1/2 cups (350 ml) freshly
    grated Swiss cheese
1 egg, lightly beaten
1-1/4 cups (300 ml) milk
1 tablespoon (15 ml) safflower
    oil
1 tablespoon (15 ml) honey

Combine the mix, dry mustard, dill weed, salt and cayenne pepper and toss with cheese. Beat together remaining ingredients until well blended and stir into dry ingredients just until moistened. Spoon into 4 prepared #4 loaf pans (page 165). Bake in oven preheated to 350°F (180°C) 20 to 25 minutes or until bread tests done. Remove to wire rack, cool 10 minutes in pans, turn out onto rack, peel off waxed paper, turn right side up and cool completely.

tea loaves

CARROT-PINEAPPLE BREAD

These two are old friends from salad days—but wait until you encounter them in dark, moist, whole-wheat loaves. They thread yellows and oranges through the honey, raisins, nuts and wheat germ, through pungent spices and orange zest to accentuate flavor and moisture. We promise that you can stake your reputation on this pair (even out of the freezer where they keep very well).

Makes Two Loaves
1-1/2 cups (350 ml) sifted
  whole-wheat pastry flour
1-1/2 cups (350 ml) sifted unbleached white flour
2 teaspoons (10 ml) double-
  acting baking powder
1 teaspoon (5 ml) baking
  soda
1 teaspoon (5 ml) salt
1 tablespoon (15 ml) ground
  cinnamon
1/2 teaspoon (2.5 ml) ground
  nutmeg
1/2 cup (125 ml) untoasted
  wheat germ
3 eggs, lightly beaten
1-1/2 cups (350 ml) safflower
  oil
1 cup (250 ml) honey
1 tablespoon (15 ml) pure
  vanilla extract
1 can (8 ounces or 225 g)
  crushed pineapple, undrained
2 to 3 tablespoons (30 to 45 ml)
  freshly grated orange peel
2 cups (500 ml) firmly packed
  scraped, grated carrots
3/4 cup (175 ml) chopped
  walnuts, pecans or filberts
3/4 cup (175) golden raisins
1/3 cup (75 ml) lightly toasted
  sesame seeds

Sift together flours, baking powder, baking soda, salt and spices. Combine with wheat germ. Beat together eggs, oil, honey and vanilla extract until well blended. Stir in pineapple and its juice, orange peel and carrots. Add flour mixture and stir just until dry ingredients are moistened. Fold in nuts, raisins and sesame seeds. Spoon into 2 buttered and lightly floured #2 loaf pans. Bake in oven preheated to 350°F (180°C) 40 minutes or until bread tests done. Remove to wire racks, cool in pans 10 minutes, invert onto wire rack, turn right side up and cool completely.

BANANA-COCONUT BREAD

Banana bread, yes, but not likely one you've experienced. It's a heavy, dark, handsome loaf, just off the boat from the tropics. Spices, coconut, whole-wheat pastry flour, lemon peel, honey, eggs—the natives never had it so good. Your natives.

*Makes One Large or
Two Small Loaves*
2 eggs, lightly beaten
1/2 cup (125 ml) safflower
  oil
3/4 cup (175 ml) honey
2 tablespoons (30 ml) buttermilk, plain yoghurt or sour
  cream
1 teaspoon (5 ml) pure vanilla
  extract, or
  1/2 teaspoon (2.5 ml) almond
  extract
1 tablespoon (15 ml) freshly
  grated lemon peel
1-1/2 cups (350 ml) mashed
  ripe bananas
1-1/2 cups (350 ml) sifted
  whole-wheat pastry flour
1/4 cup (50 ml) soy flour
2 tablespoons (30 ml) non-
  instant nonfat dry milk
1/2 tablespoon (7.5 ml) double-
  acting baking powder
1/2 teaspoon (2.5 ml) baking
  soda
1/2 teaspoon (2.5 ml) salt

1/2 teaspoon (2.5 ml) ground
  cinnamon
1/2 teaspoon (2.5 ml) ground
  allspice
1/3 cup (75 ml) unsweetened
  grated coconut
2 tablespoons (30 ml) untoasted
  wheat germ
1/2 cup (125 ml) chopped
  almonds or walnuts

Beat together eggs, oil, honey,
buttermilk and vanilla extract
until well blended. Then stir in
lemon peel and bananas. Sift
together pastry flour, soy flour,
dry milk, baking powder, baking soda, salt and spices. Mix
in coconut and wheat germ and
stir into egg mixture just until
dry ingredients are moistened.
Fold in nuts and spoon into a
buttered and lightly floured #1
or 2 #3 loaf pans. Bake in
oven preheated to 350°F (180°C)
30 minutes. Lower heat to
325°F (160°C) and bake 25
minutes longer or until bread
tests done. Remove to wire
rack, cool 10 minutes in pan(s),
invert onto rack, turn right side
up and cool completely.

FRESH PEAR BREAD

A loving affair with Boscs. The
taste lingers, holds your attention; in fact, it is emphasized
with the coriander and spiked
by the lemon. It becomes a
chewy bread with wheat germ
and nuts, and slices best when
cooled. Pears and cream cheese
speak the same tongue, as do
unsalted butter and very thin
slices of Smithfield ham.

Makes One Medium Loaf
2 eggs, lightly beaten
1/4 pound (125 g) butter,
  melted and cooled
1/2 cup (125 ml) honey
2 tablespoons (30 ml) fresh
  lemon juice
4 or 5 ripe but firm Bosc
  pears, pared and grated to
  measure 1-1/2 cups (350 ml)
1-3/4 cups (425 ml) Quick-
  Bread Mix, page 161)
1 tablespoon (15 ml) ground
  coriander
1/4 cup (50 ml) untoasted
  wheat germ
2/3 cup (150 ml) chopped
  filberts

pear bread

Beat together eggs, butter
honey and lemon juice; blend
in grated pears. Combine bread
mix, coriander and wheat germ.
Stir into egg mixture just until
dry ingredients are moistened.
Fold in nuts and spoon into a
buttered #2 loaf pan. Bake in
oven preheated to 350°F (180°C)
55 minutes or until bread tests
done. Remove to wire rack,
cool in pan 10 minutes, invert
onto wire rack, turn right side
up and cool completely.

163

*Filberts: To remove skin,
place in a 350°F (180°C)
oven for 10 to 15 minutes;
rub with rough towel and
skins will come off easily.*

FRESH APRICOT BREAD

Good ol' summertime breads, when the baking's easy, and the apricots, peaches and mangoes are full of juices. These are slightly sweet loaves to serve with iced fruit bowls or a cold fruit soup. They make a fresh replacement for school-lunch sandwiches (loaves will keep up to four months in the freezer, so that summer's bake is October's treat).

Makes Two Small Loaves
1/4 pound (125 g) butter, softened
2/3 cup (150 ml) firmly packed brown sugar
2 eggs
1 teaspoon (5 ml) pure vanilla extract
1 tablespoon (15 ml) fresh orange juice
1 cup (250 ml) chopped very ripe apricots and juices
1 cup (250 ml) unbleached white flour
3/4 cup (175 ml) whole-wheat pastry flour
1/2 tablespoon (7.5 ml) double-acting baking powder
1/2 teaspoon (2.5 ml) salt
1 teaspoon (5 ml) ground cinnamon
1/4 teaspoon (1.2 ml) ground nutmeg
1/4 teaspoon (1.2 ml) ground cloves

5 tablespoons (75 ml) ground unprocessed rolled oats (see Note)
1/2 cup (125 ml) raisins, chopped
1/3 cup (75 ml) chopped pecans, walnuts or almonds (optional)

Cream together butter and sugar; blend in eggs, one at a time. Stir in vanilla extract, orange juice and apricots. Sift together flours, baking powder, salt and spices. Stir in oats and blend into butter mixture just until dry ingredients are moistened. Spoon into 2 buttered #3 loaf pans and bake in oven preheated to 350°F (180°C) 45 to 50 minutes or until bread tests done. Remove to wire rack, cool in pans 10 minutes, invert onto rack, turn right side up and cool completely.

PEACH OR MANGO BREAD Substitute for apricots lightly mashed, ripe peaches and their juices, or thoroughly mashed ripe mangoes and an additional 1 tablespoon (15 ml) orange juice; sift with dry ingredients 1/2 teaspoon (2.5 ml) ground cardamom.

NOTE Rolled oats can be ground into flour in a blender. Blend for 5 seconds, remove container and loosen particles around blade, then blend 10 seconds longer. Texture will be like meal.

CRANBERRY BREAD

The acid bogs of New England are responsible for our lovely tart winter berry, which abounds in vitamin C as well as charisma. This jolly bread is a refreshing tempter, the cranberry singing in chorus with the orange (high C), and with chopped pecans and wheat germ joining in to give it body.

Makes One Medium Loaf
1 cup (250 ml) halved cranberries
1/3 cup (75 ml) honey
1 cup (225 ml) sifted whole-wheat flour
1 cup (250 ml) sifted unbleached white flour
1/2 tablespoon (7.5 ml) double-acting baking powder
1/2 teaspoon (2.5 ml) baking soda
1/4 teaspoon (1.2 ml) salt
1 medium to large orange
1 egg, lightly beaten
2 tablespoons (30 ml) butter, cut in bits
Boiling water
1/4 cup (50 ml) untoasted wheat germ
1/2 cup (125 ml) chopped pecans, walnuts or filberts

Soak cranberries overnight in honey. Combine flours, baking powder, baking soda and salt and set aside. Grate the peel of the orange and add to egg. Squeeze juice from orange into a cup to

164

measure 1/3 cup (75 ml); do not strain. Place butter in another measuring cup and pour boiling water in to measure 3/4 cup (175 ml). Stir to melt butter and combine with orange juice. Cool slightly and blend into egg mixture. Add wheat germ and gradually stir in flour mixture just until dry ingredients are moistened. Fold in cranberries and nuts and spoon into a buttered #2 loaf pan. Bake in oven preheated to 350°F (180°C) 55 minutes or until bread tests done. Remove to wire rack, cool in pan 10 minutes, turn out onto wire rack, turn right side up and cool completely.

DATE-OATMEAL BREAD

A nice simple loaf with no inhibitions. Thinly slice it and spread with cream cheese, or cut in thick slabs and then into half-inch strips that can be rolled in powdered sugar for a quick dessert. The sly ingredients you won't guess—whole-wheat pastry flour, rolled oats and elusive nutmeg—give this bread organic clout, as the copywriters say. We think it just plain tastes good.

If you want to experiment, substitute fruit juices—orange, cranberry or apple—for the water.

Makes One Large Loaf

1 cup (250 ml) boiling water
1 package (8-ounce or 227 g) pitted dates, coarsely chopped (approximately 1-1/4 cups or 300 ml)
1/2 cup (125 ml) unprocessed rolled oats
2-1/4 cups (525 ml) sifted whole-wheat pastry flour
2 teaspoons (10 ml) double-acting baking powder
1/2 teaspoon (2.5 ml) baking soda
1/2 teaspoon (2.5 ml) salt
1/4 teaspoon (1.2 ml) ground nutmeg
3/4 cup (175 ml) firmly packed brown sugar
1 egg, lightly beaten
2 tablespoons (30 ml) butter, melted and cooled
1 teaspoon (5 ml) pure vanilla extract
1 tablespoon (15 ml) freshly grated orange peel
1/2 cup (125 ml) chopped walnuts

Pour boiling water over dates and oats; let stand 10 minutes. Sift together flour, baking powder, baking soda, salt and nutmeg. Blend in sugar. Beat together egg, butter, vanilla extract and orange peel, stir in date mixture and add flour mixture. Mix just until dry ingredients are moistened. Fold in nuts and spoon into buttered and lightly floured #1 loaf pan. Bake in oven preheated to 350°F (180°C) 1 hour or until bread tests done. Remove to wire rack, cool in pan 10 minutes, invert onto rack, turn right side up and cool completely.

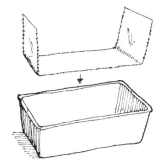

to keep quick breads from sticking to pan, line pan with strip of waxed paper; oil pan, place paper & then invert paper so batter is on oiled surface 165

always cool quick breads 10 minutes before removing from pan

LEMON-PINEAPPLE BREAD

A fine textured, cakelike loaf, only mildly honey-sweet. The whole-wheat pastry flour (available in natural-foods stores) makes a lighter batter than whole-wheat flour, but the addition of wheat germ promises good firm slices and a high luncheon rating with a fruit compote or sliced fresh peaches.

Makes One Medium Loaf

4 tablespoons (60 ml) butter, softened
1/2 cup (125 ml) honey
1 egg
2 tablespoons (30 ml) sour cream
1 can (8 ounces or 225 g) crushed pineapple, undrained
3 tablespoons (45 ml) freshly grated lemon peel
3/4 cup (175 ml) unbleached white flour
3/4 cup (175 ml) whole-wheat pastry flour
1/4 cup (60 ml) soy flour
2 teaspoons (10 ml) double-acting baking powder
1/2 teaspoon (2.5 ml) baking soda
3/4 teaspoon (3.6 ml) salt
1/4 cup (50 ml) untoasted wheat germ
3/4 cup (175 ml) raisins
3/4 cup (175 ml) chopped walnuts, pecans or almonds

Cream together butter and honey until fluffy. Beat in egg, then sour cream, pineapple and lemon peel. Sift together flours, baking powder, baking soda and salt. Mix in wheat germ and stir into pineapple mixture just until dry ingredients are moistened. Fold in raisins and nuts and spoon into buttered and lightly floured #2 loaf pan. Bake in oven preheated to 350°F (180°C) 55 minutes or until bread tests done. Remove to wire rack, cool in pan 10 minutes, invert onto wire rack, turn right side up and cool completely.

To shell pecans, freeze overnight and you can remove nutmeats whole.

ORANGE-NUT BREAD

If any of these quick breads could be called classic, this is it: straightforward citrus stringency, fragrant as orange blossoms, and unaffected by any distractions. Bake it as a single loaf, as suggested, or divide into three miniature loaf pans (#4) for mini-sandwiches. Nice served with frozen yoghurt and herb tea.

Makes One Large Loaf

1 egg, lightly beaten
1-1/4 cups (300 ml) milk
1/4 cup (50 ml) fresh orange juice
2 tablespoons (30 ml) safflower oil
2/3 cup (150 ml) honey
3 tablespoons (45 ml) freshly grated orange peel
1-1/2 cups (350 ml) unbleached white flour
1-1/2 cups (350 ml) whole-wheat pastry flour
4 teaspoons (20 ml) double-acting baking powder
1 teaspoon (5 ml) salt
1 cup (250 ml) chopped walnuts

Beat together egg, milk, orange juice, oil and honey until well blended. Add orange peel. Sift together flours, baking powder and salt. Stir into egg mixture just until dry ingredients are moistened. Fold in nuts and spoon into buttered and lightly floured #1 loaf pan. Bake in oven preheated to 350°F (180°C) 1 hour or until bread tests done. Remove to wire rack, cool in pan 10 minutes, invert onto wire rack, turn right side up and cool completely.

PUMPKIN-NUT BREAD

Of course you could use canned pumpkin here, but this is such an endowed loaf, it deserves better. Rescue Halloween's leftover, steam and puree the "punkin" in your own kitchen. The spices, dried fruit and nuts carry all the nostalgia of pumpkin pie, but adding bran flakes, buttermilk and sunflower seeds puts it in a bread heaven all by itself. This could become a tradition.

Makes Three Miniature Loaves
1/4 cup (60 ml) unprocessed bran
1/3 cup (75 ml) buttermilk
1 egg, lightly beaten
1/2 cup (125 ml) honey
4 tablespoons (60 ml) butter, melted and cooled
1 cup (250 ml) pureed cooked pumpkin
3/4 cup (175 ml) whole-wheat pastry flour
1/2 cup (125 ml) unbleached white flour
2 teaspoons (10 ml) double-acting baking powder
1/2 teaspoon (2.5 ml) baking soda
1/2 teaspoon (2.5 ml) salt
1 to 1-1/2 teaspoons (5 to 7.5 ml) pumpkin pie spice

3 tablespoons (45 ml) untoasted wheat germ
2/3 cup (175 ml) chopped dates, raisins or currants
2/3 cup (175 ml) chopped pecans, walnuts or filberts
2 tablespoons (30 ml) sunflower seeds

Soak bran in buttermilk 10 minutes. Beat together egg, honey, butter and pumpkin until well blended. Stir in bran mixture. Sift together flours, baking powder, baking soda, salt and spice. Stir into egg mixture just until dry ingredients are moistened. Combine all remaining ingredients and fold into batter. Spoon into 3 buttered #4 loaf pans. Bake in oven preheated to 350°F (180°C) 35 minutes or until bread tests done. Remove to wire rack, cool in pans 10 minutes, invert onto wire rack, turn right side up and cool completely.

BUTTERNUT SQUASH BREAD Substitute for pumpkin butternut squash; substitute for pumpkin pie spice 1/2 teaspoon (2.5 ml) ground ginger and 1/4 teaspoon (1.2 ml) each ground cloves and nutmeg.

SWEET POTATO BREAD Substitute for pumpkin yam or sweet potato; substitute for pumpkin pie spice 1/2 teaspoon (2.5 ml) ground cinnamon and 1/4 teaspoon (1.2 ml) each ground cloves and nutmeg.

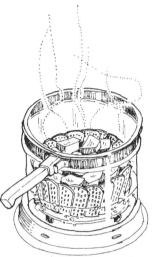

steam pumpkin or squash chunks until tender, remove rind & mash or puree in blender

The sweet potato produces more food value than any other garden plant in a given amount of space.

ZUCCHINI BREAD

The prolific vegetable that jogs away with all the honors from the rest of the bunch. Entire books have been written about its many talents at the table. We'd like to present one for you to try that you haven't found before. It's moist, it's colorful, and it's crunchy when you expect it to be soft. Zucchini is very high in water content, so grate it *just before* adding.

Makes One Large Loaf
3 eggs, lightly beaten
2/3 cup (150 ml) honey
1/2 cup (125 ml) safflower oil
1 teaspoon (5 ml) pure vanilla extract
2 cups (500 ml) whole-wheat pastry flour
2 teaspoons (10 ml) double-acting baking powder
1/2 teaspoon (2.5 ml) baking soda
1/2 teaspoon (2.5 ml) salt
1/2 teaspoon (2.5 ml) ground cinnamon
1/4 teaspoon (1.2 ml) ground ginger
1/4 teaspoon (1.2 ml) ground nutmeg
2 tablespoons (30 ml) untoasted wheat germ
2/3 cup (150 ml) raisins
2/3 cup (150 ml) chopped walnuts
2 tablespoons (30 ml) sunflower seeds
2 cups (500 ml) grated zucchini

Beat together eggs, honey, oil and vanilla extract. Sift together flour, baking powder, baking soda, salt and spices and mix in wheat germ. Combine raisins, walnuts and sunflower seeds. Stir the freshly grated zucchini into egg mixture and blend in flour mixture just until dry ingredients are moistened. Fold in raisin mixture and spoon into a buttered and lightly floured #1 loaf pan. Bake in oven preheated to 350°F (180°C) 1 hour and 10 minutes or until bread tests done. Remove to wire rack, cool in pan 10 minutes, invert onto wire rack, turn right side up and cool completely.

RHUBARB BREAD

Lovers of early morning pampering look to this quick little bread. It's not sweet, just barely tinged with the tartness of rhubarb and sour cream, and nicely moist. You can stew the fruit the day before: slice stalks into one-inch (2.5 cm) diagonal chunks and cook in a little water just long enough to soften. Don't try to use frozen rhubarb as it is too watery. Add only enough brown sugar to the stewed fruit to make it palatable —the tarter, the better.

Makes Two Small Loaves
2-2/3 cups (625 ml) whole-wheat flour
2 teaspoons (10 ml) double-acting baking powder
1 teaspoon (5 ml) baking soda
1 teaspoon (5 ml) ground cinnamon
1/2 teaspoon (2.5 ml) ground cloves
1/4 teaspoon (1.2 ml) salt
1/2 cup (125 ml) unprocessed bran
2 eggs, at room temperature
2 teaspoons (10 ml) fresh lemon juice
1 to 2 teaspoons (5 to 10 ml) freshly grated lemon peel
1 cup (250 ml) sour cream, at room temperature
1 cup (250 ml) cooked rhubarb, at room temperature
1/4 pound (125 g) butter, melted and cooled

Combine all dry ingredients and blend well. In large mixing bowl, beat eggs lightly and blend in lemon juice and peel, sour cream, rhubarb and butter. Stir in dry ingredients just until moistened and spoon into 2 well-buttered #3 loaf pans. Bake in oven preheated to 350°F (180°C) 35 minutes or until bread tests done. Transfer to wire rack, cool in pans 10 minutes, turn out onto rack, turn right side up and cool completely.

BOSTON BROWN BREAD

As native to America as the New England baked beans it's usually served with, brown bread is steamed in water on top of the stove. The acidy buttermilk or yoghurt and soda, the molasses and wheat germ, make short work of conjuring up a dark, moist cylinder of indescribable fragrance; hankering for a slice is as natural as craving pie for breakfast, in Boston. Brown bread is rightly steamed in coffee or juice cans, and the taller the loaf, the more slices it will deliver. (A dull knife will mutilate the warm loaf; cut it with a string.) Top of loaf should be firm when tested. If still sticky, steam for 20 to 30 minutes longer. When the bread is removed from the can, you can dry it slightly in a 350°F (180°C) oven for ten minutes. Always eat it warm, with lots of butter or creamed cheese, with or without beans.

Makes One Loaf

1 cup (250 ml) plain yoghurt or buttermilk
1/2 cup (125 ml) molasses
1/2 cup (125 ml) whole-wheat pastry flour
1/2 cup (125 ml) unbleached white flour
1/4 cup (60 ml) non-instant nonfat dry milk
2 teaspoons (10 ml) double-acting baking powder
1/2 teaspoon (2.5 ml) baking soda
1/2 teaspoon (2.5 ml) salt
1/2 cup (125 ml) nondegerminated yellow cornmeal
1/4 cup (50 ml) untoasted wheat germ
3/4 cup (175 ml) chopped raisins

Combine yoghurt and molasses. Sift together flours, dry milk, baking powder, baking soda and salt. Mix in cornmeal and wheat germ and stir into yoghurt mixture just until dry ingredients are moistened. Fold in raisins and spoon into a buttered and lightly floured 1-1/2-quart (1.5 L) juice can. Tie a foil cover over the top of the can. Place on rack in large kettle with tightly fitting lid. Add boiling water to reach halfway up can, being careful not to pour water over can. Steam at gentle boil 3 hours, adding boiling water as needed to keep original level. Remove can from kettle and loosen edges with long spatula. Turn upside down over rack and slowly ease bread out of can. Cool 8 to 10 minutes before slicing.

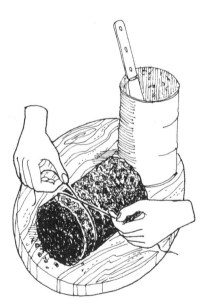

wrap thread around loaf, pull slowly; thread will penetrate and "cut" a slice

for a change, bake quick breads in a tube pan --1 large #1 pan will equal 1-9" tube

---

Check the date on the can of baking powder to be sure it is still fresh.

BRAN-OATMEAL BREAD

This is a nutritionist's special, moist but not a lightweight and packed with enough zest to carry you from Monday to Friday. It is loaded with bran, rolled oats, wheat germ, whole wheat, raisins, molasses and buttermilk—a roll call of Adelle Davis ingredients with the flavor of old-fashioned oatmeal cookies.

Makes One Large Loaf
1 cup (250 ml) unprocessed bran
1/2 cup (125 ml) unprocessed rolled oats
1-1/3 cups (325 ml) buttermilk
2 cups (500 ml *sifted*) whole-wheat pastry flour
1/2 teaspoon (2.5 ml) salt
2 teaspoons (10 ml) double-acting baking powder
1/2 teaspoon (2.5 ml) baking soda
1 teaspoon (5 ml) ground cinnamon
1/2 teaspoon (2.5 ml) ground allspice
1/2 teaspoon (2.5 ml) ground nutmeg
1/3 cup (75 ml) firmly packed brown sugar
1/4 cup (50 ml) untoasted wheat germ
2 eggs, lightly beaten
1/2 cup (125 ml) blackstrap molasses
1/4 cup (50 ml) fresh lemon juice
1 cup (250 ml) raisins

Soak bran and oats in buttermilk 10 minutes. Sift together flour, salt, baking powder, baking soda and spices. Mix in sugar and wheat germ. Beat eggs with molasses and lemon juice and blend in bran mixture. Add flour mixture and mix just until dry ingredients are moistened. Fold in raisins and spoon into buttered and lightly floured #1 loaf pan. Bake in oven preheated to 350°F (180°C) 45 minutes or until bread tests done. Remove to wire rack, cool in pan 10 minutes, invert onto wire rack, turn right side up and cool completely.

Call them coffee cakes, *Kuchen,* breakfast breads, these are special ways to warm sleepy tongues in the morning, to set bored board members purring, to bring occasional bliss to frantic after-school regulars. We've run the gamut from A to Yoghurt, and you can pick any flavor letter in between for a variation of your own. These are put together in ways different from those quick breads in this section: an upside-down fresh cranberry (or cherry) coffee cake; a Viennese-style apple layered with regiment-straight rows of thin slices and glazed with melted currant jelly; rich streuseled sour cream squares, hiding lovely fresh blueberries; a nutty, crusty whole-wheat buttermilk-soy cake made without sugar, sweet with wild honey.

THOUGHTS ON SUCCESSFUL QUICK COFFEE CAKES

• As with all baking powder and soda recipes, gather all ingredients before you start, and preheat oven for quick entry; make sure all the parts are room temperature.
• Butter pans well for easy removal.
• When measuring flour, remember that what's in the bottom of the bag or storage can has compacted. Stir with fork to loosen particles before measuring.
• Quick breads baked in loaf pans normally crack in the center because the crust forms before the middle is finished reacting to the baking powder or soda. These coffee cakes are baked in flat pans, so they shouldn't have cracked tops because thay bake more evenly.
• Test to see if cake is done with a toothpick or cake tester. If it comes out clean, remove pan to wire rack. Another good sign that it's ready: the edges will have shrunk away from the pan sides.
• Serving warm from the pan is quite acceptable—it won't last long enough to annoy purists (you can always camouflage crumbled edges with a square basket and a fresh daisy in one corner).

171

APPLE COFFEE CAKE

One clear-cut favorite of Viennese coffee houses is *Apfel Kuchen*—a thin layer of dough covered with regimental rows of overlapping apple slices, dusted with sugar and cinnamon and topped with a sloshing of melted butter. The baked *Kuchen* is glazed while hot with heated currant jelly or apricot preserves that have been sieved and thinned with Kirsch or applejack.

   Note: If apples lack tartness, sprinkle cut slices with lemon juice and let stand for 10 minutes before arranging on dough. This same base will work well under sliced fresh peaches, plums or apricots, with more sugar added if desired. Use a sheet of foil over top if the cake browns too rapidly.

Makes One Six- by Nine-inch Cake

1 cup (250 ml) sifted unbleached white flour
1/2 teaspoon (2.5 ml) double-acting baking powder
1/4 teaspoon (1.2 ml) salt
3 tablespoons (45 ml) granulated sugar
4 tablespoons (60 ml) butter, softened
2 eggs, well beaten
2 tablespoons (30 ml) milk
1 cup (250 ml) sliced green apples
2 tablespoons (30 ml) brown sugar
Ground cinnamon
Melted jelly or preserves

Sift together flour, baking powder, salt and granulated sugar. Work 3 tablespoons (45 ml) of the butter into flour mixture until it is the consistency of coarse cornmeal. Gently stir in eggs and milk to make a thick, sticky dough. With spatula, ease dough into a buttered 6- by 9-inch (15 by 23 cm) shallow baking pan and smooth top. Starting at one narrow end at edge farthest from you, arrange apples in lengthwise rows, pressing lightly into dough and overlapping them so dough is completely covered. Scatter brown sugar over apples, sprinkle generously with cinnamon and dot evenly with remaining butter. Bake in oven preheated to 425°F (220°C) 30 minutes or until apples can be pierced easily with a fork but are still firm. Remove from the oven and brush apples with melted preserves. Serve warm.

172

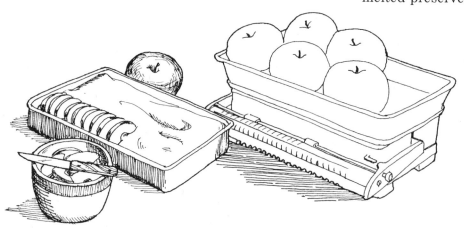

SOUR CREAM COFFEE CAKE

The composer Hadyn's wife lined her cake pans with his music. She never did learn to appreciate his talent. It's safe to guess her cakes were sour notes. We've done a little composing ourselves—a sour cream batter, titillated with vanilla and coriander and crowned with a satisfying streusel that will bring a round of appreciation from any audience. Particularly if you fold in fresh blueberries to make it company cake.

Makes One Eight-inch Square
2 eggs, lightly beaten
1 cup (250 ml) sour cream, at room temperature
1 teaspoon (5 ml) pure vanilla extract
3/4 cup (200 ml) sifted unbleached white flour
3/4 cup (175 ml) sifted whole-wheat pastry flour
2 teaspoons (10 ml) double-acting baking powder
1/2 teaspoon (2.5 ml) baking soda
1/4 teaspoon (1.2 ml) salt
1/2 teaspoon (2.5 ml) ground coriander
1 cup (250 ml) firmly packed brown sugar
Streusel, page 224

Beat together eggs, sour cream and vanilla extract. Sift together flours, baking powder, baking soda, salt and coriander. Mix in sugar until well blended and stir into egg mixture just until dry ingredients are moistened. Spoon into buttered 8-inch (20 cm) square baking pan. Evenly sprinkle Streusel over and bake in oven preheated to 350°F (180°C) 25 minutes or until cake tests done. Remove pan to wire rack. Serve warm or at room temperature.

BLUEBERRY-SOUR CREAM COFFEE CAKE Fold into batter 2/3 cup (150 ml) fresh blueberries dusted with a little flour.

RICH SOUR CREAM COFFEE CAKE

This is similar to the Sour Cream Coffee Cake, but it is enriched and assembled differently. It is a showoff, streaked with layers of brown sugar, cinnamon and nuts, so that when you cut it, it's a very pretty slice to see. Fragrant and rich, it should be eaten warm the day it is baked, or else quickly frozen and saved for future applause.

Makes One Eight-inch Square
4 to 8 tablespoons (60 to 120 ml) butter, softened
1 cup (250 ml) firmly packed brown sugar
2 eggs
1 cup (250 ml) sour cream, at room temperature
1 teaspoon (5 ml) pure vanilla extract
3/4 cup (200 ml) sifted unbleached white flour
3/4 cup (175 ml) sifted whole-wheat pastry flour
2 teaspoons (10 ml) double-acting baking powder
1/2 teaspoon (2.5 ml) baking soda
1/2 teaspoon (2.5 ml) ground allspice
1/4 teaspoon (1.2 ml) ground nutmeg
Brown sugar
Ground cinnamon
Chopped pecans, walnuts, almonds or filberts

Cream together butter and the 1 cup (250 ml) sugar. Blend in eggs, one at a time. Add sour cream and vanilla extract and blend well. Sift together flours, baking powder, baking soda and spices. Stir into butter mixture just until dry ingredients are moistened. Spoon half the batter into a buttered 8-inch (20 cm) square baking pan. Cover evenly with brown sugar, sprinkle with cinnamon and strew chopped nuts over all. Spoon remaining batter over and repeat topping. Bake in oven preheated to 350°F (180°C) 25 minutes or until cake tests done. Remove pan to wire rack. Serve warm or at room temperature.

old cranberry picker

CRANBERRY UPSIDE-DOWN COFFEE CAKE

Cranberries will store fresh for months in the refrigerator (not the freezer), so you can spring this coffee cake on your menu several times during the winter months (always being careful to pick over and cull out tired berries). This is a particularly impressive tart-sweet combination; its shiny red berries, nuts and orange peel make any moment of sharing festive. Also, it makes a great Fourth of July coffee cake in cherry-pie country by merely substituting pitted fresh cherries for the cranberries.

Fresh berries used in coffee cakes should not be washed until the very last minute.

Makes One Eight-inch Square

2 cups (500 ml) whole cranberries
2/3 cup (150 ml) honey
3 tablespoons (45 ml) freshly grated orange peel
2 tablespoons (30 ml) fresh orange juice
1/2 teaspoon (2.5 ml) ground mace or allspice
2/3 cup (150 ml) chopped pecans
1 egg, lightly beaten
3/4 cup (175 ml) buttermilk
5 tablespoons (75 ml) butter, melted and cooled
2 teaspoons (10 ml) freshly grated lemon peel
1-1/2 cups (350 ml) unbleached white flour
1/2 cup (125 ml) whole-wheat pastry flour
1 tablespoon (15 ml) double-acting baking powder
1/2 teaspoon (2.5 ml) baking soda
3/4 teaspoon (3.6 ml) salt

In saucepan, combine cranberries, 1/3 cup (75 ml) of the honey, 2 tablespoons (30 ml) of the orange peel, orange juice and mace. Bring to boil, lower heat and simmer 5 minutes. Cool slightly and stir in pecans. Set aside. Beat together egg, buttermilk, melted butter, remaining honey, lemon peel and remaining orange peel. Sift together flours, baking powder, baking soda and salt. Stir into egg mixture just until dry ingredients are moistened. Spread cranberry mixture in bottom of buttered 8-inch (20 cm) square baking pan. Spoon batter evenly over and bake in oven preheated to 375°F (190°C) 30 minutes or until coffee cake tests done. Cool in pan on wire rack 2 to 3 minutes, then invert onto rack to cool.

WHOLE-WHEAT COFFEE CAKE

Want to impress your Whole Earth friends? Just trot out this nutrition-charged offering on a wooden bread paddle and watch it vanish, leaving only a shadow where it stood. It's faintly sweet, a hearty chewy sort, just right with hot mulled red wine or cider, or a pot of freshly brewed espresso. Note: If you lean toward crusty coffee cakes, bake this 25 minutes at 375°F (190°C).

174

Makes One Nine-inch Square
2 eggs
1 cup (250 ml) buttermilk
1/4 cup (60 ml) safflower oil
3/4 cup (175 ml) honey
2 cups (500 ml) whole-wheat
flour
1/4 cup (50 ml) soy flour
1 teaspoon (5 ml) double-
acting baking powder
1 teaspoon (5 ml) baking
soda
1/2 teaspoon (2.5 ml) salt
2 teaspoons (10 ml) ground
cinnamon
1/2 teaspoon (2.5 ml) ground
nutmeg or coriander
3 tablespoons (45 ml) untoasted
wheat germ
1/2 cup (125 ml) raisins
1/3 cup (75 ml) chopped pecans,
walnuts, almonds or filberts

Beat eggs and blend in buttermilk, oil and honey. Sift together flours, baking powder, baking soda, salt and spices; add
kernels left in sifter to flour
mixture and stir in wheat germ.
Stir into egg mixture just until
dry ingredients are moistened.
Fold in raisins and nuts. Spoon
into a buttered 9-inch (23 cm)
square baking pan and bake in
oven preheated to 350°F (180°C)
30 to 35 minutes or until cake
tests done. Remove to wire
rack. Serve warm or at room
temperature.

YOGHURT-CURRANT COFFEE CAKE

Polka dots and moonbeams. No
matter how you slice it, currants scattered through the batter give this streusel coffee
cake a party life of its own. It's
one of those handy, spur-of-
the-moment put-togethers, thanks
to the Quick-Bread Mix—less
than an hour's time to taking it
out of the oven. It's moist,
compact and discreetly sweet.
Make it days before you need
it and freeze. It will come out
fresh and perky.

---

*The area of a round pan is
three-fourths that of a square
pan of the same diameter.*

nutmeg grater

Makes One Eight-inch Round
1-1/4 cups (300 ml) Quick-
Bread Mix, page 161
1/4 cup (60 ml) untoasted
wheat germ
4 tablespoons (60 ml) butter,
softened
1/2 cup (125 ml) firmly packed
brown sugar
1 egg, lightly beaten
3/4 cup (175 ml) plain yoghurt
1 teaspoon (5 ml) pure vanilla
extract
1/4 cup (50 ml) dried currants
Streusel, page 224
1/4 teaspoon (1.2 ml) ground
cardamom

Combine bread mix and wheat
germ. Cream together butter
and sugar and blend in egg,
yoghurt and vanilla extract. Stir
in dry ingredients until just
moistened and fold in currants.
Spoon into a buttered 8-inch
(20 cm) round baking pan.
Combine Streusel and cardamom and crumble amount desired over batter. Bake in oven
preheated to 350°F (180°C) 30
minutes or until cake tests
done. Remove to wire rack and
cool in pan. Serve warm or at
room temperature.

Corn Breads

America's amazing maize (Old Columbus named it from the Indian *mahiz,* and reputedly took seeds back to introduce to Europe where it is still called maize): The Indians in North America had a corner on the corn market when the Pilgrims stopped off in Massachusetts; the newcomers probably wouldn't have survived to see the next reruns if it hadn't been for that grain. Colonial wives ingeniously made yeast from potatoes, hops and even with water from soaked hardwood ashes, to give their breads a lift. So corn bread is truly a native Yankee, even if white corn is supreme in the South: grits, hominy, snack food.

Cornmeal (called Indian meal if very coarsely ground) is made from the yellow kernel, has lots of vitamin A and is also the source of corn oil. White meal has a nuttier, sweeter flavor, and when finely ground becomes cornstarch. Cornmeal has no gluten and lapses into a crumbly bread unless blended with wheat flours.

But the important factor is *how* the corn is ground. Stone-ground whole kernel is most nutritious, and can be found in natural-foods stores or from mail-order grist mills or you can grind it on a small kitchen mill. The meal in grocer's packages is much finer, almost a flour and it is bland, degerminated, leaving flavor but no texture or nutrients.

THOUGHTS ON BAKING WITH CORNMEAL

- Store stone-ground cornmeal in refrigerator or freezer; always bring to room temperature before using.
- Adding whole-wheat or unbleached white flour provides the gluten needed for a non-crumbly bread; whole-wheat pastry flour gives a rich darker color, a firm substance.
- Preheat oven 20 minutes before you start; cornmeal breads need a hot oven.
- Use the muffin method to prepare batter: Combine dry ingredients, add eggs and liquids, and stir just enough to moisten.
- Spoon bread procedure is nontypical. Read the recipe carefully; it is baked in a casserole and served like a souffle.
- All corn breads are at their best piping hot from the oven.

CORN BREAD

Packaged cornmeal bread may have been the only way you had to judge this classic. Away with bland pap and humdrum flavor. It's time you're introduced to *real* corn bread—an ear off a different stalk! Buttermilk and bacon drippings give it true southern character.

Makes One Eight-inch Square
1 cup (250 ml *sifted*) whole-wheat pastry flour
4 teaspoons (20 ml) double-acting baking powder
1/2 teaspoon (2.5 ml) baking soda
3/4 teaspoon (3.6 ml) salt
1 cup (250 ml) nonde-germinated yellow cornmeal
2 eggs, lightly beaten
1 cup (250 ml) buttermilk
4 tablespoons (60 ml) melted and cooled lard, or 2 table-spoons (30 ml) *each* lard and bacon drippings
3 tablespoons (45 ml) honey or molasses

Sift together flour, baking powder, baking soda and salt; combine with cornmeal. Beat together eggs, buttermilk, lard and honey until well blended. Stir in dry ingredients just until moistened. Spoon into a well-buttered 8-inch (20 cm) square baking pan. Bake in oven pre-heated to 425°F (220°C) 20 minutes or until cake tester inserted in center comes out clean and bread has pulled away from sides of pan.

NUTRITIOUS CORN BREAD Substitute for 2 tablespoons (30 ml) of the whole-wheat pastry flour 2 tablespoons (30 ml) lightly toasted wheat germ, non-instant nonfat dry milk or soy flour.

BACON OR HAM CORN BREAD Add to wet ingredients 2 to 3 strips bacon, crisply cooked and crumbled, or 3 tablespoons (45 ml) minced cooked ham.

CARAWAY CORN BREAD Add to wet ingredients 1 teaspoon (5 ml) caraway seeds.

PECAN CORN BREAD For the honey, substitute 1/4 cup (60 ml) brown sugar; fold into batter 1/2 cup (125 ml) chopped pecans.

CHEESE CORN BREAD Add to wet ingredients 1/2 cup (125 ml) grated sharp cheddar cheese.

ONION CORN BREAD Add to wet ingredients 1/2 cup (125 ml) chopped onion.

corn bread can be baked in muffin shape too, as in this copy of an old cast-iron pan; bake 15 min.

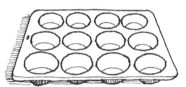

or, in mini-muffin tins, 10-12 minutes; fill either only 2/3 full

or, it can be baked in a pre-heated cast-iron kettle (without lid)

QUICK CORN BREAD

Fresh corn kernels flirting with hot peppers and pimiento, but gently cooled by the eggs and sour cream—a real Sunday-morning awakener to make you feel well fed and strong enough for any Monday. Serve this snappy fresh corn bread with little sausages and a bowl of chilled, fat purple plums that have been stewed in a honey-and-stick-cinnamon sauce, and a big pot of Guatemalan coffee.

Makes One Nine- or Ten-inch Round
4 tablespoons (60 ml) butter
2 eggs, lightly beaten
1/2 cup (125 ml) sour cream
1 cup (250 ml) self-rising yellow or white cornmeal
1 cup (250 ml) cooked fresh corn kernels (page 32)
2 to 3 tablespoons (30 to 45 ml) diced hot peppers (optional)
2 tablespoons (30 ml) diced pimiento

Preheat oven to 450°F (230°C). In a 9- or 10-inch (23 or 25 cm) iron skillet, melt the butter. Beat together eggs, sour cream and 2 tablespoons of the butter. Place skillet with the remaining butter in oven. Stir cornmeal into egg mixture just to moisten and fold in corn kernels, hot peppers and pimientos. Pour batter into skillet of bubbling butter, distribute evenly and bake 20 minutes until edges are lightly browned and center is cooked through. Cool several minutes before cutting into wedges. Bottom will be crusty.

QUICK MAYONNAISE CORN BREAD

Before you turn the page with a loud "Ridiculous," let us reassure you that, out of context, something familiar can be downright intriguing—and that's just what happens when mayonnaise meets corn bread. This is a light, fluffy corn bread whose parentage you'll *never* guess when you sample the first hot slice. The result is a good conversation gambit for any party supper.

Makes One Eight- or Nine-inch Round
1 egg, lightly beaten
3 tablespoons (45 ml) mayonnaise
1 cup (250 ml) buttermilk
1 cup (250 ml) self-rising cornmeal

In oven preheated to 450°F (230°C), heat a well-buttered 8- or 9-inch (20 or 23 cm) iron skillet until butter is bubbly. Beat together egg and mayonnaise and blend in buttermilk. Stir in cornmeal and pour into heated skillet, distributing evenly. Bake 20 to 25 minutes or until bread tests done.

MEXICAN CORN BREAD

A bread to warm the cockles, yet not throat-searing hot, it is high in eye appeal, with colorful corn and cheese yellows, pimiento reds, olive blacks and pepper greens. Again, home-ground corn-meal gives just the right rough crumb to match the chunky bits baked in this popular Mexican treat. The result is firm and crisp around the browned edges, moist in the center. If you don't have a kitchen mill, look for stone-ground cornmeal in a natural-foods store.

Makes One Eight-inch Square
2 eggs, lightly beaten
1/2 cup (125 ml) sour cream
1/4 cup (60 ml) corn oil or melted and cooled lard
1 cup (250 ml) fresh corn kernels (see page 32)
1 cup (250 ml) coarsely grated sharp cheddar cheese
2 to 4 jalapeno peppers, seeded and minced
5 pimientos, chopped
3 tablespoons (45 ml) minced onion
3 tablespoons (45 ml) minced black olives
1 cup (250 ml) nondegerminated yellow cornmeal
2 teaspoons (10 ml) double-acting baking powder
1/2 teaspoon (2.5 ml) baking soda

1/2 teaspoon (2.5 ml) salt
1/2 teaspoon (2.5 ml) crumbled
  dried oregano
1/3 cup (75 ml) finely grated
  sharp cheddar cheese

Thoroughly combine eggs, sour cream, oil, corn kernels, coarsely grated cheese, peppers, pimientos, onion and olives. Sift together all dry ingredients, tipping sifter to shake any remaining particles back into cornmeal mixture. Stir into egg mixture just until dry ingredients are moistened. Transfer to well-buttered 8-inch (20 cm) square baking pan. Sprinkle evenly with finely grated cheese. Bake in oven preheated to 350°F (180°C) 50 minutes or until toothpick inserted in center comes out clean and bread pulls away slightly from sides of pan.

To prevent corn bread from sticking to the pan, grease pan well, sprinkle with cornmeal.

SPOON BREAD

Spoon bread and Anadama (page 90) are very old corn relatives—one out of the South, the other from the North and both illustrious decendants of Indian corn. Spoon bread is rich and mellow, a kind of souffle that must be served quickly and piping hot with butter or with juices from a roast pork or a fruited corned beef. Though traditionally made with white cornmeal, try grinding some of your own yellow for a slightly heavier version.

Serves Six to Eight
3 cups (700 ml) milk
1 cup (250 ml) white cornmeal
2 tablespoons (30 ml) butter,
  softened
1 to 2 tablespoons (15 to 30 ml)
  honey (optional)
3 eggs, separated
1 teaspoon (5 ml) double-
  acting baking powder
1 teaspoon (5 ml) salt
1/8 teaspoon (.8 ml) cream
  of tartar

In heavy saucepan scald 2 cups (450 ml) of the milk. Gradually add cornmeal; lower heat and cook, stirring, until smooth and thickened. Remove from heat and blend in butter and optional honey. Beat together egg yolks, remaining milk, baking powder and salt. Blend into cornmeal mixture. Beat egg whites and cream of tartar until stiff but not dry. Fold 1 cup (250 ml) of the cornmeal mixture into egg whites, then fold into remaining cornmeal mixture. Spoon into well-buttered 2-quart (2 L) casserole and bake in oven preheated to 325°F (160°C) 1 hour until puffy and lightly browned. To serve spoon from casserole, adding butter, pan juices, honey or maple syrup.

179

Soda Breads

SODA BREADS TO THE RESCUE

Time schedules and flexibility run head on all too often. When there's nothing in the breadbox and three extras coming for supper, pull a rare bit out of your green hat: Toss together an Irish soda bread and spread a little blarney over the table. It should not take more than 45 or 50 minutes from scratch to finish, and you can serve up a warm, crusty-brown pacifier.

Our Buttermilk Bread is another menu-saver—earthy, wholesome. It can wear different hats and change personality with the flip of a spice-can lid, a teaspoon (5 ml) of dill weed and a half cup (125 ml) of chopped walnuts, a tablespoon (15 ml) of freshly grated lemon peel and one of poppy seeds, or a handful of raisins with dollop of chopped citron and some ground cardamom. After much testing, we found we liked the breads "as is," but don't let that stop *you* from being adventurous.

Baking soda is a chemical leavening agent. It reacts the same way on buttermilk, sour milk and cream, and yoghurt—alkali and acid convert the energy into carbon dioxide gas, and the batter must go into the oven as fast as possible before the gas fizzles.

THOUGHTS ON BAKING WITH SODA

● Soda doughs are handled just the opposite of yeast: high-speed action rather than patience, light handling rather than furious beating and kneading.
● Re-read the recipe; assemble all ingredients, measuring cups and spoons so you can race the bread to oven without obstacles.
● Preheat oven and prepare baking pans before you start.
● Don't use a heavy hand with soda; too much may turn your bread into a turkey.
● Don't beat vigorously; stir and turn bowl as you mix.
● The crisscross cut on the top before going into oven is to keep it from cracking (some say it's to annoy the devil).
● If the bottom crust seems soft when you remove loaf from pan, return bread to the oven for another ten minutes.
● Freeze in a tightly sealed plastic bag for up to six months; to thaw, leave wrapped at room temperature for two hours, remove wrapping and place in a hot oven to crisp again.

BROWN SODA BREAD

A new challenge for Irish soda bread fans: This coarse, chewy brown bread is made with freshly ground wheat, wheat germ, rolled oats and buttermilk—obviously a very healthful loaf. It is pitted and patted and marked with a shallow cross in the center, just as for the Irish regular. It will feed no more than four hungry mouths when baked, and is especially endearing when the quarters are split and buttered, then set under the broiler for a quick edge-browning.

Makes One Loaf

1 cup (250 ml) unbleached white flour
2 tablespoons (30 ml) firmly packed brown sugar
1 teaspoon (5 ml) double-acting baking powder
1 teaspoon (5 ml) baking soda
1/2 teaspoon (2.5 ml) salt
1-1/2 tablespoons (22.5 ml) butter
2 cups (500 ml) freshly ground whole-wheat flour
1/4 cup (50 ml) unprocessed rolled oats
2 tablespoons (30 ml) untoasted wheat germ
1-1/2 cups (375 ml) buttermilk
1 tablespoon (15 ml) butter, melted

Combine unbleached flour, sugar, baking powder, baking soda and salt. With your fingertips, crumble in butter until mixture is the consistency of coarse cornmeal. Toss in whole-wheat flour, oats and wheat germ, mix well, and with fork, stir in buttermilk just until dry ingredients are moistened. Turn out onto floured board and knead gently 6 or 8 strokes or until smooth. On a well-buttered baking sheet, pat into a 7-inch (18 cm) circle. With a sharp knife, make a shallow 4-inch (10 cm) cross in center and bake in oven preheated to 375°F (190°C) 40 minutes, or until loaf is nicely browned and sounds hollow when tapped. Transfer to wire rack and brush with melted butter. Cool slightly before breaking into serving pieces.

CORNMEAL BROWN SODA BREAD
Substitute for 1/2 cup (125 ml) whole-wheat flour, 1/2 cup (125 ml) freshly ground cornmeal.

cover with foil or a deep tin to make loaf rise more; remove the last 10 minutes

IRISH SODA BREAD

In Ireland, this bread, which they call cake, is made with meal ground from soft Irish wheat and then baked over a peat fire, a combination reputedly unsurpassed for flavor. As long as you don't have peat or their wheat, we suggest our soda bread with currants and caraway to comfort your yearning. A deep cake tin inverted over the bread while it is baking helps it rise and make a lighter loaf. Remove the tin the last 10 minutes to encourage browning of top.

Makes One Nine-inch Loaf
2 cups (500 ml) sifted unbleached white flour
1 teaspoon (5 ml) baking soda
1/2 teaspoon (2.5 ml) salt
2 tablespoons (30 ml) butter, chilled and cut in bits
1 tablespoon (15 ml) caraway seeds (optional)
1/4 cup (60 ml) dried currants
3/4 cup (200 ml) buttermilk

Sift together flour, soda and salt. With fingers, 2 knives or pastry blender, work in butter until mixture is the consistency of coarse cornmeal. Toss in caraway seeds and currants. With fork, stir in buttermilk and mix until just blended. Turn out onto lightly floured board and knead gently 20 to 30 strokes just until smooth. Do not overwork dough. Pat into a well-buttered 9-inch (23 cm) round baking pan. Make a shallow 4-inch (10 cm) cross in center and bake in oven preheated to 375°F (190°C) 25 minutes or until lightly golden. When tapped, round should sound hollow. Transfer to wire rack. Serve warm, broken into wedges.

BRAN SODA BREAD

Soda breads have chewy crusts that appeal to the child in us—that first slice is the all-crusty one for which small hands (and big) grab before others can. This bran bread also benefits from wheat germ, sesame seeds and a basis of whole-wheat flour, making it wholesome and bracing for the diet. You might note that it is simple to make and a good way to introduce baking to a seven year old.

Makes One Medium Loaf
2 cups plus 1 tablespoon (250 ml) buttermilk, at room temperature
1/4 cup (60 ml) firmly packed brown sugar
1 teaspoon (5 ml) salt
2 tablespoons (30 ml) untoasted wheat germ
2 tablespoons (30 ml) sesame seeds
2 teaspoons (10 ml) freshly grated orange peel
1-1/4 teaspoons (6.2 ml) baking soda
1 cup (250 ml) unprocessed bran
3 cups (700 ml) whole-wheat flour

Pour buttermilk into large mixing bowl. In order given, stir in remaining ingredients, mixing well after each addition. Do not beat vigorously. Spoon into a well-greased #2 loaf pan. Bake in oven preheated to 350°F (180°C) 1 hour or until bread pulls away from sides of pan and sounds hollow when tapped on top and bottom. Invert onto wire rack, turn right side up and cool.

Baking soda is a handy fire extinguisher. Keep a box within reach of stove.

BUTTERMILK BREAD

This is a little bread, just right for two hungry Indians or three weary cowpersons. It is unusual in that it is kneaded like yeast dough, but is dependent on soda to lift it in the range. You'll find it satisfying, cut in wedges or sliced, or even toasted and served with wild honey—provided you can lasso a sample before it disappears.

Makes One Round Loaf
3/4 cup (175 ml) buttermilk
1 to 2 tablespoons (15 to 30 ml) butter, melted and cooled
1 tablespoon (15 ml) molasses
1 cup (250 ml *sifted*) unbleached white flour, or as needed
3/4 cup (175 ml) whole-wheat pastry flour
1 teaspoon (5 ml) baking soda
1 teaspoon (5 ml) salt

Thoroughly combine buttermilk, butter and molasses. Sift together dry ingredients and stir into buttermilk mixture, beating well until dough forms a ball. Turn out onto floured board and knead, adding only enough additional flour to prevent sticking. Knead 3 to 5 minutes until dough is smooth and pliable and no longer sticky. Pat or roll out lightly into a circle approximately 6 inches (15 cm) in diameter and approximately 1 inch (3 cm) thick. Place on buttered baking sheet and bake in oven preheated to 375°F (190°C) 30 minutes or until lightly golden. When tapped, round should sound hollow. Transfer to wire rack. Serve warm or at room temperature, cut into wedges.

YOGHURT BREAD

Yoghurt reacts to soda in the same manner as buttermilk, but we think it makes a moister loaf. This one is dark and heavy, but with a worthy flavor and a texture quite different from the other soda breads. This is our adaptation of an original recipe from South Africa (reproduced here).

Makes One Medium Loaf
2 cups (500 ml) kuhne meal*
2 teaspoons (10 ml) sugar
1 teaspoon (5 ml) salt
1 heaping teaspoon (7 ml) baking soda
2 cups (500 ml) unbleached white flour**
2 cups (500 ml) plain yoghurt

Combine kuhne meal, sugar, salt, baking soda and flour; mix in yoghurt. Place in greased #2 loaf pan and bake in oven preheated to 350°F (180°C) 1 hour. If top browns too quickly, cover loosely with aluminum foil last 10 minutes. Turn out onto rack, turn right side up and cool slightly before slicing.

*Kuhne meal, a special grind of the wheat berry, is not available in the United States. Substitute 1 cup (250 ml) *fine* bulghur and 1 cup (250 ml) wheat flakes, which have been lightly ground in a blender. Soak the bulghur and wheat flakes in the yoghurt for 1 hour, then combine with dry ingredients.

**White flour in South Africa is softer than in the United States. To obtain the best results, substitute 2 tablespoons (30 ml) cornstarch for 2 tablespoons (30 ml) of the unbleached flour.

183

Yoghurt bread

2 cups of flour
2 cups Kuhne meal
500ml natural yoghurt
Big tsp sugar
Big tsp salt
Heaped tsp Bicarb of soda

Put it all in a basin and mix in the yoghurt. Put mixture in greased bread tin. Cook at 350°E for 1 hour

Self-rising Flour Breads

PUT SELF-RISING FLOUR ON YOUR SHOPPING LIST

Supermarkets and independent grocers are finally coming around to realizing that home baking is *big,* and are filling shelves with ethnic flours (like Mexican *masa,* used in tortillas), stone-ground whole-wheat, rice and barley flours. And now, a "manufactured" flour, self-rising, has been dredged up; General Mills offers this enriched blend of wheat and malted barley flours, with baking soda and leavening, a form of baking powder, and throws in some vitamins for good measure. There are a few others, usually made of bleached and presifted flours. And there's a self-rising cornmeal sold in many parts of the country.

For a culture dependent on "instant this" and "instant that," you'd think everyone would jump on this bread wagon, but we know better. One of the main reasons for wanting to make bread is to avoid gimmicks, to make it for the good feeling of accomplishment—from scratch. So, we're not pushing self-rising flour. What we do agree, though, is that there can be exceptions and it would be a mistake not to include the two in this section, novelties winning instant acceptance, a pair so unique they'll be conversation every time you share.

THOUGHTS ABOUT MAKING SELF-RISING BREADS

- As with any of the quick breads, do not beat, just stir until dry ingredients are moistened. If brown sugar has lumps, they will bake out as brown spots in the bread. Pressing sugar through a strainer before mixing into flour will break them up.
- Breads may be baked in mini-muffin tins (12 minutes) and kept warm on a hot tray for a party; makes four to six dozen.
- They will have a very rough crust, a quick-bread texture—and the aroma will take advantage of anyone within a ten-foot radius.

BEER BREAD

Doctor, lawyer, Indian chief—this is a popular Saturday-morning exercise for the man of the family. It's a one-bowl quick bread that never gets a chance to thoroughly cool because it's all gone so fast. Though there are several recipes floating around, we like this dilly one. It always turns out with a good rough crust and a real nice bread inside. Don't cut corners. Use a hearty brew.

Makes One Round Loaf
3-1/2 cups (825 ml) self-rising
 white flour
1/4 cup (60 ml) firmly packed
 brown sugar
1/2 tablespoon (7.5 ml) dried
 dill weed
12 ounces (355 ml) beer, at room
 temperature
1 egg, at room temperature

In large bowl, mix together flour, brown sugar and dill weed. Make a well in center, pour beer in and break egg on top. Stir just until dry ingredients are moistened. Turn into a 9-inch (23 cm) oiled pie plate. With a tablespoon or spatula dipped in water, shape the dough into a round mound, pushing in from sides to get a high loaf. Bake in oven preheated to 375°F (190°C) 1 hour or until bread tests done. Turn out onto wire rack, turn right side up and cool at least 1 hour before breaking or slicing.

VARIATION Substitute 1/2 tablespoon (7.5 ml) caraway seeds or 1-1/2 tablespoons (22.5 ml) dried onion flakes for the dill weed.

MINCEMEAT MINI-LOAVES

An easy "if-someone-comes" treat. Take bread directly from the refrigerator, slice thinly and serve with whipped cream cheese.

Makes Three Miniature Loaves
1 package (9 ounces or 252 g)
 dehydrated mincemeat
1 cup (250 ml) fresh orange
 juice
1/4 cup (60 ml) firmly packed
 brown sugar
4 tablespoons (60 ml) butter
1 egg, beaten until light and
 frothy
1/2 cup (125 ml) chopped
 walnuts
2-1/2 cups (600 ml) self-rising
 white flour

Crumble mincemeat into a saucepan, add 1/2 cup (125 ml) of the orange juice and simmer over low heat, stirring constantly, until mixture is a sticky, barely moist consistency. Set aside and let cool. Cream together sugar and butter, add egg and stir until smooth. Add mincemeat mixture and nuts; blend well. Alternately add flour and remaining orange juice. Divide dough into thirds and place in 3 prepared #4 loaf pans (page 165). Bake in oven preheated to 350°F (180°C) approximately 1 hour or until cake tester inserted in center comes out clean. Turn out onto wire rack, peel off waxed paper, turn right side up and cool completely before wrapping in foil to refrigerate or freeze.

BISCUITS RISE TO THE OCCASION

In mother's day, women were judged by their peers on three scores. You had to make your starch clear, you could never be late for church and your biscuits must never fail. Today, most mothers depend on packages of ready-to-make biscuits from the supermarket refrigerator case, and never give a thought about who judges whom, or how they judge.

But no commercial magic can ever match a batch of buttermilks popped into your own oven, particularly when you have such a cast of characters: whole wheat, wheat germ, herb, cheese, bacon or ham, curry, honey-maple, sesame, raisin-nut pinwheel (are you out of breath?), cheese pinwheel, onion, and, of course, square biscuits and twists. And one basic recipe can do all this for the equivalent of two packages of biscuits, and at a cost of less than one. A neat saving. Oh yes, you do get bigger, richer, lighter, crustier, tastier results, too.

Scones have been sadly neglected in most lives, and what a sad vacancy. With our recipe we hope to reawaken awareness, to tempt you, to dare you to make a batch. Scones are dear to the heart of the English and Scots for afternoon tea, wonderfully comforting with Devonshire cream and strawberry preserves. Or they are a currant delight at the breakfast table, hot and heart warming.

THOUGHTS ABOUT NEVER-FAIL BISCUITS

- Preheat oven to 450°F (230°C) for 15 minutes before baking.
- Assemble all the ingredients and utensils; measure exact amounts and sift dry ingredients together.
- To measure shortening, fill a cup measure (250 ml) three fourths full of cold water, add shortening until water reaches top (four tablespoons [60 ml] equals a quarter cup). Then work in the chilled lard or butter with fingers, two knives or pastry blender until mixture resembles coarse cornmeal.
- Add milk or cream all at once and stir gently with fork to make a soft, moist dough that is not sticky. Don't overmix.
- Turn out onto lightly floured board; dust hands with flour and knead the dough for about 20 seconds.
- Pat or press down lightly with flat of hand to desired thickness and cut; don't twist the biscuit cutter or sides will pinch together and the biscuits won't rise much. For high, fluffy

Biscuits

186

biscuits do not have to be one size or shape

slice pinwheels with a thread (see jelly-roll sketch)

ones, roll dough a half to three-quarters inch (1.5 to 2 cm) thick; for crisp ones, roll three-eighths inch (1 cm) thick.
● Place on ungreased baking sheet; for soft, higher biscuits, place close together; for crusty ones, space farther apart. Brush tops with milk or half-and-half before baking.
● Bake 10 to 15 minutes, depending on size of biscuits.
● Serve hot in a basket lined with pretty napkin.
● Sour cream and/or plain yoghurt (half of each) may be substituted for buttermilk in recipe.
● Shortening: Lard (homemade, if possible) or butter gives these baking-powder breads their special flavor and rich flaky texture. We prefer them over other fats for *real* biscuits.
● Biscuits and scones may be frozen in plastic bags; defrost for two hours at room temperature and then reheat. Wrap in foil and place in oven preheated to 375°F (190°C) 15 minutes. Or put two tablespoons (30 ml) water in a large skillet placed over low heat; set wrapped biscuits on rack over water. Cover and heat eight to ten minutes. You can also split thawed biscuits, spread them with butter and sprinkle with grated cheese, cinnamon and sugar.

SCONES

● Preheat oven to 425°F (220°C) for 15 minutes before baking.
● Proceed as for biscuits.
● Scones traditionally are shaped into a round bun, five to six inches (13 to 15 cm) across, and cut into four pieces but not separated; they are broken apart after baking, leaving a soft ragged edge. They may be cut like biscuits, too.

PINWHEELS, SQUARES AND DROPS

● Pinwheel biscuits: Pat dough out into a rectangle, brush with melted butter and spread with filling (see individual recipes); starting at long edge, roll like a jelly roll, seal seam and cut into half-inch (1.5 cm) slices, placing cut side down on pan.
● Square biscuits: Pat dough out into a rectangle and cut into two and a half-inch (6 cm) squares.
● Drop biscuits: Increase liquid slightly so dough drops easily from a dessert-size spoon.

antique 3-minute bread mixer

seal fruit squares by moistening edges & pressing closed with back of fork

fold

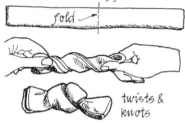

twists & knots

BUTTERMILK BISCUITS

Makes Ten to Twelve Biscuits

2 cups (500 ml *sifted*) unbleached white flour
4 teaspoons (20 ml) double-acting baking powder
1/2 teaspoon (2.5 ml) baking soda
1/2 teaspoon (2.5 ml) salt
2 teaspoons (10 ml) sugar (optional)
1/4 to 1/2 cup (50 to 125 ml) lard, chilled
2/3 cup (175 ml) buttermilk, or as needed

Sift together dry ingredients into mixing bowl. Crumble lard in with fingers, 2 knives or pastry blender until mixture is the consistency of coarse cornmeal. Add buttermilk all at once and stir gently with fork to form a soft dough that is moist enough to hold together but not sticky. Do not overmix; dry ingredients should be just moistened. Turn out onto lightly floured board and gently knead 15 to 20 times. Pat or gently roll out to desired thickness and cut into 3-1/2-inch (9 cm) rounds (or size desired). Place on ungreased baking sheet and bake in oven preheated to 450°F (230°C) 10 to 15 minutes, depending upon thickness of biscuits.

WHOLE-WHEAT BISCUITS Substitute 1 cup (250 ml) whole-wheat pastry flour for 1 cup (250 ml) of the unbleached white flour.

WHEAT-GERM BISCUITS Substitute 3 tablespoons (45 ml) lightly toasted wheat germ for 3 tablespoons (45 ml) of the flour.

HERB BISCUITS Sift with dry ingredients 1/2 teaspoon (2.5 ml) dry mustard and mix in 3/4 teaspoon (3.6 ml) crumbled dried sage and 1/2 teaspoon (2.5 ml) celery seed. Or mix into sifted dry ingredients 1 teaspoon (5 ml) caraway seeds or dill seeds and/or 2 tablespoons (30 ml) chopped fresh parsley or 1 tablespoon (15 ml) chopped fresh chives.

CHEESE BISCUITS Mix into sifted dry ingredients 1/2 teaspoon (2.5 ml) celery seeds, 1/2 cup (125 ml) grated dry cheese, such as sharp cheddar, and dash of cayenne pepper.

BACON OR HAM BISCUITS Mix into sifted dry ingredients 1/3 cup (75 ml) crumbled crisply cooked bacon or finely minced cooked ham.

CURRY BISCUITS Sift with dry ingredients 1 teaspoon (5 ml) curry powder; mix in 3 table-spoons (45 ml) finely minced cooked chicken or ham.

HONEY OR MAPLE BISCUITS Before baking, brush biscuits with melted butter and drizzle honey or maple syrup over.

SESAME BISCUITS Mix into sifted dry ingredients 1/2 cup (125 ml) lightly toasted sesame seeds.

RAISIN-NUT PINWHEEL BISCUITS Pat or gently roll out biscuit dough into a rectangle 1/2 inch (1.5 cm) thick. Brush with melted butter and sprinkle with sugar and ground cinnamon. Sprinkle evenly with raisins and/or chopped pecans, walnuts or almonds. Roll, slice and bake as directed for Pinwheel Biscuits, page 187.

CHEESE PINWHEELS Sift with dry ingredients 1/2 teaspoon (2.5 ml) dry mustard and 1/8 teaspoon (.6 ml) cayenne pepper. Roll as for pinwheels above and sprinkle evenly with grated sharp cheddar cheese. Roll, slice and bake as directed.

ONION BISCUITS Mix into sifted dry ingredients 3 tablespoons (45 ml) finely minced onion.

BISCUIT FRUIT SQUARES Pat or gently roll out 1/3 inch (1 cm) thick. Sprinkle with chopped fresh fruit, bits of butter and sugar and cut into 2-1/2-inch (6 cm) squares. Fold to make triangles and pinch edges to seal.

BISCUIT CHEESE TWISTS Pat or gently roll out 1/4 inch (6 mm) thick. Sprinkle with grated dry cheese and cayenne pepper. Cut into strips and twist each strip or form into a loose knot.

SCONES

Makes Approximately One Dozen
2 cups (475 ml) sifted
   unbleached white flour
1 tablespoon (15 ml) double-
   acting baking powder
1 to 2 tablespoons (15 to 30 ml)
   granulated sugar
1/2 teaspoon (2.5 ml) salt
4 tablespoons (60 ml) lard or
   butter, chilled
1/3 cup (75 ml) dried currants
2 eggs, lightly beaten
1/2 cup (125 ml) sour cream

Sift together flour, baking powder, sugar and salt. With fingers, 2 knives, or pastry blender, cut in lard until mixture is the consistency of coarse cornmeal. Toss in currants. Beat together eggs and sour cream and with fork mix into flour mixture. Turn out onto lightly floured board and knead gently until smooth; do not overknead. With hands, press down and out to make a round or rectangle 1/2 inch (1.5 cm) thick and cut into 2-1/2-inch (6 cm) rounds. Place rounds on ungreased baking sheet 1 inch (3 cm) apart and bake in oven preheated to 425°F (220°C) 12 to 15 minutes. Or heat ungreased griddle or skillet to 325°F (160°C) and cook slowly, 10 minutes per side, turning once. Scones will be lightly browned. Serve immediately with butter and honey.

CHEESE SCONES Omit currants and toss 2/3 cup (150 ml) grated sharp cheddar cheese into flour-lard mixture.

WHOLE-WHEAT SCONES Substitute 1 cup (250 ml) whole-wheat pastry flour for 1 cup (250 ml) of the unbleached white flour.

OAT SCONES Substitute 1/2 cup (125 ml) oat flour for 1/2 cup (125 ml) of the unbleached white flour.

WHEAT GERM SCONES Substitute 1/2 cup (125 ml) untoasted wheat germ for 1/2 cup (125 ml) of the unbleached white flour.

CORNMEAL SCONES Substitute 1 cup (250 ml) nondegerminated yellow cornmeal for 1 cup (250 ml) of the unbleached white flour.

No pastry blender?
Use your fingers.

press down & out to 1/2" thickness

cut or score part way through each round with sharp knife

189

Mother called them "gems" and baked them in pattypans. The English had their muffin man who carried his wares and tinkling bell from door to door (an early Avon man). George Bernard Shaw wrote, in *Man and Superman,* "You don't get tired of muffins, but you don't find inspiration in them."

Balderdash! Muffins properly made and served exude a Liza Doolittle charm. Who would not be perked up by a basketful of warm apple-cheese muffins and a crock of cold butter, brown rice muffins drowning in a jigger of bitter orange marmalade, or a graham-cracker muffin snuggling up to whipped chive cream cheese? What hunger is not inspired by the maddening fragrances from pans of blueberry muffins finishing in the oven? How sad, Mr. Shaw, you were born too soon. You would have loved our wheat Blue Bread of Happiness!

Muffins are about the simplest bread you can make, provided you master the sleight of hand of getting them together fast. If your time is very limited, you can bake mini-muffins in less than 35 minutes from scratch, even allowing for the oven to heat.

Muffins

THOUGHTS ON MAKING MUFFINS

- Read the recipe and assemble all the ingredients before you start.
- Don't try to double a recipe.
- Preheat oven to 375°F (190°C) before you start.
- Spray tins with vegetable cooking spray to prevent sticking.
- For lighter muffins, separate eggs and then fold in beaten whites last.
- When stirring dry ingredients into wet, blend only until just moistened; batter will be lumpy, not smooth. Too much stirring will develop tunnels and muffins will have pointy, volcano tops.
- All whole-wheat flour may be used, though the muffins will be heavier.
- Fold in nuts and dried fruits after everything else is in.
- Whether making muffins standard or mini-size, do not fill cups more than two thirds full, unless otherwise specified.
- If there are unfilled wells in a muffin tin, half fill with water.
- Cool two minutes before loosening; turn each on its side in pan to release steam. Keep warm in oven or on a hot tray.
- Always serve hot in a napkin-lined tray or basket.
- To reheat, split in half, butter and toast under broiler.

FRESH CORN MUFFINS

Quite moist, crunchy and overwhelmingly corn, these are a surprise and an uncommonly good luncheon addition to omelets, souffles, soups, tossed salads, casseroles. Bacon drippings, a smidgen of cayenne and sage lend them a subtle presence you can't ignore. It's a fresh experience for muffins. Try it and you'll be besieged by requests for the recipe.

Makes Twelve to Sixteen Muffins

2 eggs, lightly beaten
1 cup (250 ml) buttermilk
1/4 cup (50 ml) lard, melted and cooled, or 2 tablespoons (30 ml) *each* lard and bacon drippings
3 tablespoons (45 ml) honey or molasses
1 cup (250 ml) fresh corn kernels (page 32)
1 cup (250 ml *sifted*) whole-wheat pastry flour
1/4 cup (60 ml) unbleached white flour
4 teaspoons (20 ml) double-acting baking powder
1/2 teaspoon (2.5 ml) baking soda
3/4 to 1 teaspoon (3.6 to 5 ml) salt
1/2 teaspoon (2.5 ml) ground sage
Dash black pepper
Dash cayenne pepper
1 cup (250 ml) nondegerminated yellow cornmeal

Beat together eggs, buttermilk, lard and honey until well blended. Stir in corn kernels. Sift together flours, baking powder, baking soda, salt, sage and peppers. Combine with cornmeal and stir into corn mixture just until dry ingredients are moistened. Spoon into 12 to 16 buttered muffin-tin wells and bake in oven preheated to 375°F (190°C) 15 minutes or until muffins test done.

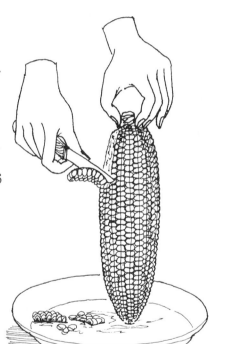

191

BROWN-RICE MUFFINS

The outer cover of a rice kernel is a bran, and like that of wheat, is very rich in vitamin B (so is molasses)—good news for bodily cell replacements. That's why we chose brown rice for these moist chewy muffins. This recipe is a good place to put leftovers, but if you start from scratch, use short-grain brown rice. Cook it the same as you would white, except use one and a third cups (325 ml) water to one cup (250 ml) rice, and steam for about 35 minutes, or until crunchy but not mushy. Fluff with a fork as it cools to room temperature.

Makes Twelve to Sixteen Muffins

2 eggs, separated
1 cup (250 ml) plain yoghurt
1/4 cup (50 ml) honey or molasses
2 tablespoons (30 ml) safflower oil
2 tablespoons (30 ml) minced fresh parsley
4 teaspoons (20 ml) minced fresh chives
4 teaspoons (20 ml) finely minced onion
1 teaspoon (5 ml) minced fresh oregano
2/3 cup (150 ml) cooked brown rice
1-1/2 cups (350 ml) sifted whole-wheat pastry flour
3 tablespoons (45 ml) non-instant nonfat dry milk
1 tablespoon (15 ml) double-acting baking powder
3/4 teaspoon (3.6 ml) salt
1/2 cup (125 ml) untoasted wheat germ

Beat together egg yolks, yoghurt, honey and oil until well blended. Stir in herbs and rice. Sift together flour, dry milk, baking powder and salt; combine with wheat germ. Beat egg whites until stiff but not dry. Stir dry ingredients into rice mixture just until moistened. Fold in egg whites and spoon into 12 to 16 buttered muffin-tin wells, filling almost full. Bake in oven preheated to 375°F (190°C) 15 to 20 minutes or until muffins test done.

BRAN MUFFINS

If you have your mouth fixed for a hearty natural, warm bran muffins will reach into every nook and cranny of your appetite. Just look at the list of ingredients. They belong together like strawberries and cream, or corned beef and cabbage. What this particular recipe does to the good things is carry overtones of dried apricots and toasted sesame seeds. Freeze any leftovers; they reheat or toast back to oven freshness.

Makes Twelve to Sixteen Muffins
1 cup (250 ml) unprocessed bran
1 cup (250 ml) buttermilk
1-1/3 cups (325 ml) whole-wheat pastry flour
3 tablespoons (45 ml) soy flour
3 tablespoons (45 ml) non-instant nonfat dry milk
2 teaspoons (10 ml) double-acting baking powder
1/2 teaspoon (2.5 ml) baking soda
3/4 teaspoon (3.6 ml) salt
1/2 teaspoon (2.5 ml) ground cinnamon
1/4 teaspoon (1.2 ml) ground ginger
1/4 teaspoon (1.2 ml) ground allspice
1/3 cup (75 ml) untoasted wheat germ
2 eggs, lightly beaten
2 tablespoons (30 ml) safflower oil
1/4 cup (60 ml) honey or light molasses
2 teaspoons (10 ml) freshly grated orange peel
1/3 cup (75 ml) raisins or finely chopped dried apricots (optional)
1/4 cup (60 ml) chopped walnuts (optional)
2 tablespoons (30 ml) lightly toasted sesame seeds (optional)

Soak bran in buttermilk 10 minutes. Sift together flours, dry milk, baking powder, baking soda, salt and spices; combine with wheat germ. Beat together eggs, oil and honey and combine with bran mixture. Stir in flour mixture just until moistened. Fold in raisins, nuts and/or sesame seeds. Spoon into 12 to 16 buttered muffin-tin wells. Bake in oven preheated to 375°F (190°C) 15 to 20 minutes or until muffins test done.

GRAHAM CRACKER MUFFINS

Slightly sweet and especially complementary to roast pork or ham, or as an after-school treat with apple or pear butter. Cracker crumbs can be made in a blender, or by placing the crackers between two sheets of waxed paper and crushing them with a rolling pin. If nuts are chopped in a blender, add one tablespoon (15 ml) granulated sugar and they won't compact around blades. (Subtract a tablespoon from the amount of brown sugar indicated.)

Makes Ten to Twelve Muffins
2 tablespoons (30 ml) butter, softened
1/3 cup (75 ml) firmly packed brown sugar
2 eggs
1 cup (250 ml) milk
1/2 teaspon (2.5 ml) pure vanilla extract
1 teaspoon (5 ml) freshly grated orange peel
1 cup (250 ml) honey graham cracker crumbs
1 cup (250 ml *sifted*) whole-wheat pastry flour
1 tablespoon (15 ml) double-acting baking powder
1/2 teaspoon (2.5 ml) salt
1/2 cup (125 ml) chopped walnuts, pecans, almonds or filberts

Cream together butter and sugar. Beat in eggs, one at a time. Blend in milk, vanilla extract, orange peel and graham cracker crumbs. Sift together flour, baking powder and salt; stir into egg mixture just until dry ingredients are moistened. Fold in nuts and spoon into 10 to 12 buttered muffin-tin wells. Bake in oven preheated to 375°F (190°C) 15 minutes or until muffins test done.

WHEAT BERRY MUFFINS

Wheat berries are the very hard dry fruit or seed of wheat. They have all the nutrients—vitamins E, B₁, proteins and enzymes—but they can be hazardous to the health of your molars. That's why they must be cooked as you would rice or barley, until they are chewable but not mushy. It's that distinctive, chewable part that transforms muffins into performers on the breakfast circuit. Rye or triticale berries add their special family flavor if you want to substitute.

Makes Twelve to Sixteen Muffins

194

2 eggs, lightly beaten
2/3 cup (150 ml) buttermilk or plain yoghurt
1/3 cup (75 ml) safflower oil
2/3 cup (150 ml) cooked wheat berries, page 73
3/4 cup (175 ml) whole-wheat pastry flour
3/4 cup (175 ml) unbleached white flour
1 tablespoon (15 ml) double-acting baking powder
1/2 teaspoon (2.5 ml) baking soda
1/2 teaspoon (2.5 ml) salt

Beat together eggs, buttermilk and oil until well blended. Stir in wheat berries. Sift together dry ingredients and stir into egg mixture just until dry ingredients are moistened. Spoon into 12 to 16 buttered muffin-tin wells and bake in oven preheated to 375°F (190°C) 20 minutes or until muffins test done.

RAISIN-WHEAT BERRY MUFFINS
Toss 1/4 cup (60 ml) raisins with a little of the flour mixture to coat well; fold into batter.

GLAZED WHEAT BERRY MUFFINS
Heat equal amounts of butter and honey, with or without lightly toasted sesame seeds or fresh lemon juice. Spread over muffins before or after baking.

DRIED PRUNE MUFFINS

This is the year when much is written and said about drying fresh fruit. Kitchen-size dryers are advertised in home service magazines. The new ovens, particularly convection types, give instructions on drying. Certainly it cuts the sky-rocketing cost of commercially dried prunes, pears, peaches and apricots—all of which make these muffins so desirable. Home drying has no additives—the flavor of the fruit dominates. All we've added to these muffins is lemon peel, that marvelous catalyst to point up the flavor.

Makes Twelve to Sixteen Muffins

1/3 cup (75 ml) unprocessed rolled oats
1/2 cup (125 ml) buttermilk, plain yoghurt or sour milk
2 tablespoons (30 ml) butter, softened
1/3 cup (75 ml) honey
2 tablespoons (30 ml) firmly packed brown sugar
2 eggs
2 tablespoons (30 ml) juice from cooking prunes
1/2 tablespoon (7.5 ml) freshly grated lemon peel
2/3 cup (150 ml) chopped unsweetened cooked prunes
1-1/3 cups (325 ml) sifted whole-wheat pastry flour
1-1/2 teaspoons (7.5 ml) double-acting baking powder
1/2 teaspoon (2.5 ml) baking soda
1/2 teaspoon (2.5 ml) salt
1/2 cup (125 ml) chopped almonds, walnuts, pecans or filberts

Soak oats in buttermilk 10 minutes. Cream together butter, honey and sugar. Beat in eggs, one at a time. Blend in oats and buttermilk, prune juice, lemon peel and prunes. Sift together flour, baking powder, baking soda and salt. Stir into prune mixture just until dry ingredients are moistened. Fold in nuts and spoon into 12 to 16 buttered muffin-tin wells. Place in oven preheated to 375°F (190°C) and bake 15 minutes or until muffins test done.

PEAR MUFFINS Substitute cooked unsweetened dried pears and juice for prunes and juice; add to dry ingredients 1/2 teaspoon (2.5 ml) anise seed.

PEACH MUFFINS Substitute cooked unsweetened dried peaches and juice for dried prunes and juice; sift with dry ingredients 1 teaspoon (5 ml) ground allspice.

APRICOT MUFFINS Substitute cooked unsweetened dried apricots and juice for dried prunes and juice; sift with dry ingredients 1/2 teaspoon (2.5 ml) ground cinnamon and 1/4 teaspoon (1.2 ml) ground nutmeg.

APPLE-CHEESE MUFFINS

A quirk of taste is the very-American union of apple pie and cheese: two completely different tastes and textures, but what a fusion! Now try apple-cheese muffins made with spices, nuts and honey for a nifty non-pie treat. Just be sure to use Pippins, Greenings, Gravensteins, Spitzenbergs or any of the tarts of appledom, and an outstanding cheddar, to make the most of this delicious apple-chunky small bread. Serve with cheese slices.

Makes Twelve to Sixteen Muffins
1 egg, lightly beaten
1/3 cup (75 ml) safflower oil
3/4 cup (175 ml) honey
1 teaspoon (5 ml) pure vanilla extract
2 cups (475 ml) sifted whole-wheat pastry flour
2 tablespoons (30 ml) soy flour
2 tablespoons (30 ml) non-instant nonfat dry milk
2 teaspoons (10 ml) double-acting baking powder
1/2 teaspoon (2.5 ml) baking soda
1/2 teaspoon (2.5 ml) salt

1 teaspoon (5 ml) ground cinnamon
1/2 teaspoon (2.5 ml) ground allspice
1/4 teaspoon (1.2 ml) ground nutmeg
2 tablespoons (30 ml) untoasted wheat germ
1/3 cup (75 ml) firmly packed grated sharp cheddar cheese
2 cups (500 ml) chopped unpared tart apples
1/2 cup (125 ml) chopped pecans, walnuts or almonds

Beat together egg, oil, honey and vanilla extract until well blended. Sift together flours, dry milk, baking powder, baking soda, salt and spices. Combine with wheat germ and stir into egg mixture just until dry ingredients are moistened. Fold in cheese, apples and nuts and spoon into 12 to 16 buttered muffin-tin wells. Bake in oven preheated to 375°F (190°C) 15 minutes or until muffins test done.

195

To keep cut fruit from turning brown, sprinkle with fresh lemon juice.

BLUEBERRY MUFFINS

Our Blue Bread of Happiness! Given a choice of muffins, hands always reach out for warm blueberry over others. It could be that a slightly tart-sweet memory lingers, the taste buds recalling with pleasure the first buttered bite. We've given them new energy with yoghurt, whole wheat, rolled oats, and emphasized them with lemon peel, nutmeg and cinnamon. When fresh berries are not in season, substitute canned ones, well-drained and dried on paper toweling. If neither is available, substitute white raisins and nuts.

Makes Twelve to Sixteen Muffins

1 to 1-1/4 cups (250 to 300 ml) fresh blueberries
2 eggs, lightly beaten
1 cup (250 ml) buttermilk, plain yoghurt or sour milk
2 tablespoons (30 ml) safflower oil
1/2 teaspoon (2.5 ml) pure vanilla extract
2 teaspoons (10 ml) freshly grated lemon peel
1-1/2 cups (350 ml) sifted whole-wheat pastry flour
3 tablespoons (45 ml) non-instant nonfat dry milk
1 tablespoon (15 ml) double-acting baking powder
1 teaspoon (5 ml) salt
1/2 teaspoon (2.5 ml) ground cinnamon
1/4 teaspoon (1.2 ml) ground nutmeg
1/3 cup (75 ml) firmly packed brown sugar
1/2 cup (125 ml) lightly toasted wheat germ
1/4 cup (60 ml) ground unprocessed rolled oats (see Note, page 164)

Carefully wash berries, drain in colander and pat dry; set aside. Beat together eggs, buttermilk, oil, vanilla extract and lemon peel until well blended. Sift together flour, dry milk, baking powder, salt and spices. Reserve 3 tablespoons (45 ml) of the flour mixture and combine remaining with sugar, wheat germ and oats. Stir into egg mixture just until dry ingredients are moistened. Toss reserved flour mixture with berries to coat well and gently fold into batter. Spoon into 12 to 16 buttered muffin-tin wells. Bake in oven preheated to 375°F (190°C) 20 minutes or until muffins test done.

Unleavened Breads

We've corraled a quartet of unusual breads in this section, misunderstood breads considered tricky by experts and scary by newly addicted bakers, but so winning that each may become part of your bread circuit once you've discovered that making doesn't need to be complex or troublesome.

They are unusual in that two are flat earthy breads, mostly flour and water and baked on top of the stove, and two have a hen's fortune in eggs to make things go *puff* in the oven—all without help from outside leaveners.

Both tortillas and chapatis are " instinctual" bakings—ancient methods handed down from mother to daughter. Perhaps this is why they seem tricky. The tortilla flour is a special grind of corn mixed with lime, while the chapati, from India, translates best with whole-wheat and white flours. We set out to find workable ways to make them, to eliminate the uncertainties, by going directly to the source to watch, to record measurements and methods. Then we made them ourselves, easily and successfully.

We baked egg popovers . . . over . . . and over, and found the sure way to make those big fat ones with crisp outer crust and a light inner bread around a hollow center, as well as a new twist—terrific whole-wheat popovers. Yorkshire pudding, a handsome eggy bread usually served with roast beef, is also a memorable breakfast bread with homemade preserves, and definitely not tricky.

These unleavened breads freeze well, can be thawed at room temperature and reheated. The popovers are delicately crisp if sliced in half and toasted under the broiler.

popovers

yorkshire pudding

chapatis & tortillas

POPOVERS

There are two different schools of thought on popovers: the start-them-in-a-cold-oven school, and the start-them-in-a-hot-oven, then reduce-heat-to-moderate school. Your particular oven may do one better than the other, so try both, just don't say "popovers are too difficult." They're quick to whip up and the crisp, air-filled puffs are a delight to nose and eye. Use a heavy iron popover pan or six-ounce (175 ml) custard cups set on a heavy baking sheet, which will make larger popovers. Remember, if using pyrex set heat 25°F (12.5°C) lower. Peeking is forbidden, so if you don't have a window in your oven you'll just have to take your chances and learn through experimentation. When you remove the popovers from the oven, prick them in several places to release the steam.

pierce hot popovers with fork or knife to release steam

COLD-OVEN POPOVERS

Makes Five Large Popovers
1 cup (250 ml *sifted*) unbleached white flour
1/4 to 1/2 teaspoon (1.2 to 2.5 ml) salt
1 cup minus 2 tablespoons (215 ml) milk, at room temperature
2 eggs, at room temperature

Sift together flour and salt twice. Blend in milk until smooth. Beat eggs and whisk into flour-milk mixture, beating until smooth. With 1/3-cup (75 ml) measure, ladle into 5 well-buttered pyrex custard cups, distributing any remaining batter evenly among them. Set cups on heavy baking sheet and place on middle rack of oven. Set oven at 425°F (220°C); when up to heat, bake 15 minutes. Lower heat to 325°F (160°C) and bake another 15 minutes. Serve hot.

HOT-OVEN POPOVERS

Makes Eleven Medium Popovers
3 eggs, at room temperature
1 cup (250 ml) milk, at room temperature
1 cup (250 ml *sifted*) unbleached white flour
1/2 teaspoon (2.5 ml) salt
1/8 teaspoon (.8 ml) ground nutmeg
2 tablespoons (30 ml) butter, melted

Heat oven to 450°F (230°C) and place a heavy iron popover pan or eleven 4-ounce (125 ml) custard cups on heavy baking sheet to preheat. With rotary beater, beat eggs well, add milk and continue beating until thoroughly blended. Combine flour, salt and nutmeg and sift over egg mixture. Continue beating 1 minute, adding melted butter slowly. Remove pan or cups from oven, brush liberally with melted butter and fill cups two thirds full. Quickly return to oven and bake 20 minutes (if you could peek at this time, popovers would be double in size and lightly browned). Reduce heat to 350°F (180°C) and continue baking 20 to 25 minutes longer (by this time peeking is okay). Serve hot.

WHOLE-WHEAT POPOVERS

Makes Eleven Medium Popovers
1/2 cup (125 ml) *sifted* unbleached white flour
1/2 cup (125 ml) *unsifted*
   whole-wheat flour
1/2 teaspoon (2.5 ml) salt
1 cup (250 ml) evaporated
   milk
1 tablespoon (15 ml) butter,
   melted
2 eggs, well beaten

In bowl, combine flours and salt. Beat milk and butter into eggs and pour over flours. Beat at high speed with electric hand mixer until thoroughly blended, at least 1 minute. Proceed as for Hot-Oven Popovers, preceding.

Always warm flour that has been refrigerated before using; ten minutes in a 300°F (150°C) oven.

YORKSHIRE PUDDING

In the long-gone days of great beef roasts turning on spits, drippings of fat were caught in pans below and Yorkshire pudding was baked in the pan. Fortunately for our cholesterol count, both roasts and drippings rarely appear on the menu any longer, but the pudding—not a sweet dessert as we know the word, but an eggy substitute for bread with a main course or as a Sunday brunch treat—is baked in a small amount of rendered beef fat or butter. The secret of achieving the puffy center is to have all ingredients at room temperature.

Serves Four to Six
1 cup (250 ml) sifted
   unbleached white flour
1/2 teaspoon (2.5 ml) salt
1/4 teaspoon (1.2 ml) ground
   thyme or oregano (optional)
1 cup (250 ml) milk, or
   1/2 cup (125 ml) *each* milk
   and half-and-half or
   evaporated milk
2 eggs
3 to 4 tablespoons (45 to 60 ml)
   beef drippings, rendered
   beef fat or butter

Sift together flour, salt and thyme into mixing bowl. With egg beater, gradually add milk, beating until smooth. One at a time, beat in eggs, beating at least 1 minute after each addition. Cover bowl tightly with plastic wrap and refrigerate at least 2 hours. Put beef drippings in a shallow 6- by 10-inch (15 by 25 cm) baking pan, place in oven and turn heat to 450°F (230°C). When oven is up to heat and drippings are sizzling, pour in batter. Bake 15 minutes; do not open oven door. Lower heat to 375°F (190°C) and bake an additional 10 to 15 minutes until edges are crispy and golden and center puffed. Serve immediately, cut in squares.

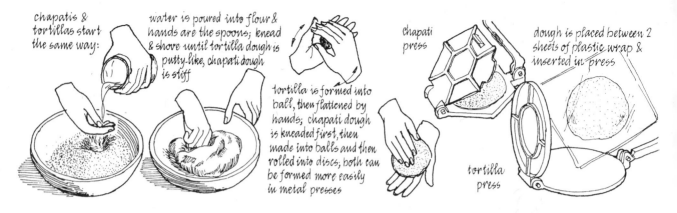

chapatis & tortillas start the same way:

water is poured into flour & hands are the spoons; knead & shove until tortilla dough is putty-like, chapati dough is stiff

tortilla is formed into ball, then flattened by hands; chapati dough is kneaded first, then made into balls and then rolled into discs; both can be formed more easily in metal presses

chapati press

tortilla press

dough is placed between 2 sheets of plastic wrap & inserted in press

CHAPATIS

Here is the staple bread of India, much as the tortilla is part of Mexican culture, but it is made with wheat flours instead of corn, and results in a much more yielding texture. One of the high points of being a guest in an Indian household is to be served throughout dinner with these slim rounds of piping hot bread dripping with ghee, or butter (the woman of the house eats *after* the men and guests and devotes herself to making more chapatis so they arrive continuously). When *you* serve them, bake them beforehand, just before everyone sits down—so that you can sit too. A hot tray at the table, with dampened tea towel under the chapatis, will make them readily handy—and hot. Reheating can also be done in a hot frying pan; a few seconds on each side will do the job, but don't let them dry out.

Makes 12

2 cups (500 ml) whole-wheat pastry flour, or 1 cup (250 ml) *each* whole-wheat flour and unbleached white flour
1/2 teaspoon (2.5 ml) salt (optional)
2 tablespoons (30 ml) vegetable oil
1/2 to 3/4 cup (125 ml to 175 ml) water
Clarified butter as needed

In large mixing bowl, combine the flours, salt and oil. With your fingers, rub the oil into the flour until oil is evenly distributed throughout. Add 1/2 cup (125 ml) of the water, and with your hands, knead the mixture in the bowl to form a solid mass. If the mixture is too crumbly, add more water, 1 tablespoon (15 ml) at a time, until it is the proper consistency. Transfer to lightly oiled wooden surface and knead for 10 to 15 minutes, or until

dough is stiff but smooth. (It should have the consistency of a stiff pizza dough.) Form into a ball and divide into 12 equal portions. Working with 3 portions at a time and keeping the remaining portions covered, form each into a ball. Press each ball flat between the palms of your hands into a disc about 2 inches (5 cm) in diameter. On a lightly floured board, roll out each flattened ball into a round 6 inches (15 cm) in diameter. Heat a heavy skillet over medium heat and place one of the rounds in it. Cook on the first side for 30 seconds, then turn with a spatula and cook on the second side 30 seconds. Turn over again, and with a towel, press down lightly on the surface of the round. The bread should swell slightly at this point. (If it doesn't, don't worry. It will with practice.) Turn the round over again and continue to cook and turn a few times until lightly browned on both sides. Remove from the pan and spread with clarified butter. Repeat with remaining rounds and dough.

TORTILLAS

What is a tortilla? Judging by the ones in the freezer box of your friendly grocer, it might be a corn-flavored cardboard pancake.

Real tortillas are the bread of Mexico, abiding comfort through peace and plenty, famine and wars, for peons and presidents: Corn and water, that's what a tortilla is. Hands pat the dough into thin circles which are baked quickly on very hot iron sheets until they speckle golden brown and puff up—still soft and ready for outstretched hands.

Tortillas can be addictive. While very hot, eat one with butter dripping or wrap it around meats, beans and cheese and devastate it with chili-laden *salsa.* It can be fried to become the plate for a *tostada,* and if it's stale, it can be cut into triangles and fried as scoops for *guacamole.* North America has adopted the tortilla with gusto, and you can start right now to make your reputation— to master the technique that small Mexican children learn when they are knee-high to a *taco.*

Makes One Dozen
1-1/2 cups (350 ml) *masa harina*
3/4 cup (175 ml) water, or as
     needed

Measure the *masa harina* into a bowl and add 1/2 cup (125 ml) water. Holding bowl firmly with one hand, shove the other hand into the bowl to start mixing. Keep squeezing dough through fingers, turning bowl, shoving and kneading, adding more water very carefully until a firm dough that holds together is formed. Kneading with the heel of your hand against the dough in the bowl is very important, and you should continue for 4 to 5 minutes. Dough should become the consistency of putty: To test, take a small piece of dough, roll it into a ball between your hands, pressing in slightly and causing dough to rotate as it gets thinner. In a practiced hand this flattening is like a ballet of the fingers, but it takes much practice to learn. If there are small cracks at the edge of the dough, continue mixing and adding water a teaspoon (5 ml) at a time. Test again, and again. Consistency must be just right. While forming and baking, if dough starts to dry out in bowl, add a little more water.

To form tortillas, cut 2 sheets of plastic wrap each about 10

inches (25 cm) square. Place 1 square on tortilla press, place a ball of dough the size of a small walnut in center and top with second square of plastic wrap. Press down to form a finished circle approximately 5 to 5-1/2 inches (13 to 14 cm) in diameter. Peel plastic off dough, *not* dough off plastic. Heat a large ungreased iron skillet or griddle (when drops of water sizzle and sputter, skillet is hot enough) and place 2 or 3 circles in skillet. Continually turn the circles over in the skillet, lifting them quickly with fingers. When they begin to get golden-brown speckles, using your 3 middle fingers press the center of each down gently and quickly, and the tortillas will start to puff. Top and bottom must separate to be done. (If left too long on one side, they won't puff.) Turn over one last time and bake *briefly* on second side. Remove to a dampened towel spread on a cookie sheet. Stack in a spiral, cover with dampened cloth and keep warm in 200°F (90°C) oven until serving time. Or cool, wrap individually in foil and freeze. Then unwrap, stack, rewrap together and return to the freezer. To thaw, dip individual tortillas in cold water and immediately reheat on hot iron griddle.

Crackers

Crackers are not the easiest bread to construct, so why risk frustration when they're handy on your grocer's shelf, at least 50 different types? We asked ourselves that question. Challenge? Partly. But then we came upon five, after lots of experimenting, that you can't buy anyplace and that friends will beg for. They are worth the concentration and careful handling; set aside a morning and "do" at least three kinds. They store well in tightly covered tins and can be reheated quickly in a toaster oven.

Our curry-wheat wafers are a surprise, a delightful cheese or soup mate. The thyme-scented squares go well with thick winter soups and hearty salads, and the wheat-nut rounds are bursting with vitamins and organic stuff. Our natural cheese wafers are so delicate that they melt in your mouth, plus there are friendly Scandinavian flat breads for uncontrolled nibbling.

THOUGHTS ON MAKING CRACKERS

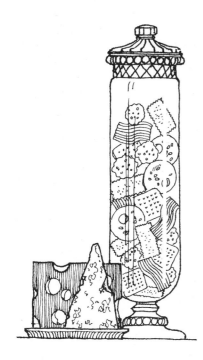

- Bake on a day when humidity is not high; crackers like low-working moisture. When handling dough, however, always keep unworked portions set aside covered with a clean towel so they won't dry out.
- Cutting crackers: A sharp knife or cookie cutter shapes will give personality so they don't look bought. A pastry wheel with "pinking" edge dresses up a simple square or rectangle. To mark a cracker surface, prick with fork, or press a wooden meat tenderizer into dough to make evenly spaced indentations.
- An old clean cotton sock fitted over the rolling pin will make rolling out easier. Getting dough thin is the big job with crackers. We even tried rolling them in the baking sheet and then scoring with a floured pastry wheel.
- Seeds can be mixed in the dough or sprinkled on before baking.
- Watch baking carefully; turn pan around in oven halfway through baking to insure even browning. Crackers should be *delicately* browned.
- Lift very carefully from pan after baking (broken ones are freebies) and cool on wire rack. Store in airtight container in a cool place.

THYME SQUARES

You may think making crackers is for the birds, but this one is so easy and has such distinctive flair, it's a shame not to try. Thyme is well spent with cheese, pates and smoked fish for hors d'oeuvre, but the herb needs to be full of vigor. Don't use an old can of thyme that has been in the back of the cupboard for ten years.

Makes Sixty-four
2 cups (500 ml minus 15 ml) unbleached white flour
1/4 cup (60 ml) granulated sugar
1 teaspoon (5 ml) salt
1/2 teaspoon (2.5 ml) double-acting baking powder
1/2 teaspoon (2.5 ml) baking soda
1 teaspoon (5 ml) ground thyme
4 tablespoons (60 ml) butter, chilled
1 cup (250 ml) buttermilk or plain yoghurt

mark dough with wooden meat mallet

Sift together dry ingredients into medium-sized bowl. Cut in butter with fingers, 2 knives or pastry blender until mixture is the consistency of coarse cornmeal. All at once, add buttermilk and stir with fork to form into a ball. Turn out onto floured board and knead gently 15 to 20 strokes. Form into ball, wrap in foil and chill in freezer 15 minutes. Remove dough from freezer (it will be soft but not sticky) and divide into 2 equal portions. Rewrap 1 portion and place in refrigerator. Divide first portion in half and roll out each half into an 8-inch (20 cm) square approximately 1/8 inch (3 mm) thick. With fluted pie edger or pizza cutter, cut each square into 16 2-inch (5 cm) squares. Carefully transfer to greased baking sheet and repeat with second half. Dip the points of a wooden meat mallet into flour, shake off excess and press hard into each square, piercing through to pan and making a neat pattern of holes. Bake in oven preheated to 450°F (230°C) 10 minutes or until puffed and nicely golden. Cool on wire rack. Repeat with second portion of dough.

NATURAL CHEESE CRACKERS

Very rich, very fragile, very good. The amount of cheese indicated may seem to overwhelm the rest of the ingredients, but the result is like eating crisp dill-flavored cheddar, and that can't be bad. These are a natural accompaniment for luncheon salads or a tall cool brew.

Makes Approximately Five Dozen
2 cups (500 ml) grated cheddar cheese
1/4 pound (125 g) butter
1/2 cup (125 ml) whole-wheat flour
1 teaspoon (5 ml) dried dill weed
1/2 teaspoon (2.5 ml) salt

203

Combine all ingredients, shape into rolls approximately 1-1/2 inches (4 cm) in diameter and 6 or 7 inches (12 to 15 cm) long and wrap in waxed paper. Chill at least 2 hours or until firm. Slice as thinly as possible and place on an ungreased baking sheet. Bake in oven preheated to 350°F (180°C) 10 minutes or until crisp. Cool on wire rack.

use 1/2" nozzle end of pastry bag to cut hole

serve stacked on a wood skewer

CURRY-WHEAT CRACKERS

These wafers with a hole will make an event out of a modest soup or Saturday's salad. They stack on a wooden skewer anchored into a chunk of cheese, and the tiny cutouts masquerade as croutons.

Makes Thirty to Thirty-six
1 cup (250 ml) unbleached
　　white flour
1/2 cup (125 ml) fine bulghur
1/4 teaspoon (1.2 ml) salt
1/4 teaspoon (1.2 ml) baking
　　soda
4 tablespoons (60 ml) butter,
　　chilled
1/2 cup (125 ml) plain yoghurt
1 teaspoon (5 ml) curry powder
1/4 cup (60 ml) lightly toasted
　　sesame seeds

In mixing bowl, combine flour, bulghur, salt and baking soda. With fingers, 2 knives or pastry blender, work in butter until mixture is the consistency of coarse cornmeal. Stir in yoghurt and curry powder and form dough into a ball. Divide ball into 4 equal portions. Working with 1 portion at a time and keeping others covered to prevent drying out, roll out on floured board as thinly as possible into a rectangle. With 3-inch (8 cm) cutter, cut into rounds. With plain metal tip of pastry bag, cut out a 1/2-inch (1.5 cm) hole from each round, positioning it slightly off center. Lift rounds and tiny circles onto ungreased baking sheet. Repeat with remaining portions of dough. Sprinkle with sesame seeds and bake in oven preheated to 400°F (210°C) 5 to 7 minutes or until lightly browned. Cool on wire rack.

SOFT RYE CRACKERS

Scandinavians spend their long, dark winters thinking up wonderful foods, and one of the little wonders is a cracker called *lefse*. Some like it soft, rolled around butter; others bake a crisp version. Both are slightly sweet, strongly rye and hard to leave alone. We've put together a kind of compromise—a crusty, chewy cracker with soft center to serve with fruits, cheeses or iced juices. To make them more interesting, the Swedes use a grooved rolling pin; we duplicated the pattern by using a butter paddle.

use butter paddle to mark lines

place on oiled pan & gently shape with fingers

grooved Scandinavian rolling pin

*Makes Approximately
Five Dozen*

1/2 cup (125 ml) buttermilk
2 tablespoons (30 ml) fresh
  orange juice
2 tablespoons (30 ml) light
  corn syrup
1 egg, lightly beaten
1-3/4 cups (425 ml) unbleached
  white flour, or as needed
1/2 cup (125 ml) rye flour
1/4 cup (60 ml) rye flakes
1/2 teaspoon (2.5 ml) salt
2 tablespoons (30 ml) granulated sugar
1/2 teaspoon (2.5 ml) baking
  soda

Melted butter

Combine liquids and blend
thoroughly. In another bowl stir
dry ingredients together until
well blended and add all at
once to liquids. Continue stirring until dough leaves sides of
bowl. Turn out onto floured
board and knead briefly, adding more flour if needed to
make a workable dough. Roll
out as thinly as possible into a
rectangle. With your fingers,
continue stretching dough until
it is as thin as you can make it.
With pizza cutter or sharp
knife, cut into 1- by 3-inch (2.5
by 7.5 cm) strips. Shape into
modified S, place on oiled

baking sheets and bake in oven
preheated to 425°F (220°C) for
10 to 12 minutes. Transfer to
wire rack and brush with melted
butter.

WHEAT-NUT CRACKERS

This recipe is shared by a
woman whose life has revolved
around nutrition. Her crackers
are wholesome and delicious in
the old-fashioned meaning of
the words—before advertizers
used them to label store-bought,
stuffed-with-additives items.

*Makes Approximately
Seven to Eight Dozen*

2 cups (500 ml) whole-wheat
  flour
1 tablespoon (15 ml) granulated
  sugar
1/2 teaspoon (2.5 ml) salt
1 teaspoon (5 ml) baking
  soda
1 cup (250 ml) coarsely ground
  sunflower seeds, filberts or
  almonds, or 2/3 cup (150 ml)
  sesame seeds and 1/3 cup
  (75 ml) untoasted wheat germ
5 tablespoons (75 ml) butter,
  cut in bits
3/4 cup (175 ml) buttermilk

In large bowl, combine dry
ingredients. With fingers, 2
knives or pastry blender, work

*use a pastry jagger
and ruler to cut uniform-
size crackers*

in butter until mixture is the
consistency of coarse cornmeal.
Pour buttermilk over and, using your hands, work until
dough forms a ball and leaves
sides of bowl clean. Turn out
onto lightly floured board and
knead 15 seconds to be sure
dough is thoroughly mixed. Divide into 3 portions. Set 2
aside covered with a towel and
roll out third portion as thinly
as possible. With ruler and
fluted pie edger or pizza cutter,
cut strips 1-inch (3 cm) wide.
Place ruler across cuts and cut
strips into 3-1/2-inch (9 cm)
lengths. Repeat with remaining
dough. Place on ungreased baking sheet and bake in oven preheated to 400°F (210°C) 10
minutes. Cool on wire rack.

Stove~top Breads

GRIDDLECAKES & WAFFLES
FRIED BREADS
DUMPLINGS
TRAIL & SAIL BREADS

Call them pancakes, hotcakes, a "stack" or flapjacks (from California's intrepid gold miners). No one knows who invented this endearing morning booster, snack, lunch-filler or even late, late-movie commercial break. It appears in almost every country in some form, but we've concentrated on 17 back-home variations we think you'll find refreshingly adequate, with extra energy boosts of whole wheat, bran, cooked rice, cottage cheese or berries. We've also included what we've learned about their antics. You can bake a different batch every day of the week and never be bored.

THOUGHTS ON MAKING GRIDDLECAKES WITHOUT A FLAP

- Don't overbeat. Stir only until dry ingredients are well-blended; fold egg whites in gently at the last.
- Lumpy? That's natural for the batter.
- Heat griddle to 425°F (220°C) or until water sizzles and dances when sprinkled on a griddle that has been greased lightly. If water disappears, griddle is too hot.
- If batter is too thick, thin with a little water; always test by baking one small pancake alone the first time.
- To make a good round pancake, pour about one-fourth cup (60 ml) of batter from tip of a large spoon held close to griddle. It will be two to three minutes before bubbles appear on top—your sign to turn it over. Lift edge to be sure it has browned, but not too much; and turn only once. The underside is never attractive, so serve with best side up.
- If you can't serve at once, keep pancakes warm in the oven on a baking sheet covered with a tea towel. Don't stack; it makes them limp.

SUGGESTIONS

- Substitute sour cream or yoghurt for part of the buttermilk.
- In high altitudes, use one fourth less baking soda or baking powder than indicated in recipe.
- Before you pour the batter, sprinkle griddle with poppy, sunflower or sesame seeds.
- Use half butter, half oil to grease griddle.
- Don't crowd the griddle; pancakes should not touch.
- For a thicker pancake, add a tablespoon (15 ml) more flour.

Griddle-cakes

COTTAGE CHEESE PANCAKES

Pancakes are not just for breakfast. They can substitute for rice under creamed finnan haddie or shrimp jambalaya. They can double for a shortcake under scrumptious strawberries and whipped cream. Don't short change them. Also, don't divulge the secret ingredient. Just let your guests know they're high in gastronomical pluses.

Makes Approximately Two Dozen Four-Inch (10 cm) Pancakes
2 eggs, lightly beaten
2/3 cup (150 ml) plain yoghurt
2 to 3 teaspoons (10 to 15 ml) brown sugar
1 tablespoon (15 ml) butter, melted and cooled
1 cup (250 ml) sieved low-fat cottage cheese
1/2 cup (125 ml) unbleached white flour
1/2 cup (125 ml) whole-wheat flour
1 tablespoon (15 ml) double-acting baking powder
1/2 teaspoon (2.5 ml) baking soda
1 tablespoon (15 ml) lightly toasted wheat germ
Buttermilk as needed

Thoroughly combine eggs, yoghurt, brown sugar, butter and cottage cheese. Mix all dry ingredients together and stir into egg mixture just until moistened. Thin to desired consistency with buttermilk and cook according to general directions for griddlecakes.

RICE PANCAKES

Make a point of baking a batch of these hearty pancakes the next time you have a cup of leftover cooked brown or white rice. The rice slips a nutritive bounty into a familiar "bread" we take for granted as we rush through breakfast. Pancakes should be drummed off the fast-food list. They deserve to be savored, enjoyed leisurely, whether for Saturday breakfast or lunch (try them with curried chicken) or Sunday night supper after a heavy day of TV football.

Makes Approximately Sixteen Four-inch (10 cm) Pancakes
2 eggs, separated
1 cup (250 ml) sour cream
1 cup (250 ml) milk
3 tablespoons (45 ml) butter, melted and cooled
1/2 teaspoon (2.5 ml) pure vanilla extract (optional)
1/2 teaspoon (2.5 ml) ground cinnamon (optional)
1/2 teaspoon (2.5 ml) salt
1 cup (250 ml) cooked brown or white rice
1 cup (250 ml) whole-wheat flour, or as needed

Beat egg yolks until light. Blend in sour cream, milk, butter, vanilla extract, cinnamon and salt. Stir in rice and then flour, adding more flour as needed to create desired consistency. Beat egg whites until stiff but not dry. Fold in one third of the batter and then fold mixture into remaining batter. Thin to desired consistency with milk and cook according to general directions for griddlecakes.

To keep bowl in place on a slick work counter, fold a damp towel and place underneath.

BUTTERMILK GRIDDLECAKES

Makes Approximately Fourteen Four-inch (10 cm) Griddlecakes

2 eggs, separated
1 cup (250 ml) buttermilk, or as needed
1 teaspoon (5 ml) corn or safflower oil
2 to 3 teaspoons (10 to 15 ml) honey
1-1/2 cups (350 ml) unbleached white flour
1/2 teaspoon (2.5 ml) baking soda
1/2 teaspoon (2.5 ml) salt

Combine egg yolks, buttermilk, oil and honey. Sift together flour, baking soda and salt and stir into egg mixture until just blended. Beat egg whites until very stiff and fold into batter. Thin to desired consistency with buttermilk and cook according to general directions for griddlecakes.

WHOLE-WHEAT GRIDDLECAKES Substitute 3/4 cup (175 ml) whole-wheat flour for 3/4 cup (175 ml) of the unbleached white flour.

BUCKWHEAT GRIDDLECAKES Substitute 1/2 cup (125 ml) buckwheat flour for 1/2 cup (125 ml) of the unbleached white flour.

FRUIT GRIDDLECAKES Substitute 1/4 cup (50 ml) fresh orange juice for 1/4 cup (50 ml) of the buttermilk; add to batter 2/3 to 3/4 cup (150 to 175 ml) fresh berries, drained crushed pineapple or mashed banana.

BRAN GRIDDLECAKES Add to batter 3 tablespoons (45 ml) unprocessed bran soaked 10 minutes in 1/4 cup (60 ml) additional buttermilk.

WHEAT GERM GRIDDLECAKES Add to batter 3 tablespoons (45 ml) lightly toasted wheat germ; adjust buttermilk measurement to desired consistency.

NUT GRIDDLECAKES Add to batter 1/4 cup (50 ml) finely chopped peanuts, pecans or walnuts.

CORNMEAL GRIDDLECAKES Substitute cornmeal for up to one half of the flour measurement.

FORTIFIED GRIDDLECAKES Substitute 1/3 cup (75 ml) soy, garbanzo or oat flour for 1/3 cup (75 ml) unbleached white flour; add 2 to 3 tablespoons (30 to 45 ml) non-instant non-fat milk and adjust buttermilk measurement to desired consistency.

SPROUT GRIDDLECAKES Add to batter 1/3 cup (75 ml) sprouted wheat or rye berries (page 73).

GRAIN GRIDDLECAKES Add to batter 1/2 cup (125 ml) cooked grain, such as bulghur or brown rice.

OATMEAL GRIDDLECAKES Soak 1/2 cup (125 ml) unprocessed rolled oats in an additional 1/2 cup (125 ml) buttermilk 10 minutes. Add to batter before folding in egg whites.

SESAME GRIDDLECAKES Add to batter 1/2 teaspoon (2.5 ml) Oriental sesame oil and 3 tablespoons (45 ml) lightly toasted sesame seeds.

MEAT GRIDDLECAKES Add to batter 1/4 cup (50 ml) diced cooked ham or 3 tablespoons (45 ml) crumbled crisply cooked bacon or sausage meat.

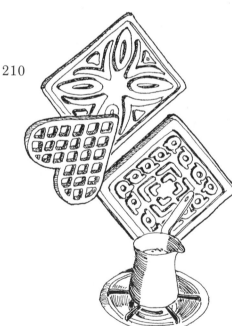

Waffles have been around for a long, long time. The colonials baked them in long-handled irons that they held over the coals in the fireplace. The Belgians invented a very deeply indented waffle, the *gaufres,* that is served with whipped cream and berries or dusted with powdered sugar. Today's electric irons, with patterns as well as grid indents, are round and square and long, nonstick, and have accurate heat controls. All you need is a superior recipe. It just so happens there is this whole-wheat one with yoghurt just awaiting your experimentation. Good morning!

THOUGHTS ON WAFTING WAFFLES

- A new waffle iron will probably need to be seasoned. *Read* the manufacturer's instructions before you start (you have no idea how many good pieces of equipment are ruined for want of reading the booklet that is furnished).
- Once the iron is seasoned and has been used, don't grease or wash it; just use a small stiff brush to remove crumbs.
- Heat iron until indicator shows it is ready to use, or test by putting a drop of water on griddle. When it sizzles, griddle is ready.
- Never add hot butter to batter; always let it cool first.
- Fold in egg whites last, but not completely. Little white fluffs should still show. Overmixing makes waffles tough.
- Batter may be stored briefly in refrigerator.
- Pour or spoon batter to cover about two thirds of grid, close lid and wait about four minutes before checking; if lid will not lift easily, it may not be done. To be sure, wait until all steam has stopped and waffle is a rich golden brown.
- When taking out of iron, hold waffle on fork five to ten seconds. This encourages a crisp crust. (For an even crisper crust, add more yoghurt to our recipe.)
- Waffles may be frozen; bake entire batch (to save reheating, and energy), cool leftovers and wrap individually in foil. To warm, drop in toaster.

YOGHURT WAFFLES

As with a child who has never seen a cow and knows milk comes from a carton, many breakfast-getters still think waffles come out of a biscuit-mix package. Our job was cut out for us. We couldn't let that go on. There is no mystique to making waffles—just whole-wheat flour, honey, eggs, yoghurt and a couple other things wrapped up in a no-fail recipe. Once *you* start making waffles, you'll know where they come from.

Makes Two Large Waffles
2 eggs, separated
1-1/3 cups (300 ml) plain
   yoghurt
4 teaspoons (20 ml) honey
4 tablespoons (60 ml) butter,
   melted and cooled, or
   safflower or corn oil
2/3 cup (150 ml) unbleached
   white flour
2/3 cup (150 ml) whole-wheat
   flour
2 teaspoons (10 ml) double-
   acting baking powder
1/2 teaspoon (2.5 ml) baking
   soda
1/2 teaspoon (2.5 ml) salt

Beat together egg yolks, yoghurt, honey and butter. Sift together dry ingredients, adding kernels left in sifter to flour mixture, and blend into egg-yolk mixture. Beat egg whites until stiff but not dry and fold into batter. Bake according to general directions for waffles and serve with any of the topping suggestions (page 225).

ROMAN MEAL WAFFLES Substitute 2/3 cup (150 ml) Roman Meal cereal for the 2/3 cup (150 ml) of whole-wheat flour.

WHEAT GERM WAFFLES Substitute 3 tablespoons (45 ml) soy flour for 3 tablespoons (45 ml) of the unbleached white flour. Increase yoghurt measurement by 2 tablespoons (30 ml) and fold into batter with egg whites 3 tablespoons (45 ml) lightly toasted wheat germ.

CORNMEAL WAFFLES Substitute 1/2 cup (125 ml) yellow or white cornmeal for 1/2 cup (125 ml) unbleached or whole-wheat flour.

BERRY OR NUT WAFFLES Add to batter just before folding in egg whites 1 cup (250 ml) rinsed and drained fresh berries or chopped pecans or walnuts, 1/2 teaspoon (2.5 ml) ground cinnamon and 1/4 teaspoon (1.2 ml) freshly grated lemon peel.

CHEESE WAFFLES Add to batter before folding in egg whites 2/3 cup (150 ml) grated cheddar, Monterey Jack, Edam or other mild cheese, 2 to 3 slices bacon, crisply cooked and crumbled, and 1/2 teaspoon (2.5 ml) dry mustard (optional).

BRAN WAFFLES Soak 1/3 cup (75 ml) unprocessed bran in the yoghurt 10 minutes. Reduce whole-wheat flour measurement to 1/3 cup (75 ml).

add nuts
last: they
slow the
rising

pine nut
pistachio
filbert
almond
walnut

Fried Breads

These are small pieces of dough browned in deep oil in a heavy kettle (as opposed to pancakes, English muffins, tortillas, etc., which are griddle-fried with just enough oil to keep them from sticking). We've included what we found to be the most seductive of fried breads—spicy doughnuts, Colonial-style fried bread, Hungarian *langos,* New Mexican *sopaipillas* and South African *koesisters.*

THOUGHTS ON SUCCESSFUL DEEP FRYING

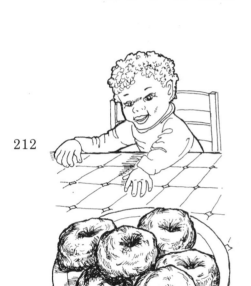

212

- Heat three to four inches (8 to 10 cm) of peanut oil to 375°F (190°C) in a fryer or heavy, deep kettle; check temperature with candy thermometer, attached to side of fryer for constant control. Use the bread cube test if a thermometer is not available: A small cube of bread dropped in hot oil should brown in 60 seconds.
- The dough is fragile, so lift each piece very gently with wide spatula and slide into oil.
- Don't crowd the pan, even if you're in a hurry. These breads need space to expand. Fry on one side three to four minutes until nicely browned; turn over for another three to four minutes. Turn only once.
- Lift out the golden bread with tongs or slotted spoon, allowing it to drip over oil momentarily, and place on brown paper or paper toweling to drain completely.
- Continue until all dough has been fried. Another pair of tongs will make quick work of dipping warm pieces in syrup glaze.

REUSING OIL

Call in your friendly potato after you've finished "bread frying": Three or four thick slices dropped into the hot oil will clarify it, that is, make it clear and tasteless, so that you can reuse it several times. Remove the potato slices, cool oil and strain it through two layers of cheesecloth into a clean coffee can with lid, and store in the refrigerator. Use this batch for bread *only.* If you stray and share it with batter-fried squid, brain fritters or vegetable tempura, spare the next batch of doughnuts and start fresh. "Used" fat has the memory of an elephant's mother.

RAISED DOUGHNUTS

How many raised doughnuts are eaten daily in lieu of breakfast? Tens of millions, no doubt! They rate tops on the finger-food list, and are often completely naked of nourishment. Not so these: tender, loaded with flavor doughnuts, with a goodly dash of cinnamon, nutmeg and lemon peel, eggs and milk—chock full of good morning starters. They reheat nicely on a hot tray or in a toaster oven, too.

Makes Approximately Two Dozen
1 tablespoon (15 ml) active
  dry yeast
3 tablespoons (45 ml)
  lukewarm water
1/2 cup (125 ml) milk, scalded
2 tablespoons (30 ml) butter,
  cut in bits
3 tablespoons (45 ml) firmly
  packed brown sugar
1-1/2 cups (350 ml) unbleached
  white flour, or as needed
1 egg, lightly beaten
1/2 teaspoon (2.5 ml) freshly
  grated lemon peel
3/4 teaspoon (3.6 ml) salt
1/2 teaspoon (2.5 ml) ground
  cinnamon
1/4 teaspoon (1.2 ml) ground
  nutmeg

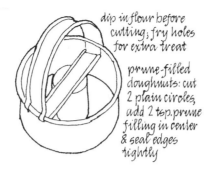

dip in flour before cutting; fry holes for extra treat

prune-filled doughnuts: cut 2 plain circles, add 2 tsp. prune filling in center & seal edges tightly

In medium bowl, sprinkle yeast over water, stir to dissolve and let stand until foamy. Combine milk, butter and sugar and stir to melt butter and dissolve sugar; cool to lukewarm. Add to proofed yeast with 1 cup (250 ml) of the flour. Beat vigorously about 3 minutes until air bubbles form. Stir in egg, lemon peel, salt and spices. Gradually add remaining flour, beating well. Turn out onto floured board and knead, adding additional flour only as needed to prevent sticking, 5 minutes. Form into smooth ball, place in oiled bowl, turn to coat all surfaces, cover with tea towel and let rise in warm place 45 minutes or until double in bulk. Punch down and let rise 40 minutes or until double in bulk. Punch down, knead briefly and roll out 3/8 inch (1 cm) thick. Cut with doughnut cutter, place rings and holes on floured baking sheet, cover with tea towel and let rise in warm place 30 minutes or until almost double in size. Invert and slip into hot oil. (This gives the underside a chance to rise evenly with the top side.) Deep fry according to general directions.

GLAZED DOUGHNUTS Combine 1 cup (250 ml) powdered sugar and 1/3 cup (75 ml) boiling water, stir in 1/2 teaspoon (2.5 ml) freshly grated lemon peel or 1/2 teaspoon (2.5 ml) pure vanilla extract and dip hot doughnuts into mixture, one at a time; transfer to wire rack. Roll in chopped nuts or grated coconut for variety.

SUGARED DOUGHNUTS Shake hot doughnuts, one at a time, in paper bag with granulated or powdered sugar seasoned to taste with ground cinnamon or other spices.

If you forget to add salt, sift it into flour used for kneading, and work in thoroughly.

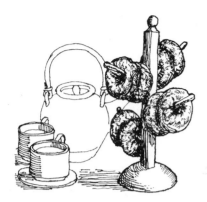

CAKE DOUGHNUTS

There's nothing quite like a freshly made doughnut. They bake in their hot oil and the fragrance floats through the rooms, unnerving diets, denting resolves. Sour-cream cake doughnuts are considered unbeatable and practically non-fail. The chilling period keeps them from absorbing oil.

Makes Approximately Fourteen
1 egg, lightly beaten
1/3 cup (75 ml) granulated sugar
1/3 cup (75 ml) sour cream, at room temperature
1/2 teaspoon (2.5 ml) freshly grated lemon or orange peel
1 cup plus 3 tablespoons (275 ml sifted) unbleached white flour
1 tablespoon (15 ml) cornstarch
1/2 heaping teaspoon (3 ml) double-acting baking powder
1/4 heaping teaspoon (1.5 ml) baking soda
1/8 teaspoon (.8 ml) salt
1/8 teaspoon (.8 ml) ground cinnamon or cardamom
Dash ground cloves
Dash ground nutmeg
Peanut oil for deep frying
Powdered or granulated sugar for dusting

Beat together egg and sugar until creamy and blend in sour cream and lemon peel. Sift together dry ingredients and stir into egg mixture until blended. Knead briefly, form into ball, wrap in waxed paper and chill several hours. Preheat oil. Roll out dough approximately 3/8 inch (1 cm) thick. Cut into rounds with doughnut cutter and deep fry according to general directions. Dust with sugar.

KOESISTERS

A happy addition to this group of seductive finger foods, thanks to friends in South Africa, is the *koesister.* It is a narrow strip of dough folded over on itself and then twisted into a figure eight, fried and dipped in a gingery syrup—a Quixotic delight! It is a simpler, quicker version of yeast fried bread, equally welcome at the breakfast table or a tea break. Dress them up a little by rolling them in grated coconut after they are dipped in syrup.

Makes Approximately Two Dozen

Dough
1-3/4 cups (425 ml) unbleached white flour
1/2 tablespoon (7.5 ml) double-acting baking powder
1/4 teaspoon (1.2 ml) salt
1 egg, lightly beaten
1/2 cup (125 ml) water, or as needed

Syrup
1 cup (250 ml) granulated sugar
1/2 cup (125 ml) water
1/2 teaspoon (2.5 ml) fresh lemon juice
1/2 teaspoon (2.5 ml) light corn syrup
1/8 teaspoon (.8 ml) salt
1/8 teaspoon (.8 ml) ground ginger
1/8 teaspoon (.8 ml) cream of tartar

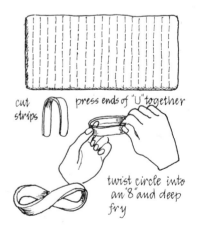

cut strips

press ends of "U" together

twist circle into an "8" and deep fry

To make dough, sift together dry ingredients into mixing bowl. Beat together egg and water and pour onto flour mixture. Stirring with fork, combine, gradually adding additional water as needed to make a workable dough. Knead briefly to blend well, cover with tea towel and let rest 1 hour.

While dough is resting, make syrup. In saucepan, combine sugar, water, lemon juice, corn syrup, salt and ginger. Stir well, bring to boil and, stirring occasionally, boil 7 minutes. Stir in cream of tartar and cool.

Without using any flour on board, roll out dough thinly into a rectangle. Cut into strips approximately 1/2 inch (1.5 cm) wide and 7 inches (18 cm) long. Fold strip in half lengthwise, seal ends together and then twist to make a figure eight. Deep fry according to general directions. Drain and, using a second pair of tongs, dip breads into syrup for approximately 30 seconds, or until they have absorbed the syrup. Let drain on wire rack briefly and serve warm.

COLONIAL FRIED BREAD

Many years B.D. (before doughnuts), mothers improvised treats for hungry young mouths by saving small pieces of dough from the day's bake and frying them in hot lard to a crisp brown, then loading each with honey or jam. This recipe, inspired by that idea, can be formed into balls, pretzels or just pulled and stretched before dropping in the hot oil. It also makes an excellent basic loaf using caraway or sesame seeds for variations. After deep-frying according to general directions, dip the bread into Sugar Syrup, page 214, or sprinkle with powdered sugar and cinnamon.

Makes Approximately Two Dozen
1/2 pound (225 g) baking
   potatoes
3 cups plus 1 tablespoon (725
   ml) unbleached white flour
3 tablespoons (45 ml) cornstarch
2 teaspoons (10 ml) active
   dry yeast
1/2 tablespoon (7.5 ml) salt
Peanut oil for deep frying

Scrub potatoes, slice, cover with water and boil until soft. Drain, reserving water; rice or sieve the potato and set aside. Into large bowl, sift together flour and cornstarch. Make a well in center and pour in 3/4 cup (175 ml) of reserved potato water. Cool to lukewarm and sprinkle yeast over. Stir lightly, incorporating a little of the flour, cover with tea towel and

let stand in warm place 20 to 30 minutes. Blend in remaining flour in bowl and then beat in reserved potato and salt. Adding additional potato cooking water or water as needed, mix with wooden spoon and then hands to make a pliable, soft dough. Knead briefly, form into smooth ball, place in oiled bowl, turn to coat all surfaces, cover with tea towel and let rise in warm place 1-1/2 hours or until double in bulk. Punch down, turn out onto board and knead, adding additional flour only as needed to prevent excessive sticking, 10 minutes. Dough will be slightly sticky. Form into shapes or balls, approximately 2 ounces (56 g) each, place on oiled baking sheet, cover with tea towel and let rise in warm place 40 minutes or until almost double in size. Deep fry according to general directions and serve hot.

fried bread can also be formed into bows: roll dough 1/4" thick, cut diamonds with pastry jagger, 4 to 6" long, 1/2" wide; slit as shown

3" slit

slip one end through slit & pull

SOPAIPILLAS

These puffs, originating in New Mexico, make an excellent accompaniment to highly seasoned Mexican food. Break off a corner of one and fill with honey, or serve them with fillings as you would pita bread. No need to worry if the shapes are not quite perfect or if they do not all puff. They will vanish and leave no trace.

Makes Approximately Sixteen
1 cup (250 ml) unbleached
    white flour
1/2 cup (125 ml) whole-wheat
    pastry flour
1 tablespoon (15 ml) double-
    acting baking powder
3/4 teaspoon (3.6 ml) salt
2-1/2 tablespoons (22.5 ml)
    lard, chilled
1/3 cup (75 ml) water, or as
    needed
Peanut oil for deep frying

In mixing bowl, combine flours, baking powder and salt. With fingers, 2 knives or pastry blender, work in lard until mixture is the consistency of coarse cornmeal. With fork, stir in water, adding more by the teaspoonful until dough is workable and holds together. Knead gently in bowl to form a ball, then knead *briefly* on board until dough is smooth. Roll out 1/8 inch (3 mm) thick and cut into rectangles approximately 3 by 4 inches (8 by 10 cm). Deep fry according to general directions. Serve immediately.

LANGOS

Hungarians, those bold and fearless cooks, lend wings to this puffy golden bread by serving it piping hot and offering a cut clove of garlic to rub vigorously on both sides (meanwhile you're trying not to burn your fingers). The result? An instant love affair between bread and paprika-hot soups or cold lettuce salad. However, we suggest something different for Sunday breakfast: forego the usual sweet roll and try one hot with scrambled eggs—a new appetite bender.

Makes Sixteen
1 recipe Colonial Fried Bread
    dough, page 215
1/2 teaspoon (2.5 ml) ground
    ginger
1/2 teaspoon (2.5 ml) baking
    soda
Peanut oil for deep frying
Garlic cloves, halved lengthwise

Prepare Fried Bread dough, adding the ginger and baking soda with the salt. After dividing and rising, reshape balls into flat rectangles as shown. Make slits with sharp knife all the way through, place on oiled baking sheets and let rise 45 minutes or until half again as large. Deep fry according to general directions.

shape balls of dough into flat rectangles by pulling out with hands; make slits with knife or fingers

lift from oil & let drip briefly; drain on paper toweling set on wire rack; serve very hot, with garlic

Dumplings

White bread clouds float on a stew or in a soup. Dumplings are delicate bread "baked" in liquid, but never browned. In fact, you test to see if they're done by inserting a cake tester or toothpick; if it comes out clean, they're ready to serve. The secret is to keep them simmering and steaming on top of the liquid, and never to let the liquid boil. What you're after is a fluffy tender dumpling with a light bready texture, and we've included three ways to achieve just that: wheat germ herb, caraway and stew.

THOUGHTS ON MAKING DUMPLINGS

● Use a large pot so that dumplings will not be crowded; there should be adequate liquid for them to float in.
● It is possible to simmer dumplings in clear broth or water.
● The dough should be soft-biscuit texture, with ingredients mixed until just moistened—not runny but just holding shape.
● To shape, dip medium-sized serving spoon in liquid, then into dough. A cup (250 ml) of dough should yield six large dumplings (up to 18 one-inch [3 cm] size); space large ones one and a half to two inches (4 to 5 cm) apart to allow for expansion.
● Chopped fresh or dried crumbled herbs can be sprinkled on dough before steaming.
● As soon as dough floats, cover pot and set timer for time indicated. Liquid should simmer, never boil.
● Remove with slotted spoon and serve alongside stew, or in soups or broths. Dumplings don't reheat well.
● They should be added to stew the last 20 minutes of cooking. The lid must not be lifted during that period; if you're lucky enough to have a tightly fitting glass lid, you can spy occasionally on their progress.

rely on a cake tester or toothpick to be sure dumplings are done

217

CARAWAY DUMPLINGS

Caraway seeds and a wee bit of dry mustard add lilt to veal and lamb. If you're planning a ragout, add small teaspoon-sized balls to the pot about seven to eight minutes before you're ready to serve. Remember, they must be cooked under a tight lid, and the liquid must not boil or it will toughen the protein in the egg. They can also be cooked in broth or water and added to the serving dish as a ring around the edge of the entree.

Serves Six
1-1/2 cups (350 ml) unbleached white flour
2 teaspoons (10 ml) double-acting baking powder
1/2 teaspoon (2.5 ml) salt
1/4 to 1/2 teaspoon (1.2 to 2.5 ml) dry mustard
1 teaspoon (10 ml) caraway seeds, or to taste
1 egg, lightly beaten
1/2 cup (125 ml) milk, or as needed
2 tablespoons (30 ml) butter, melted and cooled slightly

Sift together flour, baking powder and salt. Toss in mustard and caraway seeds. Mix egg, milk and butter, and with fork, stir into dry ingredients just until moistened, adding additional milk if need to make a

soft dough. According to general directions for dumplings, drop by spoonfuls into gently simmering salted water and cook 4 to 8 minutes or until dumplings test done.

STEW DUMPLINGS

Serves Six
2 cups (500 ml *sifted*) unbleached white flour
2-1/2 teaspoons (12.5 ml) double-acting baking powder
1 to 2 teaspoons (5 to 10 ml) granulated sugar
1 teaspoon (5 ml) salt
5 tablespoons (75 ml) butter, chilled and cut in bits
1-1/2 cups (350 ml) milk

Sift together dry ingredients into large bowl. With fingers, 2 knives or pastry blender, work in butter until mixture is the consistency of coarse cornmeal. With fork, stir in milk to make a fairly soft, moist dough. According to general directions for dumplings, drop by medium-sized spoonfuls onto simmering stew and cook 20 minutes or until dumplings test done.

Note   One cup (250 ml) whole-wheat pastry flour may be substituted for 1 cup (250 ml) of the unbleached white flour.

WHEAT GERM-HERB DUMPLINGS

The introduction of wheat germ and whole-wheat flour adds a new dimension to dumplings, and should be put on your must-try-some-day list. They can be cooked in gently simmering water and served separately with gravy.

Serves Four
1 cup (250 ml) Quick-Bread Mix, page 161
2 to 3 tablespoons (30 to 45 ml) lightly toasted wheat germ
1/4 teaspoon (1.2 ml) salt
1/8 teaspoon (.8 ml) ground mace
Dash black pepper
1 tablespoon (15 ml) minced fresh chives
1/2 cup (125 ml) milk, or as needed
2 tablespoons (30 ml) safflower oil or melted and cooled butter

In large bowl, combine bread mix, wheat germ, seasonings and herbs. Mix together milk and oil, and with fork, stir into dry ingredients just to moisten, adding additional milk if needed to make a soft dough that will hold its shape. According to general directions for dumplings, drop by spoonfuls into gently simmering salted water and cook 4 to 8 minutes or until dumplings test done.

Trail & Sail Breads

Finding comfort in the great outdoors after a long day's hike or rough seas is a lot simpler than even ten years ago. When warm bed and warm bread beckon, you've got the best of two worlds.

The bedroll is down filled and the bannock bread, an old reliable, is filled down with good things in dry form at home and secured in a plastic bag that becomes mixing bowl when water is added at the campsite or in the galley. Working batter with fingers and dropping it into a hot greased skillet is more fun than mudpies—and the hot bread with its heavy crust is pure creature comfort. (Note: The dryer the dough, the better the results when baking over campfire; add chopped nuts, fresh wild berries, dried fruits for energy-restoring goodness.)

The pressure cooker, or iron-pot bread, is somewhat more complicated because of the yeast, the kneading and rising, but it produces a substantial crunchy whole-wheat loaf you won't forget. Part of the joy of "getting away from it all" is the planning and preparation. Put the makings of several breads in your sea bag or rucksack.

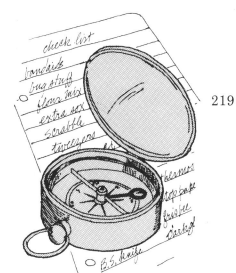

TRAIL BANNOCK BREAD

Ah wilderness . . . and the plastic bag. These weightless small food bags have changed the eating limitations of campers and hikers. They store all the dry ingredients—the makings of bannock bread as well as spices, tea, and matches—and they become mixing bowls when you add water and oil. Tightly tie the top of the bag, squeeze it and twist it until the dry ingredients are moistened and out comes a batter all ready to be baked. We suggest you carry oil in a lightweight plastic bottle, and that you wash out the plastic bag and reuse to return your litter to city garbage swallowers.

The best utensil for outdoor baking is a deep skillet with metal lid. No plastic because it will melt.

Makes One Round Loaf

1-1/2 cups (350 ml) whole-wheat flour
3/4 cup (175 ml) unbleached white flour
1 cup (250 ml) nondegerminated yellow cornmeal
1/2 cup (125 ml) unprocessed rolled oats
1/4 cup (60 ml) non-instant nonfat dry milk
1/2 tablespoon (7.5 ml) double-acting baking powder
2 tablespoons (30 ml) firmly packed brown sugar
3 tablespoons (45 ml) corn oil
1 cup (250 ml) water

Mix together dry ingredients thoroughly, stir in oil and mix well. Stir-in water. The dough will be rather dry. Pat into a well-oiled 9-inch (23 cm), straight-sided baking pan. Bake in oven preheated to 350°F (180°C) 25 to 30 minutes.

If using on trail, premix all ingredients except oil and water, bag tightly and when ready to bake, add the oil and water. Pat into cured and well-oiled skillet or lid to a camping cook set. Place over fire, cover and cook 10 to 15 minutes. If done correctly, dough should not stick to pan. Flip and cook other side for 10 minutes. Cut into sections or break off pieces and eat with lots of jam.

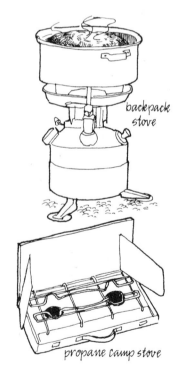

backpack stove

propane camp stove

220

to invert bread being baked on top of stove:

place oiled plate over pan and invert partially-baked bread onto plate ➡

slide loaf back so top is now on the bottom

finish baking & cool on wire rack

PRESSURE-COOKER OR IRON-POT WHEEL

Remarkably good bread can be made without an oven. We tried a four-quart (4 L) pressure cooker and invented the wheel, of bread, that is, and it's a runaway success, a great boon if you're a sailor. We even made it with sea water (boiled for 10 minutes to eliminate any stray foreign agents, and cooled to 115°F or 46°C). The recipe indicates how much salt to substitute if you're starting with fresh water. Plan ahead to simplify "baking": Prepare a plastic bag of measured flour and salt (if using), a measuring cup to hold yeast and sugar, bowl and spoon for mixing, and place all in pressure cooker or iron pot with lid. You're ready to make bread wherever you can find an adjustable stove.

Makes One Round Loaf

1 tablespoon (15 ml) active dry yeast
1-1/2 cups (350 ml) lukewarm water
1 tablespoon (15 ml) granulated sugar
1-1/4 teaspoons (6 ml) salt (omit if using sea water)
1 cup (250 ml) whole-wheat flour
1/2 cup (125 ml) untoasted wheat germ
2-1/2 cups (600 ml) unbleached white flour, or as needed

Grease the inside of a 4-quart (4 L) pressure cooker or iron pot and dust lightly with flour. Place in a shallow pan of hot water temporarily so pan will be warmed.

Sprinkle yeast over 1/2 cup (125 ml) of the water, stir in sugar and let stand until foamy. Add remaining water, salt, whole-wheat flour, wheat germ and 2 cups (500 ml) of the unbleached flour. Beat well, adding additional unbleached flour to make a stiff dough. Turn out onto floured board and knead, adding additional flour as needed to prevent sticking, 5 minutes or until smooth and pliable. Form into a smooth ball and coat surface lightly with oil. Place in prewarmed cooker and cover with lid. Let rise in warm place 1 hour. (If no specific warm place is available, wrap pan in heavy bath towels and place out of draft for 2 hours.) Remove towels and place cooker, with lid on, over a low-medium (325°F or 160°C) burner on stove top for 20 minutes. (Remember to leave valve opening of pressure cooker free for steam to escape.) Reduce heat to low (275°F or 135°C) and continue "baking" 15 minutes longer. Remove lid, place plate over top of pan and invert bread onto plate. Slide back into pan so top is now on the bottom, replace lid and continue to "bake" 30 minutes or until bread tests done. Remove to wire rack and cool 1 hour before serving.

221

Topping Off Breads

One aspect of baking we have neglected is the matter of *visual* taste. Next time you're in a bakery, looking at all the breads spread out for your choice, ask yourself which ones draw the eye back for seconds. Is it the shiny sourdough rye, deeply slashed and tempting under a sprinkling of coarse cornmeal? Is it the egg bread and the brioche glistening with an egg wash that baked daringly dark and tantalizing? Or is it the iced sweet roll, the poppyseed twist, the coffee cake thickly streuseled, even the earthen oatmeal with creamy oat flakes broadcast on top?

Eye appeal, that's what! There's something seductive about these breads that a plain loaf misses; it may be the same bread but never underestimate the eye's connection to the stomach.

We've included a dependable list of ways to add makeup to your baking efforts, to give them that high-eye cue boost.

WASHES

CORNSTARCH WASH Combine and cook over medium heat, stirring constantly, 1/2 cup (125 ml) water and 1 teaspoon (5 ml) cornstarch. When boiling, continue to cook and stir until thickened and translucent.

EGG WASH Beat together 1 egg and 1 tablespoon (15 ml) water; add 1/2 teaspoon (2.5 ml) salt (optional).

EGG WHITE WASH Beat together 1 egg white and 1 tablespoon (15 ml) water until slightly frothy.

MILK WASH Combine 1 tablespoon (15 ml) warm milk and 1/2 tablespoon (7.5 ml) melted butter; brush top surface of bread before baking to create shiny appearance.

MOLASSES WASH Combine 1 tablespoon (15 ml) molasses and 2 tablespoons (30 ml) water. Brush top surface of bread halfway through baking and again 4 minutes before bread is done.

SALT WASH Dissolve 1 tablespoon (15 ml) salt in 1/4 cup (60 ml) water; brush on bread after 20 minutes of baking.

GLAZES

BROWN SUGAR GLAZE Over low heat, cook and stir 4 tablespoons (60 ml) each butter and brown sugar until sugar is dissolved. Add freshly grated orange peel, ground cinnamon, and/or ground nutmeg, if desired.

COFFEE GLAZE Cream together 1 tablespoon (15 ml) butter, softened, and 6 tablespoons (90 ml) powdered sugar. Thin with 2 teaspoons (10 ml) strong brewed coffee, or as needed for proper consistency.

LEMON GLAZE Cream 1 tablespoon (15 ml) butter, softened, with 6 tablespoons (90 ml) powdered sugar. Thin with 2 teaspoons (10 ml) fresh lemon juice, or as needed for proper consistency. Add freshly grated lemon peel, if desired.

ORANGE GLAZE Cream 1 tablespoon (15 ml) butter, softened, with 1/2 cup (125 ml) powdered sugar. Thin with 4 teaspoons (20 ml) fresh orange juice, or as needed for proper consistency. Add freshly grated orange peel, if desired.

POWDERED SUGAR GLAZE Combine 1/2 cup (125 ml) powdered sugar, 2 teaspoons (10 ml) milk or water and 1/4 teaspoon (1.2 ml) pure vanilla extract, adding milk or water as needed for proper consistency.

APRICOT FILLING

*Makes Approximately
One Cup (250 ml)*
1 cup (250 ml) chopped cooked dried apricots
1/4 cup (60 ml) fresh orange juice
1/3 cup (50 ml) granulated sugar or honey
1/2 teaspoon (2.5 ml) ground coriander

In heavy saucepan, combine all ingredients. Cook and stir over medium-high heat until mixture has thickened and flavors are blended. Remove from heat and let cool. May be refrigerated in covered jar several days. Bring to room temperature before using.

APRICOT-NUT FILLING Proceed as directed for Apricot Filling. Remove mixture from heat, stir in 1/4 to 1/2 cup (60 to 125 ml) chopped walnuts, pecans, almonds or filberts.

ALMOND FILLING

Makes Approximately Three-fourths Cup (175 ml)
1 7-ounce (200 g) package almond paste
2 egg whites, unbeaten
3 tablespoons (45 ml) ground blanched almonds

Thoroughly combine all ingredients. May be refrigerated in covered jar up to 1 week. Bring to room temperature before using.

COTTAGE CHEESE FILLING

*Makes Approximately
Three-fourths Cup (175 ml)*
2/3 cup (150 ml) sieved small-curd cottage cheese
3 to 4 tablespoons (45 to 60 ml) granulated sugar
1 egg yolk
1/2 teaspoon (2.5 ml) pure vanilla extract
1/2 teaspoon (2.5 ml) ground cinnamon or allspice
1 teaspoon (5 ml) freshly grated lemon peel
1/4 cup (60 ml) dried currants

Combine all ingredients and refrigerate, covered, until ready to use. Do not keep more than 1 day.

CANDIED FRUIT FILLING

*Makes Approximately
One and One-half Cups (350 ml)*
5 tablespoons (75 ml) butter, softened
5 tablespoons (75 ml) unbleached white flour
3 tablespoons (45 ml) firmly packed brown sugar
1 teaspoon (5 ml) pure vanilla extract
2 teaspoons (10 ml) brandy
2 teaspoons (10 ml) freshly grated lemon peel
2/3 cup (150 ml) chopped mixed candied fruits
1/3 cup (75 ml) dried currants
1/2 cup (125 ml) chopped blanched almonds

Cream together butter, flour and sugar. With fork, stir in remaining ingredients. May be refrigerated in covered jar several weeks.

DATE FILLING

Makes Approximately One and One-half Cups (350 ml)

8 ounces (225 g) pitted dates, chopped (approximately 1-1/2 cups or 350 ml)

2/3 cup (150 ml) water

1 tablespoon (15 ml) fresh lemon juice

1/4 cup (60 ml) firmly packed brown sugar

1/2 teaspoon (2.5 ml) ground cinnamon

1/4 teaspoon (1.2 ml) ground cloves

1/4 teaspoon (1.2 ml) ground nutmeg

2 teaspoons (10 ml) freshly grated orange peel

1/2 cup (125 ml) grated raw apple (optional)

1/2 cup (125 ml) chopped pecans, walnuts, almonds or filberts

In heavy saucepan, combine all ingredients except nuts. Cook, stirring, over medium-high heat until mixture thickens and flavors are blended. Remove from heat, stir in nuts and let cool. May be refrigerated in covered jar several days. Bring to room temperature before using.

POPPY-SEED FILLING

Makes Approximately Three-fourths Cup (175 ml)

3 tablespoons (45 ml) butter, softened

3 tablespoons (45 ml) honey

6 tablespoons (90 ml) ground poppy seeds

6 tablespoons (90 ml) ground walnuts or pecans

1 tablespoon (15 ml) freshly grated orange peel, or 1/2 tablespoon (7.5 ml) freshly grated lemon peel

Heavy cream

Cream together butter and honey. Blend in poppy seeds, nuts, citrus peel and enough heavy cream to make spreading consistency. May be refrigerated in covered jar several days. Bring to room temperature before using.

Freeze shelled nuts to keep them from becoming rancid.

STREUSEL

Makes Approximately One and One-third Cups (300 ml)

3 tablespoons (45 ml) butter

1/3 cup (75 ml) firmly packed brown sugar

1/2 cup (125 ml) unbleached white flour

1/2 teaspoon (2.5 ml) ground cinnamon

1/4 teaspoon (1.2 ml) ground nutmeg or coriander

1/2 teaspoon (2.5 ml) freshly grated lemon peel

1/2 teaspoon (2.5 ml) pure vanilla extract

1/3 cup (75 ml) chopped pecans, walnuts, almonds or filberts, or 3 tablespoons (45 ml) unprocessed rolled oats

Cream together butter and sugar. Sift together flour and spices and crumble into butter mixture. With fork, stir in lemon peel and vanilla extract. Toss in nuts or oats. May be refrigerated in covered jar several weeks. Use as a filling or as a topping.

TAHINI FILLING

Makes Approximately
One Cup (250 ml)
3/4 cup (175 ml) tahini (sesame
    seed paste
1/4 cup (60 ml) honey

Thoroughly combine tahini and
honey. May be refrigerated in
covered jar up to 1 week. Bring
to room temperature before
using.

WALNUT-HONEY FILLING

Makes Approximately
One and One-half Cups (350 ml)
2 egg whites
1/4 cup (60 ml) ground walnuts
1/2 cup (125 ml) honey
2 tablespoons (30 ml) butter
3/4 cup (175 ml) chopped
    walnuts
2 teaspoons (10 ml) freshly
    grated orange peel
1 teaspoon (5 ml) fresh lemon
    juice

In heavy saucepan, combine
egg whites, ground walnuts,
honey and butter. Cook, stirring constantly, over medium-
high heat 5 minutes or until
thickened. Remove from heat,
stir in remaining ingredients
and let cool. May be refrigerated in covered jar 4 or 5 days.
Bring to room temperature be
fore using.

PRUNE FILLING

Makes Approximately
One Cup (250 ml)
1 cup (250 ml) finely chopped
    cooked prunes
2 teaspoons (10 ml) freshly
    grated lemon or orange peel
1/4 to 1/3 cup (60 to 75 ml)
    granulated sugar
1 to 2 tablespoons (15 to
    30 ml) butter
1/2 teaspoon (2.5 ml) ground
    cinnamon
1/2 teaspoon (2.5 ml) ground
    cloves, or 1/4 teaspoon
    (1.2 ml) ground nutmeg
3 to 4 tablespoons (45 to 60 ml)
    water, or part fresh orange
    and/or lemon juice

In heavy saucepan, combine all
ingredients. Cook over medium
heat, stirring, until mixture has
thickened and flavors are
blended. Remove from the heat
and let cool. May be refrigerated in covered jar 4 or 5 days.
Bring to room temperature before using.

Honey can be substituted
for sugar: 2/3 cup (150 ml)
for each cup (250 ml) of
sugar; then add 1/3 cup
(75 ml) more flour to the
recipe (if the amount is 1
tablespoon [15 ml], substi-
tute on a 1 to 1 basis).

TOPPING SUGGESTIONS FOR GRIDDLECAKES, WAFFLES AND FRENCH TOAST

- Creamed butter seasoned
with orange juice concentrate
and freshly grated orange peel
- Orange slices heated in orange marmalade
- Currant jelly melted with a
little hot water and seasoned
with a dash of salt and fresh
lemon juice
- Melted butter and honey,
heated and combined with
toasted unsweetened grated
coconut and/or finely chopped
or ground almonds
- Butter whipped with honey
and/or molasses
- Creamed butter combined
with chopped pecans and chut-
ney
- Creamed butter combined
with maple syrup, grated nutmeg and ground walnuts
- Applesauce or poached
pears or apples seasoned with
ground cinnamon, allspice, nutmeg or cardamom
- Lightly cooked blueberries
thickened with cornstarch and
seasoned with fresh lemon juice
- Maple syrup boiled with a
little half-and-half and seasoned
with pure vanilla extract

Leftovers

FRENCH TOAST

In France they call it *pain perdu,* "lost bread" (usually stale bread) and serve it as a dessert. America likes it for breakfast or brunch, with honey or maple syrup, or dusted with powdered sugar and cinnamon or nutmeg. Try it with Canadian bacon or sauteed chicken livers along with apples, bananas or fresh peaches heated in butter and brown sugar. For other topping suggestions, see page 225. French toast is pan fried in half butter, half oil, to a golden color, turned only once. Quick or heavy breads do not take to the egg dipping—they get soggy. But fresh sour French, sliced thick: oo-lala! In fact, almost any yeast bread, either fresh or stale and French toasted, will feed the soul.

Serves Two or Three
1 egg
1/2 tablespoon (7.5 ml) light corn syrup or honey
1/8 teaspoon (.8 ml) salt
1/4 teaspoon (1.2 ml) ground cinnamon
1/8 teaspoon (.8 ml) ground nutmeg

1/2 teaspoon (2.5 ml) freshly grated orange peel
1 cup (250 ml) milk or evaporated milk
6 to 8 slices stale bread

Beat egg lightly and combine well with corn syrup, salt, spices, orange peel and milk. One at a time, dip bread slices into batter so batter penetrates almost halfway through from each side, turning over to soak second side. If bread is very hard and dry, let soak until fork will barely penetrate with light pressure. Cook, according to directions in above introduction.

PUFFED FRENCH TOAST

Serves Four to Six
1 cup (250 ml) unbleached white flour
1/2 tablespoon (7.5 ml) double-acting baking powder
1/2 teaspoon (2.5 ml) salt
1/4 teaspoon (1.2 ml) ground cinnamon, or to taste
Dash ground nutmeg
1 cup (250 ml) milk
2 eggs, lightly beaten
1 teaspoon (5 ml) freshly grated orange peel
8 to 12 slices stale bread

Combine all dry ingredients. Beat together milk, eggs and orange peel and stir into dry ingredients until well blended. Dip bread slices in mixture according to directions for French Toast, preceding. Deep fry (page 212) in 1/2-inch peanut oil. Serve immediately, or keep warm in 300°F (150°C) oven until ready to serve.

CROUTONS

Cut bread into 1/2-inch (1.5 cm) cubes and dry in a 200°F (90°C) oven. Toss 3 cups (700 ml) of cubes with 4 tablespoons (60 ml) butter, melted and seasoned with one of the following mixtures. Place on baking sheet and, stirring frequently, lightly brown in 300°F (150°C) oven.

● 1/4 cup (50 ml) freshly grated Parmesan cheese, 1 teaspoon (5 ml) paprika, dash cayenne pepper
● 1/2 teaspoon (2.5 ml) salt, 2 teaspoons (10 ml) mixed crumbled dried herbs, pepper
● 1-1/2 tablespoons (22.5 ml) fresh lemon juice, 1 tablespoon (15 ml) freshly grated lemon peel, 1 teaspoon (5 ml) paprika
● grated or finely minced garlic, minced oregano, salt and pepper to taste

---

Make Melba toast with French bread slices. Bake at 200°F (90°C) until crisp, store in airtight container.

A different kind of dough . . .

Play Dough

No practical bread book would be complete without that *other* kind of dough, the non-edible but irresistible one that has become the favorite medium of amateur and junior sculptors—play dough. Ruth Asawa, a famous San Francisco sculptor and artist with joyful imagination, introduced the pliable modeling material in the sixties. Its unlimited potential immediately hatched a generation of kitchen and nursery shapers and bakers, molding and squeezing, twisting and painting Christmas tree ornaments, wall plaques, bread baskets, dolls and refrigerator door magnets, just to skim the list. So that you will always have the recipe at hand, we print it here:

4 parts white flour
1 part salt
1-1/2 parts water

Mix together all ingredients in a bowl and then turn out on floured board and knead a few times to get a smooth dough. Then comes the fun. Place shaped dough on a lightly greased cookie sheet and bake at 350°F (180°C) for 1 hour or until the dough is quite hard. Cool and add any color decorations using water-soluble paints. If a shiny surface is desired, apply orange shellac and let dry thoroughly.

EDIBLE PLAY DOUGH

This is full of good stuff, so don't count on its lasting like the recipe above. It's a richer dough, but shapes well and will preserve details through the baking. It does not lend itself to coloring, except with frostings, but can be glazed with egg white. Edible play dough is a fine party additive: Let guests or children do the sculpting and eating while you bake.

1/2 cup (125 ml) untoasted wheat germ
3/4 cup (175 ml) instant skim dry milk
1 cup (250 ml) smooth peanut butter
1/4 cup (60 ml) honey

Mix and knead as for inedible play dough above, then shape. Bake in a 300°F (140°C) oven 1 hour. Turn heat down to 275°F (120°C) if dough browns too rapidly. Handle with care when removing from pan.

The tail that wags this book . . .

Dog Biscuits

HEARTY DOG BISCUITS

Instead of a bare cupboard, Old Mother Hubbard missed a bet. She could have filled it with these homemade bonuses for her dog—and beat the rising cost of pet food, too. They're quick to make and filled with nutrients—something bracing for *your* canine aficionado to chew on.

228

Makes Approximately Nine Dozen

1 tablespoon (15 ml) active dry yeast
1/4 cup (60 ml) lukewarm water
2 cups (500 ml) lukewarm beef broth
2 cups (500 ml) unbleached white flour, or as needed
2 cups (500 ml) whole-wheat flour
2 cups (500 ml) fine bulghur
2 teaspoons (10 ml) salt
1/2 cup (125 ml) instant nonfat dry milk
1/3 cup (75 ml) nondegerminated yellow cornmeal
Egg Wash, page 222

In large bowl, sprinkle yeast over water, stir to dissolve and let stand until foamy. Stir in broth. Combine flours, bulghur, salt and dry milk; beat into yeast mixture to make a very stiff dough. Turn out onto floured board and knead 4 minutes. Divide into 3 equal portions; put 2 aside, covered with tea towel. Roll out remaining portion to a thickness of less than 1/4 inch (6 mm) and cut with a bone-shape cookie cutter or small circular cutter. Place on ungreased baking sheets that have been sprinkled evenly with cornmeal. Brush cutouts with wash and repeat with remaining 2 portions of dough. Set in warm place to rise for 45 minutes and bake in oven preheated to 325°F (160°C) 45 minutes. After all are baked, turn oven off and leave biscuits in cooling oven overnight to harden. Store in airtight container.

Bread Language

ADDING COLOR: Egg yolks give a yellow tinge to bread; a pinch of saffron, or dried safflower intensifies yellow. Coffee, chocolate, carob and toasted stale bread give black bread that deep, peasant brown. Molasses turns bland white yeast breads into an appealing cream tone. Bran, wheat germ and whole grains color breads darker. Chopped carrots, zucchini and pineapple enliven breads and rolls. Chopped candied fruits signify holiday sparkle. Egg washes cause breads to brown quickly and intensely.

BAGUETTE: Long, skinny, crusty French breads; measure oven to be sure loaves will fit diagonally. Should be eaten the day they are baked.

BARM: Yeast made from grains (*barm* is the old Gaelic word for yeast).

BATCH: One recipe of yeast or quick breads.

BATTER: Dough that is too moist to knead, as in batter bread. Also used to describe texture in early part of directions before all the flour has been added. To break down chilled fats and dough for croissants, the dough is "battered" with a heavy rolling pin.

BREAD FLOUR: Hard-wheat flour used by commercial bakeries, but rarely available to the home baker (unless that home baker can convince a local bakery to sell 5 or 10 pounds). It must be kneaded longer than all-purpose flour.

BOLTING: Sifting of the ground grain through linen or silk sieves to keep out bran and deliver a white flour. Nylon is now used.

BRAN: The husk of the grain.

BREWER'S YEAST: A form of yeast that is little used in recent times because active dry yeast is more dependable and more readily available. It is usually sold in solid blocks and must be well wrapped and refrigerated. Originally, it was bitter, leaving a nasty mouth, but now is "debittered." There is also another brewer's yeast, the granulated kind sold in natural-foods stores. It is not a leavener, but instead is intended for health mixtures such as tiger's milk.

CAROB: A substitute for chocolate with a low-fat profile. Comes from the pod of St. John's Bread, an evergreen tree of the Mediterranean and California. Toasting gives the chocolatelike taste.

CORNELL FORMULA: One of the early 20th-century changes in bread nutrition, developed at Cornell University by Dr. Clive McKay. It is a formula for enriching weak white flour: 1 tablespoon (15 ml) soy flour, 1 tablespoon (15 ml) non-instant low-fat dry milk and 1 teaspoon (5 ml) wheat germ. Measure these ingredients into a cup, then fill balance with all-purpose flour or unbleached white flour. Transpose any yeast recipe in this book if you want to boost enrichment.

CRUMB: Crumb has two definitions: the crumby one, which

is the mess left after slicing bread; the other refers to the baked texture inside the bread, that is, fine or coarse "crumb."

DEEP FRY: An alternative way of baking breads, usually associated with doughnuts. We recommend safflower or peanut oil for deep frying. Temperature is a primary concern: Attach a candy thermometer to the side of the fry-kettle to keep you clued in (for details on deep-frying breads, see page 212).

DOUBLE IN BULK: Refers to the expansion of gluten cells in yeast bread that has risen. It is difficult for beginners to judge, so we suggest the finger test after the allotted time has elapsed: Press two fingers into dough, and if marks remain unchanged, it is ready to be punched down.

DOUBLE IN SIZE: Refers to the final rising before bread is baked. This is a visual measurement, subject to guessing and experience. Less is better than more. Individual recipes indicate what to look for including "almost double in size," or "until half again as large."

DOUGH: The "before" of bread.

DREDGE: Adding flour by casting by hand across work surface under the dough; sprinkling flour from a sifter. Also, flouring dried fruits before adding to dough.

DUST LIGHTLY: Applying dry ingredients (flour, powdered sugar, etc.) in a limited manner.

ENDOSPERM: The white starchy center of wheat grain.

FERMENTATION: Conversion of sugar to equal parts of carbon dioxide (gas) and alcohol; essential to most baked goods.

FOLDING-IN: The gentlest action after first rising. No stirring, since tearing lessens elasticity and strength of gluten. Sprinkle ingredients (oil, salt, raisins, etc.) over top, lift up bottom over top, with wooden spoon or spatula, and work from sides of bowl, which is turned as folding goes on.

FRENCH vs ITALIAN BREAD: Italian bread is much heavier, uses more flour and is finer textured; French is desired for its tough crust and large holes. Never seal either in tight bags; they need to breathe. Eat within 24 to 48 hours of baking. Can be reheated in dampened brown

paper bag, or just on the oven rack, for crisper crust.

GLUTEN: Protein substance of grain that toughens the walls of the cells in bread.

GRITS: Hominy, with germ and hull removed. Sometimes soaked in wood-ash lye, then dried and broken into bits. Soy grits are ground the same way.

HARD-WHEAT FLOUR: High amount of gluten, harder to knead.

HEEL: Telling the bread to "sit" while you cut off the first slice—yours by rights if you baked the loaf.

KNEAD: To work dough to a smoothness and elasticity with hands or aided by a mixer.

LEAVENER: Any substance that will cause fermentation: yeast, baking powder, baking soda, sourdough starter, etc.

OLD-FASHIONED FLAVOR: Simplicity; nostalgia warmed over.

PROOF: The word descends from ancient times. A method used for assurance that yeast was still alive by dissolving in warm water. New methods of putting breads together eliminate this step—CoolRise, Rapid-Mix and One-Bowl.

230

PUNCH DOWN: With gusto push fist into center of dough that has finished rising; pull dough in from edges to center, then push edges down with fingers into center in a fork fashion. Invert dough out onto hand and continue to tuck dough under as you shift in hand. (This is a very enjoyable moment. You can forget everything except the warm round ball in your hand!)

REHEAT: Most breads benefit from reheating (see FRENCH BREAD), and if frozen, can be rejuvenated in foil wrap in oven.

REST TIME: Yeast doughs benefit from brief respites of handling; individual recipes tell you when. Always cover resting dough so a "skin" doesn't form. Turn a bowl over it or cover with tea towel.

SCALDED MILK: Heating milk to the point just before a scum appears on surface. (If it does form, remove it.) Purpose of scalding is to kill undesirable types of yeast that milk has collected in air. These undesirables produce molds and souring of bread. Raw milk must be scalded; pasteurized and dry milks have already been heat-treated, so scalding is optional.

SLACK DOUGH: Dough that does not have enough flour to retain its shape.

SLASHING DOUGH: Yeast breads that form an early crust will crack on top or sides to allow for more expansion. Slashing with a sharp razor or knife before baking relieves tension. If slashing is done before last rising, bread will spread too much and lose identity.

SOURDOUGH STARTER: Starter is a batter that is fermented and used to start other dough.

SPONGE: A method of starting bread which allows a more relaxed time schedule (see page 51).

SPROUTING: Germinating seeds or grain in moisture to force them to sprout, increasing nutritional content tremendously. They may be eaten raw in salads, cooked, or added to breads (see page 56).

STONE GROUND: Process of milling grain between two specially shaped stones, at low heat, which splits the grain to form whole meal. (Roller-grinding crushes grain.)

TOAST: Bread or seeds placed near direct heat to freshen or lightly brown. Dark toast has lower nutrition, so toast lightly.

UNLEAVENED: Breads made with no rising agent, such as flat breads. Also, breads made with eggs, such as popovers.

WASHES AND GLAZES: Washes are egg, oil, milk or water mixtures applied to the crusts of breads before placing in oven (washes also act as a kind of glue to hold sprinkling of seeds, etc.). Melted butter or oil is brushed on breads after baking to make them shiny, more appealing. Glazes are usually sugar based, like frostings (see section on washes and glazes).

WEAK FLOUR: Soft flour made from wheat with low-gluten content.

WHOLE MEAL: One hundred percent of the berry; also called whole-grain and whole-wheat flour.

ACKNOWLEDGMENTS

If this book becomes your favorite working partner in the making of real bread, it will be due in large measure to the unstinting help and enthusiasm we were favored with by experts and breadlovers. The credibility of challenging recipes like croissants and brioche was given by French-cooking expert Bobbie Greenlaw, of Bobbie's Kitchen; the simplified techniques and joy of making good earthy breads were shared by a young peripatetic baker, Meg Hutchins, who has kneaded from Alaska to Squirrel Island, Maine. Our thanks to Cheryl Farrell, who guided us over high-altitude baking; to Shanta Nimbark Sacharoff, for sharing her chapati recipe from her book, *Flavors of India;* and to Barbara Huey, for her dog biscuits. To the many who offered ideas, suggestions and criticisms, to those who bravely tested and retested, our Real Bread rises because of you.

SOURCES

FLOURS, GRAINS

Moore's Flour Mill, 1605 Shasta St., Redding CA 96001
Walnut Acres (organic foods), Penns Creek PA 17862
Applewood Seed Co., Golden CO 80401

EQUIPMENT

Williams-Sonoma, 576 Sutter St., San Francisco CA 94102
Eddie Bauer (outdoor cooking), P.O. Box 3700, Seattle WA 98124
For miscellaneous bread needs, check in your library for *Complete Food Catalog* (Holt, Rinehart & Winston).

LARGE EQUIPMENT

Convection ovens, food processors, heavy-duty mixers and blenders are available in the kitchenware sections of major department stores. Bosch Magic Mill: for sources in your vicinity, write Bosch Products, 235 West 200 South, Salt Lake City UT 84101.
All-Grain Mill is available through Horizon Marketing Div., P.O. Box 15783, Salt Lake City UT 84115.

SPECIAL BOOKLET ON QUICK-METHOD BREADS

Fleischmann's Yeast, Box 337, Teaneck NJ 07666

Index

GENERAL INFORMATION INDEX

233

234

RECIPE INDEX

238

MAGGIE BAYLIS is best known for her half-million-copy bestseller *House Plants for the Purple Thumb*. But while she was collecting kudos for this and her other plant books, she was an avid "closet baker." Actually Maggie Baylis has been baking bread since her childhood and as an adult has found breadbaking to be the answer to relieving tensions from her busy career as an artist, designer, writer, lecturer and plant consultant. Her other books include *Practicing Plant Parenthood* and the illustrations for *Greenhousing for Purple Thumbs* and *The Punctured Thumb: Cactus and Other Succulents*. Her articles have appeared in most of the nation's leading home and garden publications.

CORALIE CASTLE is the author of five other cookbooks with total sales of one-quarter million copies. Her research for *Real Bread* spanned four continents over a period of three years— acquiring recipes and testing them under varying conditions of altitude and climate. She also worked with local bakers in many regions of this country and abroad and experimented with the flours and waters peculiar to the various areas. Coralie Castle's other books include *The Art of Cooking for Two, Country Cookery: Recipes From Many Lands, The Edible, Ornamental Garden, Hors d'Oeuvre Etc.,* and *Soup.* She also was co-editor of *The Whole World Cookbook,* a collection of 1,500 recipes from 101 cookbooks published in hardcover by Scribners.

MP4L